I dedicate this book to all who need to know they matter and their story matters: you are who I wrote this book for. May you find hope and strength within these pages for your journey into a greater depth of intimacy with our precious Father, our beautiful Jesus, and our strengthening Holy Spirit.

Speak up for those who cannot speak for themselves,
for the rights of all who are destitute.
Speak up and judge fairly;
defend the rights of the poor and needy. —Proverbs 31:8–9

For Kristiana, Jack, Mariah, Peter, David and Anna.
Your story matters.

My Dance with Justice

My Dance with Justice

Lydia Rose McSweeney

RESOURCE *Publications* · Eugene, Oregon

MY DANCE WITH JUSTICE

Resource Publications
An Imprint of Wipf and Stock Publishers
199 W. 8th Ave., Suite 3
Eugene, OR 97401

www.wipfandstock.com

PAPERBACK ISBN: 979-8-3852-0533-2
HARDCOVER ISBN: 979-8-3852-0534-9
EBOOK ISBN: 979-8-3852-0535-6

VERSION NUMBER 010824

Unless otherwise indicated, Scripture quotations are from:

The Holy Bible, New International Version®, NIV®, copyright © 1973, 1978, 1984, 2011 by Biblica, Inc.™ Used by permission. All rights reserved worldwide.

The Holy Bible, New Living Translation, copyright © 1996, 2004, 2007, 2013, 2015 by Tyndale House Foundation. Used by permission of Tyndale House Publishers Inc., Carol Stream, Illinois 60188. All rights reserved.

The Holy Bible, New King James Version®, copyright © 1982 by Thomas Nelson. Used by permission. All rights reserved.

Contents

Abbreviations

AT   attachment theory

BCNZ   Bible College of New Zealand

ED   emergency department

HDU   high-dependency unit

NICU   neonatal intensive care unit

NIV   New International Version

OM   Operation Mobilization

ORT   object relations theory

PTSD   post-traumatic stress disorder

SIDS   sudden infant death syndrome

YWAM   Youth with a Mission

Introduction

I HAVE ALWAYS FELT fully alive when dancing. In my youth, I studied ballet and loved the stage and performing. As with most young dancers, life led me on to employment and travel, and unfortunately dance was laid aside. A couple of years ago, my Father imbued my passion for dance with a sense of his presence, amidst deep tragedy.

Intimacy is key to the most memorable of dances, and Torvill and Dean displayed this in their dance entitled *Bolero* in the 1994 Winter Olympics. The awe and silence as the crowd watched and the euphoria that exploded at the end of their perfect-ten scores were palpable. Torvill and Dean did not, I am sure, dance with such fluidity and intimacy when they initially began dancing together. Years of relationship, hard work and probably many tears went into preparing for their performance that day.

I have experienced beautiful intimacy in knowing and being known in my relationship with Jesus, my Father, and the Holy Spirit. The rhythms of life have choreographed our dance. Held deep within their embrace, I am safe, I am home, I belong. Through all the deep anguish and incessant questioning, I have come to know God in the confusion as more brilliant and faithful than I could confine in a theological treatise. We can never fully articulate the lived experience of the fullness of God. For this reason, I have placed my story within the concept of an all-embracing dance because this is how I have experienced the beauty of God as justice.

Growing up, I was presented through multiple avenues with a theological framework implicitly suggesting that because of what Jesus has done for me, I should automatically be able to dance in life and relationship with the Trinity with the fluidity and ease of highly trained dancers such as Torvill and Dean. Yet, there is a sense we all feel like this at times, don't we? There is often a great divide between what we know and how we are living what we know.

I once thought following Jesus meant adhering to what I believed were given instructions on how to live as a Jesus-follower, but tragedy has taught me that intimacy is different than following instructions; intimacy is born out of love, amidst deep pain and joy. Limiting our lives to an intellectual understanding of what it means to be a Jesus-follower is not what our Father wants for us. That would be like being taught the rules of dance but never actually dancing.

In an article I was reading for my Master of Applied Theology program, a phrase stood out: "Jesus is Justice." In that moment, my theological academic career, my love for dance, my passion for people, and what I had gone through myself all converged. Justice took on a deeper level of connection. If Jesus is justice, then that means he cares about giving justice to the profound wounds that life brings to our psyche, that which makes us who we are or, in some cases, distorts who we are.

There are times we will experience an injustice that will deeply impact our core psychological well-being. God cares deeply about the injustices we carry in our psyche, whether they have come through the intentional or unintentional choices of others or whether they are actions we have perpetrated against others. God is manifestly interested in bringing justice because righteousness and justice are the foundation of his throne; love and faithfulness go before him (Ps 89:14).

I am not referring to the human concept of justice within modern court systems, where the perpetrator must pay. In theological terms, justice is where God pays the price of injustice with the giving of Jesus, who takes our place. I find N. T. Wright's description of justice as where God "puts humans to rights" very helpful.[1] God wants to put right your internal world in relation to himself, others, and creation. Jesus' death and resurrection puts us right with our Father, and our mandate to bring justice flows from that. Inclusive in this understanding of justice is that we want those who have perpetrated great injustices against us to be healed, to be put right. This is the inference of Jesus' declaration that we are to bless our enemies.

The justice I formulated from my research for my master's is encapsulated in the term *psychological justice*. As this term had not yet been utilized within theological academic domains, I developed a framework where the believer's lived experience is shown to be affected by the intersection of four core components:

---

1. Wright, *Paul and the Faithfulness of God*, 934. The phrase "puts humans to rights" is unique to N. T. Wright.

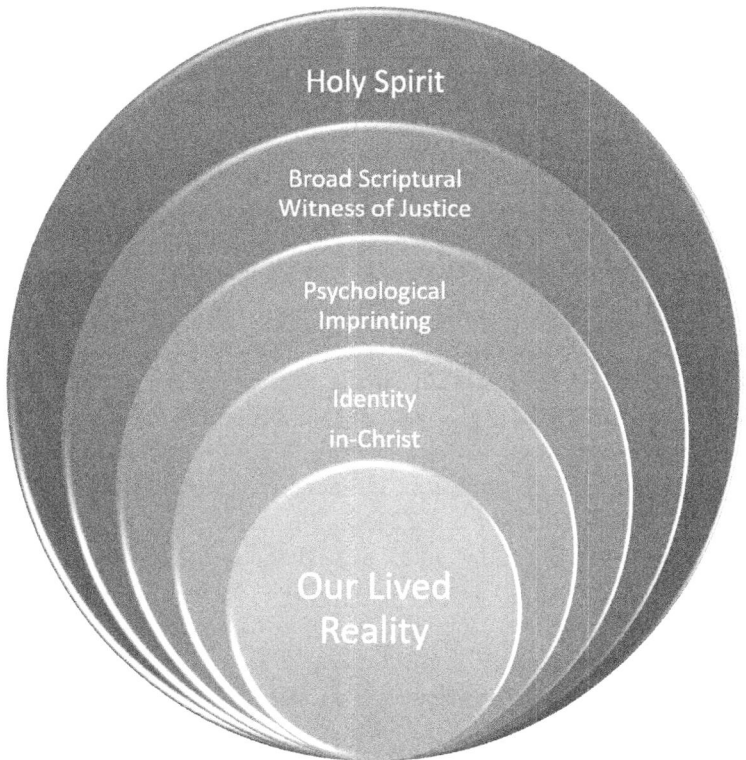

The Psychological Justice Framework

- psychological imprinting: Our psychological development and consequential imprinting from birth to the present (our psychological story);
- identity in Christ: The status that was given to us as believers upon reception of Jesus and all that he accomplished for us on the cross and in his resurrection (who we are in Christ);
- the broad scriptural revelation of God's justice as found in the Old and New Testaments; this includes a Hebraic understanding of justice (*mishpat*) and righteousness (*tsedeqah*) in the Old Testament, and an exploration of the Greek term for justice/righteousness (*dikaiosynē*) utilized by New Testament writers;
- the Holy Spirit, who is central, overarching and undergirding our lived experience, synchronizing all core components.

Even though they are independent entities, each component has a distinct and profound effect on the others. For example, fractures formed in our psyche, i.e., *psychological imprinting* through trauma or injustice, can impact our image of God and affect our connection with God. Just like a fracture in a foot or arm, when not healed, can cause weakness and disability, some events have broken something inside of us that may still not yet be healed and are affecting our present. Most of the time, we cannot see that what we carry psychologically from our past and the intellectual beliefs we hold about our *identity in Christ* has any connection to *our lived reality*. Most of us see the relevance of social, restorative, or criminal justice to our position and lived experience as believers, but not many would consider the psychological implications of what being born again means in similar ways.

The passion God has for bringing wholeness to our fullest sense of being is so important to grasp as believers. Our Father is not content for us to be satisfied with being justified. He longs for us to apprehend the richness of the *broad scriptural witness of justice*. He wants us to know him in the width, length, height, and depth of his love (Eph 3:18), to comprehend in all aspects of our lived reality through the *Holy Spirit* that we are genuinely known and deeply loved. Understanding how these four components influence our lives, we can focus more intentionally on each aspect and, with the Spirit's help and healing, develop a more Christ-centered lived reality.

The Holy Spirit has been my wonderful counselor (Isa 9:6). Throughout our dance, over and over the Holy Spirit has brought divine counsel to me so beautifully. I am in awe of his incessant compassion, wisdom, patience, and guidance. For some of you, my story (including the "Digging Deeper" and "Psychological Justice" sections) may trigger aspects of your own journey. I encourage you to not be afraid to seek the help of professional counselors. In partnership with the ever-present Holy Spirit, they can bring invaluable insight to support the process of healing the fractures in our psyche caused by past wounding.

My beautiful daughter, Jessica, painted the picture below. I cried when she presented it to me because it perfectly encapsulates my relationship with Jesus. He has been my best friend through everything. Even when I have lost the will to dance, he has picked me up and held me until I can place my feet on solid ground. The broken scales are symbolic of how our Father, in giving of his Son, through the Spirit, has broken the chains of injustice that bind us to the law. The enemy of our souls loves the law. He loves to remind us of the rules of justice. But, as my story will show, Jesus *is* Justice, so his authority breaks every chain.

I pray that as you read my story, you will feel invited into a more intimacy-filled dance with your heavenly Father. I pray the passion I have for *psychological justice* will also be borne in you, and you will gain a greater understanding of the revelation of justice within the Scriptures. This is important because our greatest mission as believers is to be bearers of justice to a broken humanity and creation.

How to Read This Book

I HAVE STRUCTURED THIS book so that it may be read in several ways. In order for you to be able to read my journey without feeling as though you are constantly being interrupted, I have separated my story from my reflections on the topics raised within each season.

I have included a section called "Digging Deeper" after each segment. This is to expand on or engage more with subjects that may have been raised. I have endeavored to provide theological and psychological support to help engender deeper growth in your own journey.

Below this, I summarize how "Psychological Justice" is exemplified to enable you to better comprehend the concept and apply the insights to your lived reality.

I then pose a couple of questions beneath the title "What's Your Story?" These questions are designed as a guide for personal reflection on subjects you may not yet have considered or as an opportunity to consider from a different perspective.

It may be easier for some of you to read the story through first and then go back and delve deeper. Others may prefer to read as is.

I encourage you not to be put off by the theological or psychological terminology used. I have, where possible, deciphered these terms with concepts that are familiar. I want to enable you to feel at ease with these terms because they will help build a framework of reference for reading other authors. Once you learn these concepts, they will help you to explain your own story more thoroughly. (They will also help immensely when reading my next book, on the *psychological justice model*.) I have included appendix 1, a vocabulary list, as a helpful, quick reference. I have gathered the questions that pertain to "What's Your Story?" and listed these in appendix 2 for ease of access. Some of you may want to have these separate to use for pondering in your own time and pace. They could also prove helpful for use in a group setting.

There is a bibliography for those who would like to do further reading.

The Lord gave me a prophetic picture as I completed my quest to write what, for me, is my epic saga. In the vision, I was speaking the words I have transcribed throughout these pages, and they became a swirling breath, similar to when you breathe out on a foggy day. The Holy Spirit came and teased out my words, and each person received what they needed. I trust our beautiful Father to give each one of you the words *you* need to help you flourish.

Our Lives, a Cosmic Battle

It was around four o'clock in the morning. The room was eerily quiet, apart from a few monitors beeping. I was sitting by the bed of my twenty-two-month-old son, Ben, where he lay in intensive care in Starship Children's Hospital (New Zealand's largest children's hospital). He was in a room with three other children who were also in critical condition.

I had been reading my Bible as I sat, keeping vigil. I had just read 2 Chronicles 20, where the Lord impressed on me that I needed only to be still to see the deliverance he would bring. I was exhausted. I had not slept for twenty-one hours at this point. Ben was lying immobile with many tubes coming out of him, surrounded by multiple monitors flashing and beeping. It was overwhelming.

Wearing only his nappy, Ben was lying on a mattress that kept his temperature very cold. The University of Auckland was researching whether this procedure would reduce the risk of brain damage. I was oscillating from quiet rest to agonizing panic. Every beep of the monitors would raise my heart rate, and my body would seize in time. The eerie quietness was intercepted by moments of sheer distress, as another drug would be injected into my baby boy's body.

He lay motionless and so helpless, having been put in an induced coma. I could not fathom the events of the day that had brought us to this point. The circumstances reeled in and out like a terrible nightmare from which I was constantly rotating and unable to wake, or a horror movie that was too terrifying to be my present reality.

Never in my wildest imagination, after all we had gone through as a family, had I ever entertained that things could get any worse. The fact that my son now lay motionless, being fed drugs to keep him alive, caused me to experience a constant stream of fierce waves of palpable terror—terror that I never imagined was possible.

I constantly viewed the monitors, though there were a lot of them, and I had no idea what many of the readings were for. There was one I understood: the blood pressure indicator. At around four o'clock in the morning, I watched it start to plummet. The nurse who was stationed permanently at the end of Ben's bed pressed a button, alerting the specialist medical registrar to come straight to her.

They injected a substance into one of Ben's numerous tubes, and his blood pressure rose again. It was only a matter of minutes, however, before his blood pressure started dropping rapidly again. My heart, already on edge, seized in my throat as I tried to breathe. Again the nurses injected him with medication. His blood pressure started rising again, but this time the medical doctor said, "We can only do this so many times. If he doesn't stabilize, he will not make it through until the morning."

I had held Ben dead by the pond the previous afternoon and had screamed out to God for mercy as his lifeless body lay in my arms. I had already witnessed the extreme coldness of death take my son from me. By a miracle, he had been revived, but now I was watching him die again and had no psychological or spiritual depth left. I had screamed it out of my soul by the pond. My heart was in deep anguish, and I was frozen in time. I wanted time to stop. I wanted to run back to the pond and change everything that had just happened.

The ability of the mind, soul, and body to disintegrate all at once was now my reality. Where was God? Why would he promise me a child and then take him from me—not only once by the pond, but now possibly in the hospital? I swirled in and out of faith, which in itself was terrifying, and in and out of reality.

They gently implored me to ring my husband and get him to the hospital so we could say goodbye to Ben together. John had gone home earlier that evening to be with our older children, Jessica and Joseph. I rang him but was unable to get through. We had both been traumatized by the day's events. My mind scrambled to think of what to do as I busily watched monitors and heard doctors and nurses murmur amongst themselves. Increasingly concerned, they asked me how I was doing at getting through to John. Trembling, panic-stricken, and with a deep sense of urgency, I rang my good friend Kathryn, who lived around the corner, and asked her to drive around and alert John of Ben's precarious state. Being a faithful friend, she did so.

Meanwhile, in hospital, Ben was teetering between this world and the next. I felt helpless and obsessively watched the monitors. They asked if I wanted a chaplain to come in. I knew this meant they were helping prepare me for his death. They cut some of Ben's hair so I would have something of him when he died. My heart was being pulled in so many directions, and my mind was whirling with dread. I was alone with my beautiful son, the one the Lord had promised me after I had already lost and buried six children.

In the midst of waiting for John and the chaplain and my wailing by Ben's bedside, the Lord spoke loudly to my heart. "Remember the dream," he said. Into my mind flashed the scene that had played out in the same dream three times in one night several years earlier. The Lord asked me, "What happens to Ben in the dream?" I replied, "He grows up to be a strong, powerful man." My Father replied, "So, believe. Believe my promise above the doctors and the reality of what is before you."

Normally, my heart would have jumped and said, "I believe, Lord!" But this was life and death. This wasn't a promise about just anything. This was my son's life. This was not about me getting something the Lord promised that had no critical and far-reaching consequences. This was no simple disparity between a promise from God and my circumstances. Like one of those movies where the end of the world is at stake, I felt like my world would shatter mercilessly and forever if Ben died in this hospital.

My heart was screaming, and it was so hard to hear the promise and the voice of God as my mind raced between what the nurses and doctors were saying and my Father's voice. It felt like I was caught in some terrible celestial scene, and my son was the one being fought over. My Father then also reminded me of the promise he had just given me in 2 Chronicles 20, of the deliverance he was going to bring. It was not going to be a medical intervention that saved Ben, and this was becoming increasingly obvious to everyone in the room.

The lead medical specialist was looking gravely concerned, and the highly trained intensive care nurses wanted me to get my mind ready for the inevitable death of my son. They had seen this before and had seen it play out to the end. Because this was a consequence of my poor decisions by an idyllic pond on a beautiful winter's day, my life also lay in the balance. How could God heal my son when I had done this, when Ben was in there because of me, where my actions had precipitated this? Did God's mercies really extend that far? Why on earth had I let myself be distracted talking to a friend? These questions and many others reverberated within my soul. I had held Ben dead by the pond, and what had poured out of the depths of my being was, "Have mercy on me, God!" I had kept screaming this over and over and over. Here I was. Would God have mercy on me?

I could not ask for resurrection for my son when I was responsible, could I?

My Father's voice was insistent. His promises grew louder, as did the reality I saw with my own eyes in front of me. I just wanted to pick Ben up and cradle him back to me, but he was so hooked up and bound to machines that I could not. I wanted to go back in time and change the day but I couldn't. I was imprisoned by guilt. I was responsible for the whole situation. "My son is going to die!" I screamed inside myself. "It's my fault. What if he dies? Have I killed my own son?" I can't explain the pure horror I was experiencing. I felt like I had been trapped in a time vault, and my being was being rendered in two.

Extreme mental, physical, spiritual, and emotional trauma consumed me as I sat alone.

The chaplain arrived. A beautiful woman from the Anglican Chaplaincy Service came to Ben's bedside and asked if I wanted her to pray for Ben. I eagerly agreed, thankful there was another believer in the room with me. She anointed him with oil and started praying through a healing service for Ben, just as John arrived. I told John of the promise God had given me that night. I reminded him of the dream I had had of Ben several years earlier, and we joined with the chaplain to agree together with God about his plans for Ben. In that moment, Ben's blood pressure stabilized and did not falter from that moment on.

Our son Ben was given back to us, but there was still a very painful and fear-filled journey ahead. He had water from a one-hundred-year-old duck pond in his lungs, and we had no idea if his brain was still functioning—but he was with us and stable. My heart fell into my Father's lap, and I wept uncontrollably, physically trembling at what had just taken place.

Season 1

Identity Formation

He grew up before him like a tender shoot, and like a root out of dry ground.
He had no beauty or majesty to attract us to him, nothing in his appearance
that we should desire him. (Isa 53:2)

WRITING ABOUT MY JOURNEY with Ben was the hardest chapter of this book
to compose. It took three months before I could sit down and even attempt
to write. I went through many boxes of tissues, walked countless hours, and
hid behind glasses to conceal my bloodshot eyes.

This is part of my story, and I will fully recount the remarkable miracle
that my Father did for Ben in the following chapters. I begin telling part of
it here as one example from my life where our present reality sometimes
clashes with the reality and/or desire of what we expect from God. Another
word for this is "incongruence." I will use this word throughout the following chapters as it is a helpful definition of what happens when our circumstances shout a different voice to what we think we know. We are human,
and we live on this side of eternity. On this side, there will be pain, heartache, and sometimes the deepest anguish a soul can endure. Sometimes our
lived reality, the truths we know in the Scriptures, and the theology we hold
does not match up. Where they do not match up, are there ways they can
be bridged to bring them closer together? Can we cross this bridge back
and forth and know that there will come a day when we will know as we are
known?

The impact of my experience with Ben by the pond uncovered a deep
and crippling shame about who I was. For as long as I can remember, I

have felt shame about existing. Deep down, I have believed I am a burden to people. In light of that, this has caused me to try to prove a bit more, be more, just to be on the planet—always saying sorry for being here, for being in the way. It wasn't until I studied psychological theory that I finally understood this state of being. It is due to having a *shame-based identity*. That is, I don't feel shame about something I have done; I feel shame for being alive. The reason I explain this here in the beginning of my book, after such a profoundly miraculous story as Ben's drowning, is that what happened by that pond was precipitated by a life of believing I was a mistake. I had spent my life up until that point trying to *be* something, anything. I was doing okay at this until Ben's drowning in that pond. All of a sudden, I felt everyone knew my secret: I really wasn't good enough. I had been exposed as the fraud I had been so desperately trying to hide. Well, at least that is how I suddenly felt. Uncovered. Naked. Seen.

In the following chapters, I will write about my childhood before I get to the manifold tragedies I would face in later life. I have a purpose in this. I want to show through the eyes of my childhood how the complexity of our stories have influenced who we are today, in our successes, strengths, weaknesses, and failures. These experiences pre-empt how we may face deep darkness and tragedy. Many of the issues we struggle with in our present are rooted in the development of the stories we carry in our core being. As you read my story, ask the Father to show you where my story may echo notes or steps in your own.

From our birth through to about two years of age is probably the most important period in terms of our psychological development. In these crucial years of life, we develop an attachment style to our primary caregiver. The psychological term used to describe this is *attachment theory*. How we attach to our mother or another primary caregiver determines how we will attach to others throughout our journey. For some of us, we attach to a mother who is present and available. Others may have an anxious mother, and some may experience violent or destructive mothering. This experience becomes our primary attachment relationship template.

Templates are designed to enable multiple reproductions. We hold within our attachment template many imprints. These imprints come from a range of events. They can be life-filling, such as moments of sheer joy; or destructive, such as being abused or facing a distressing circumstance. We carry this template and our imprints around with us, and they determine our responses and our understanding of our place in the world.

I thought I had an unremarkable childhood until I had to write my biography for a paper in my master's program from a psychological perspective. All of a sudden, many things I had brushed aside, mainly due to my shame-based, inferior sense of being, started revealing a different God narrative. As you will see, there were many things that happened in my developmental years that were anything but unremarkable.

Mislaid Foundations

My story begins in what was a small city in Australia in 1966, where I was given a name different from the one I have now. My mother conveyed to me that an Anglican minister came into the hospital when I was born; he prophesied over me that I was called and appointed by God and separated for his work and that I would travel the world ministering the gospel. Mum was not a believer at the time, but she remembers feeling what he said was significant.

I came to Jesus when I was around seven and remember being so in love with him. He was my best friend and my secure place. I would go to church with my aunty because Mum had been deeply hurt by the church after a terrible upbringing and suffering under intense spiritual abuse. Her parents were given a substantial inheritance; however, my grandfather gave a considerable portion to the church in line with prosperity gospel teaching. It was such a devastating story because the church would betray them. They took the money and then subsequently abandoned my mum, her parents, and her five siblings. They were left with little money and were driven to live in a tent at the beach. You would think this would have turned my grandparents off to church, but no, it got worse for my mum. She would be beaten at night if she did not speak in tongues before bed. She only had one pair of shoes and one school dress. When she had head lice, teachers would put her in a corner of the classroom, and no one was allowed to play with her. I suspect God must have appeared frightening to Mum, and life must have been full of experiences of deep shame and public humiliation.

In my first year of school, my mum started working for a legal firm. She would leave at seven o'clock in the morning and arrive home around six o'clock at night. This is normality for many mothers now, but this was 1970, so it was unusual. I hated coming home alone. I was so jealous of my friends whose mums had made cookies and milk for them after school. Instead, I would come home and bottles of milk and bread would be outside our front door. My sister, brother, and I would eat the inside of the bread and drink most of the milk while watching our daily lineup of television shows. We would listen for Mum's Morris Minor car to come down the hill at around six o'clock at night, and we would go splash water around the bathroom to make out that we had had a bath. We joked when we got older that it would have taken less energy to actually have a bath! My father was a traveling salesman and would be away regularly for days and weeks at a time.

I was not coping at school and my confidence was dwindling. I had a difficult teacher who loved telling me how immature I was, and he would belittle anyone who could not do physical sports. I remember one day trying to cut out something, and he yelled at me in front of everyone that I was so stupid for not being able to cut in a straight line. This teacher impacted my identity at such a deep level. The shame I felt during this year changed my perception of myself and my abilities. I already had labels at this point of being "oversensitive" and "childish." I would find out later in life that this teacher was suspended because so many children had been affected by his abusive behavior. Unfortunately, this teacher's comments marked me.

I started attending ballet and jazz classes at the age of nine. In the midst of all my confusion, dance gave me such a wonderful sense of being. I felt fully alive when I danced, and it was something I was naturally gifted to do. I loved the entire experience, from the costumes to the choreography and stage settings. I loved performing and did well in my exams. My teacher was beautiful, elegant, and an outstanding dancer. She instilled such love and passion in me for dance and fostered a deep confidence in my abilities. Dance was, and always will be, my first love.

I loved watching the television show *Mary Tyler Moore* and viewed Mum as very much like her. I adored my mum. She was my heroine. This would become a problem in my later years as she could not live up to my idolization of her, but it was my way of coping with her absence, I suppose. Her absence, of course, was in order to give us a better life than she had had, but I had no idea of that at such a young age. I was so lonely. The emptiness, fear, and realization that our family was different was hard, especially considering how insecure I already felt.

Most summer vacations growing up, we would go camping as a family, and I loved it. The campsite was between a lake and a beach. We became friends with other families who also came at the same time every year. Some of these friends owned boats, so I was fortunate to go water-skiing. We would also catch prawns with our hand nets, then cook them over a small fire that Dad would light on the beach. These are great memories. My friends and I would spend our time riding our bikes around the campsite and visiting the store every day to purchase sweets and ice creams.

I remember one day riding my bike back with two ice creams in my hands, then realizing I couldn't brake properly because my hands were full. I rode full-bore into a tree! My dad found me with a twisted bike, a very sore head, and ice cream all over myself. He asked me, "Are the ice creams okay?" He was always taking the mickey out of me. He was champion of the dad jokes. I still have the scar from that accident. Dad and I would walk along the beach and up the cliff at the end of the beach to where the oysters were. I couldn't stand slimy, ugly-looking oysters, but Dad loved them, and I loved being with my dad.

Digging Deeper

By the time I reached my twelfth birthday, I had already developed and accumulated many deeply held beliefs about myself and my identity. As I mentioned above, I was rooted in a shame-based identity. I felt a deep shame about who I was. Having been labeled as immature, oversensitive, and the emotionally needy one that caused many problems in the family, I loved from a place of deficit. The labels I had accumulated made me strive incessantly to find dignity through pleasing people. The friendship I had with Jesus gave me a deep stability in the midst of my anxious personality and highly programed shame-based identity during these years, but I would also come to accumulate many spiritual labels.

I wouldn't call my mother a feminist. She had to work for our survival. But neither would I have called her a victim. She took work on and excelled. I still really admire her work ethic. I particularly loved her unbelievable lack of care for what others thought of her. She was a legal assistant and therefore a straight shooter. The black sheep of her family, I saw her as an icon of the times. Because of Mum, I have never had a sense of needing to fight as a woman in my working life, even in my academic career, and I thank her for that.

Psychological Justice

Psychological imprinting begins with how we attach with our significant caregiver (usually the mother) in the first two years of life. I have always had a felt abandonment, and this, I think, may be due to the way I attached to my mother. Having Mum work so many hours so early in my upbringing caused a perpetual state of anxiety, which I tried to replace with idolizing my mother to compensate for her not being at home with me after school.

An anxious (preoccupied) attachment with my mother meant I felt anxious to attach deeper with her. She was an amazing mum, so devoted and kind. She sacrificed her life for us, for me. Yet, I never felt secure. This was not her fault; it is, however, how I attached to her, and you will see how this influenced my decisions and responses to life and to my mother in increasingly destructive ways. Attachment styles form the basis of our attachment to God and our image of God. These early years form the psychological structures for the way we will interact with God, the world, and our self in ensuing years. I had an anxious attachment to my mother, and the consequences and effects this had on my faith development will become obvious as I outline events in my later years. The other attachment styles are secure, avoidant (dismissive or anxious-avoidant), and disorganized (or fearful-avoidant).

Dance also gave my anxious psychological self a core sense of well-being and joy. Dance touched a deep place in me where I felt fully alive. It gave me courage and confidence during these early, anxiety-filled years.

In terms of my identity in Christ (see below), this began with the prophetic word spoken over my life at infancy and was confirmed when I had a personal experience with Jesus at seven years old. My perception of God was blurry, but my relationship with Jesus was very intimate and got me through many painful situations. My relationship with Jesus gave me a sense of security amidst deeply felt psychological abandonment.

You will notice that I use this phrase "identity in Christ" throughout. By this phrase, I mean that because of what Jesus has done for us, this now defines the security we have in our relationship with the Trinity, the most secure attachment that we, on earth, have with another.

What's Your Story?

What attachment style do you think you may have had? Have a think about how that may have impacted your life, your relationships, and the image of God you hold.

Stolen Identity

You know how I talked about having an unremarkable childhood? I look at my teenage years through the eyes of my adult self, and I am alarmed at how I endured so many different types of abuse and somehow categorized them as unremarkable and normal.

The crux of it is that in my early adolescence, my mum started unraveling and as a consequence so did my image of her as my heroine. I came into my twelfth year with a deepening faith but an identity that was quickly destabilizing. I was trying to begin a move to independence from Mum, but I oscillated in my confidence. The following years seemed to compound the shame I was trying to escape, and what identity in God I had left was being repeatedly challenged.

I'll start with the spiritual abuse that I had somehow categorized as my fault. That's perhaps the definition of abuse right there—it is never anyone else's fault. Abuse, by its very nature, is to call blame on the victim. I had been attending a church with my aunty during my childhood. I really enjoyed the children's Bible club and felt at home there. I was developing in my understanding of who Jesus is beyond my friendship with him into more theological spaces. This, along with my already-formed anxious attachment template, meant I was primed for the abuse that transpired.

It was just before I turned twelve, and I was eager for more of God and for more participation in the service. When the pastor offered for people to be prayed for to be baptized in the Spirit, I willingly stepped forward. I didn't even know what this term meant. Three or four adults prayed for me for this experience for quite a while, but whatever was meant to happen didn't. I am sure they were well meaning, but in the light of nothing happening, they then decided that it must be sin in me and started praying for whatever demons were residing in me because of my sin to be bound. When that didn't happen, they informed me that unless I repented of my sin, I would continue to be filled with demons. They left the conversation hanging on that theological precipice. This was replayed in my head as: "We can't help you. God won't help you. We won't help you figure out why God won't help you. You are now cut off from God and us until you help yourself." I was twelve, for goodness' sake. I was already anxious and trying to step deeper into the only attachment relationship I felt secure in, with God, only to be notified that this relationship was no longer secure.

I no longer felt safe. I was alone. I concluded that no one could help me.

The only spiritual experience I had that day was that a deep fracture of abandonment occurred in my faith and an acute fear entered my relationship with God. God went from being a safe place in which I could harbor into a punishing God who at any moment could send me to hell. Hell was a big card that this particular church played to get you fearful enough to give your money, time, and absolute devotion to the church and pastor.

The age of twelve is an important milestone in any child's psychological development as this is where the crux of our identity is solidified, including our image of God. This was an acutely abusive situation and therefore had a critical impact on my relationship with God. As a consequence, I stopped going with my aunty to this church and sought out a church closer to home that I could attend. I was in my first year of high school when I decided I wanted to be baptized. I had grown to the point in my faith where I wanted to commit more deeply to the Lord, but I also wanted to establish boundaries with my mother in terms of my journey with God.

Why, all of a sudden, is Mum in the picture?, you may ask. Mum went through something that prompted her to receive the Lord just before I was baptized. You would think this was a great moment, right? Unfortunately, everything in our home and particularly in my relationship with my mum seemed to get worse after this. Mum's painful religious upbringing and the wounding that came from that came to the fore, needing immediate attention. This started to change the mother I had known. My free and empowering heroine was all of a sudden controlling and demanding. It felt like my relationship with God—that which had been mine—was now being judged by my mother's belief that her understanding of God was superior. This might sound confusing, but it was like I had to choose between whether my faith in God was enough or my mother's relationship with God was more accurate. This impacted me profoundly. I really missed the confident, strong mother I had known. She provided stability in my unpredictable world. Now I felt abandoned by the one who had given me the structure and ability to face a world I had been scarred by. I remember feeling anxious all the time. Her unpredictability caused me even greater insecurity.

I was trying to make tentative steps to solidify my sense of being in God and my identity. However, my mother would constantly plead that I evaluate all I had known in my relationship with God in light of her reestablished theology. This all came to a head one day. We must have been having some sort of family event in our home, and I had stated my belief about something. My mother, in front of everyone, called me out on this and ridiculed me for thinking whatever it was I had just said. I went out onto our back porch and sat frozen on the steps, feeling numb and confused. I was trying to think and reason independently from her, and all I had done was garrison her hold on my desire to separate from her. This moment is etched in my memory as a powerful disincentive to ever voice my opinion in a situation like that again. I felt shut down and unable to reply when she humiliated me among my peers and significant others. This would become a core identity structure that, to some extent, still has a hold on me at certain times. I recognize it playing out in my present more quickly now, but it can still impact me.

Why does any of this matter now? Why is it important to highlight? Because abuse affects us deeply. I had come through an abusive encounter at my aunt's church and had left to find a spiritual home independent from my family. However, my mother's spiritually abusive past was now affecting not only her, but my relationship with her and my relationship with God.

Around the same time, my uncle, who resided in America, came to visit. He was a well-known international pastor and Mum's sisters were all agog with his coming back home. At one family event, my mother got very angry at the way her "heathen" (their words) husband was being treated. After this event, my mother cut herself off from her birth family, and I did not see my cousins again until I was much older. This really hurt, as my younger cousins were my best friends and my aunty was like a mother to me. I would often spend the day with her when I was sick, as Mum was working, so she had become quite an influence in my life. My cousins and I would strategize to get "sick" on the same day so that we could all have a day off together at their house. We would raise our temperatures by sitting right next to the heaters to garrison our deceit. We didn't have internet or mobile phones, so we would spend time creating and building things. Losing my cousins was a huge grief for me that I wasn't really permitted to process.

Losing such an important extended family enforced an already high level of abandonment.

Thankfully, I have great social memories with my father growing up. My dad tried to normalize life and invest some fun into my love tank. I loved watching cricket with him throughout summer in the garage and rugby league with him in the winter. For years, Dad would take me to the V8 races regularly. We would get hot dogs and chips and watch the car derby. It was loud, smelly, and crowded, but I loved it! I am still a massive petrol head to this day. When I turned fifteen, I remember telling Dad I didn't want to go to the races anymore, and I think I broke his heart. His little girl no longer wanted to smell petrol fumes with him. As I got older, my dad started taking me on his work trips during school break. I loved this time with him. We would leave very early in the morning and get sausage rolls for breakfast, stay at lovely motels, and eat delicious roast dinners.

I was terribly afraid of thunderstorms as a child, and thunderstorms in Australia, where I lived, are epic. One day, Dad took me with him and sat me on his lap as a thunderstorm came through our city. He held me and narrated a story that God was ten-pin bowling. When the lightning would strike, he would ask me to count with him until the thunder resounded; we would know if we needed to head inside if it got to one second between the lightning and thunder, as then the storm was too close. He showed me how to manage my fear and emotions, and this led to me feeling safe and brave. To this day, I absolutely love thunderstorms. I always remember sitting with my dad watching the storms and I wish they were more violent and explosive than they are where I presently live.

For all of Dad's good intentions, however, he too was about to betray my trust in him. Another "unremarkable" event happened that, because of my abandonment issues, masked the abusive encounter for what it was.

I was about thirteen, and my dad took me to a campsite for a weekend. We had pitched the tent near the beach, and a couple were camping next to us. Dad and the gentlemen next door would stay up late drinking. Dad got so drunk one night that he took all his clothes off and started running around the beach naked. I sat in the tent in the dark, feeling unsafe and alone, and when I shared with Dad the next morning about what had happened, he feigned ignorance and made a big joke of it. The next night, the same thing happened. Dad's actions affected the safety I had always felt with him. He did not take my voice seriously, and he did not put things in place to keep us safe. I was devastated by the way he made light of what, for me, was a deeply distressing position to be in. This episode in my life created a belief in me that others can silence your voice, and there is nothing you can do about it. The one with whom I should have felt the safest disregarded my dignity and my ability to do something about a situation I felt was dangerous. This added further to the lack of voice I felt with my mother in her treatment of me.

Another time when we went camping, I met a man who told me he had just got out of prison. I told him about Jesus and how he could help him. My dad found me outside the bathroom talking to him, grabbed me by my hair, and dragged me down the middle of the campground to our tent, yelling at me to stop being so stupid. I had no idea what I had done wrong. I was so naive that I had no idea this man was not a safe person. I presume Dad feared my naivete and was trying to make a point with me, but it didn't work because I didn't have a filter for discerning sexual or precarious situations of this type. The events with Dad at the beach the previous year had put paid to that. I wish my father had sat down with me and talked me through what was happening, so I would be able to make better choices in the future. All his actions did was create self-doubt in me and humiliate me in the process.

On the same camping trip, Mum said she wanted to go and get some vegetables in town. It was a Sunday, and I queried her because none of the shops were open, but she insisted. I got in the car with her, and she drove the long road down through the bush that led to the main road. Halfway, she stopped the car and directed me to get out. I had no idea what she was doing. Mum took a belt out and led me to a dense area of bush. She started beating me with the belt. I was too petrified to resist her. This went on for quite a while. We silently walked back to the car, and she drove back to the campground. I had no idea what had just happened, and she never talked about it with me at the time. My heart and mind were swirling in disbelief, and deep trauma took hold. I must have disassociated as the event was so surreal. To this day, I wonder why I even let her hit me. My trust and idolization were now embedded with fear, and I imploded internally. Terror lodged deep within, and we never spoke about it, not even to my father. This event solidified an acute experience of violent assault in my inner being.

It wasn't until writing this book that I suddenly found myself crying uncontrollably while recounting this event. I heard my heart crying out, "How could you beat me? *Why* would you beat me? Why take me, your daughter, to an isolated place, where no one could hear me scream, where no one would see your abuse? Did you really hate me that much?"

I still don't understand why she did that. How could I even think that was okay? Just how devoid of love and hope was I that I would let myself be beaten in the middle of nowhere by my own mother and think it was my fault, and then never tell anyone? Did I have no one I could trust? Was there no one who would have believed me? How on earth did my mother so separate me from reality that I thought I had no one to turn to? That is how abusive people work. They treat you in such a way that they own you. They need to control someone. They need to have some sort of power in their lives. They need to take another person's voice because they have lost their own. The only way they know how to speak is to remove another's ability to do so.

Herein lies why I tell this story. When you get to later chapters and wonder why I do what I do, maybe remember this chapter. I was silenced at fourteen, and everything that happened after this event only makes sense when seen in the light of this violent act against a defenseless and abandoned child.

When people ask why women or men who are abused do not leave their partners, this may be one factor. They think they are less than human, and are treated this way because they believe there is something wrong with them, and they deserve it. I know what it feels like to feel so subhuman that being beaten and threatened physically, sexually, spiritually, and emotionally is because of me. Always my fault.

The tears I have shed writing this section have meant every key struck has tears staining it. I hear myself say to myself, "It is never okay to be abused—ever."

During this time, my older brother became quite protective of me. He tried to include me in his life and take me out with his friends to pick up some of the pieces that it felt like my predatory mother had shaved off of my soul. I walked in such disorientation and confusion. My brother tried so hard to fix me.

People with a shame-based identity are normally strong underneath the smokescreen of shame. Shame distorts and strangles the identity of a person through lies embedded in the soul during the formative years. Jesus knew who I was underneath all my constructs. He saw me. He saw the rose lying beneath the snow. And he sees you.

By the time I left school in 1983, at the age of sixteen, my self-identification had been crucially fractured through these events and experiences. The worst part of it all was that after all my hard work to hold some dignity throughout my high school years, I would betray myself in the following young adult years in order to keep my relationship with my mother intact.

Digging Deeper

In 2017, I would revisit the memory of the camping trip with my dad at the beach. I was sitting in the midst of many others at church, and during the worship, a pictorial memory of myself entered my conscious mind from a deeper place within me. I looked at it for ages trying to ascertain how old I was, where I was, and what I was hiding from (I was in a cupboard hiding, with absolute fear stricken across my face). Every fiber of my being was lost to everything around me as I looked at this younger version of myself. As I watched, the cupboard turned into a tent, and then the full impact of what I was seeing hit me: this was myself in the tent at the beach with my dad. The memories started swirling around me, and I saw myself in that moment. Trust in my father had been uprooted, and I was feeling overwhelmingly abandoned. This event was still raw, impacting me at a very deep level and affecting my lived experience of abandonment. My heavenly Father entered this scene and offered me an opportunity to trust again. I had been asking my Father before this encounter to increase my trust, and he answered by taking me back to the point where trust had been broken. This type of deep change is not only wrought in us by memorizing and declaring the scriptural truth that God is trustworthy. As humans, we function typically from our unconscious memory imprints. If wounds are deep, then solely declaring the truth is not going to pierce the root of the wound so it can be healed.

It wasn't until my mid-thirties that I asked my mother why she had led me to the bush to beat me that day. She said it was because I wasn't eating. I know now I disassociated during this experience of being beaten because years later I would talk about this encounter like a person reading the newspaper. I had no emotion when I would recount the story. I had internalized this abusive situation deep in the core of my being, and it was not until the Holy Spirit came and helped me face this event that deep emotion came to the surface. This is what *psychological justice* looks like to me. It is God going to those deep places and drawing out what is unspoken. I could not have processed this until later, as I would not have had the psychological resources to do so. It was only once I had found my voice with my mother that I was able to go to that place. God's timing to deal with this scenario was full of grace and mercy. It is important not to force people to deal with certain issues until they are ready. You can retraumatize a person if you ask them to heal too soon, or before they have the resources and the people around them to process it well. I love that my Father has done this for me. He has been so faithful to heal me, even where I didn't know I needed it.

I also want to touch on generational legacy a little here. I am not writing to vilify my mother. You may remember in earlier chapters how I talked about how she had been beaten at night when she did not speak in tongues. Her father also beat her mother regularly when he became terminally ill with tuberculosis. I cannot ask you to enter into my story of grief over her beating me without also entering into her story and understanding her fractured life. It is always hard when talking about systemic abuse; that is, abuse that tends to repeat in another generation. Here is the really important bit. The only way to cut off generational abuse is to deal with it properly. Understanding does not mean we sweep it under the carpet of grace. Understanding means we take grace into the very cauldron of abuse and we deal with it at the roots. For me, you will see that the Father has asked me to deal with some really traumatic situations thoroughly. This has been extremely difficult, but I knew that if I didn't fight for my kids by facing the abuse squarely, they might pass on abuse to their children. I forgive my mum thoroughly. Not only because it happened to her, but because I don't want it to happen to my children and their children.

Psychological Justice

Psychologically, many imprints are being formed in the crucial period leading up to adolescence. My mother, whom I had elevated to heroine status in my early years, started to unravel, and my secure—albeit absent—father became a person whom I felt I could no longer trust. I had grown in developing core aspects of my personality, such as enjoyment of dance, V8 cars, and creativity, but had also been affected by anxious spaces of abandonment. My treasured memories of my father were now being replaced by sexual confusion and neglect. The incident of my mother beating me arrested my psychological development. Processing this is how *psychological justice* becomes a lived experience.

Being baptized solidified my acceptance of my identity in Christ. I felt at the time the weight of the decision I was making, and I was committed to living in this new identity even if it meant being displaced by my family. However, this decision came with a host of competing figures for my loyalty. My childhood intimacy with Jesus was affronted by an image of God through a church experience that was painful and frightening. I was a young girl trying to emerge as a woman in her own right, and these conflicts over my identity in Christ only intensified as attacks on my sexuality and loyalties increased. I did not have the psychological resources to navigate these successfully, as I carried a felt abandonment and an insecure self.

What's Your Story?

What "unremarkable" events may have impacted your developing identity in childhood that you may have dismissed? They may hold the key to uncovering fractures in your psyche that are affecting your present.

Losing Hope

As already mentioned, the years of pain and abuse from my mother's past were catching up with her, as they often do when not resolved and heard. She withheld autonomy from me out of her perception that I was too immature to cope with life without her. This resulted in me perceiving myself in the same way. I know this because of the phrases she would use to minimize my voice. I started slowly handing over my freedom to think and reason out life for myself to Mum. I would constantly feel like I didn't have the capacity to make reasoned decisions, even though I have plentiful examples that I was absolutely able to do this. Resources that I needed to develop and mature were diverted to survival and constructing defenses. In psychological terms, I became stuck.

What made this situation harder was that, by this stage, my father was struggling with the fact that my mother was not coping and released the burden of her onto me. He wanted me to carry her emotionally. I could not get Mum upset. He had an absolute angst about me getting upset about anything. For example, one afternoon, Dad was making dinner, as he often did when he was not traveling for work. We had a cute dog named Muppet, and I was chasing him around the house. I came bolting into the kitchen, and the oven door was open. I hit my head on the oven door and it burned my scalp badly. It was unbelievably sore. Dad charged me to quit crying because Mum would be home soon and I better not be crying when she walked in the door. I was not allowed to tell her what had happened. We were having dinner and my scalp was burning. I was in so much pain. I tried so hard not to cry, but it was throbbing. Mum asked why I was crying, and then, well, pretty much all hell broke loose. I know that's blunt, but it absolutely is what happened. I still have the scar to this day.

I was always blamed for Mum getting upset. I felt such a huge burden not to be emotional that it made me more emotional. I was left feeling—and still felt for years—that Mum was the way she was because of me. If I could just not be a child and grow up, everyone would be happy.

You can see how this could enforce the fear that I was a mistake.

I just wanted Dad to intervene and be the safe person he had always been for me. The onus should have been on Dad to support me, not the other way around. But I also understand now my dad's reaction. Mum's behavior was erratic. We never knew when we heard her car come down the road which mother we were going to get. Whatever happened in our day, our world, or even that afternoon all hinged on how Mum was that day. The anxiety of just not knowing was awful.

I was entering adulthood ill equipped. This was my foundation, and, as you will read, events that were to transpire over the coming years were about to see me rapidly lose whatever freedom to think and reason for myself I had left. In the midst of all this, I decided to study typing and shorthand so I could become a secretary in the bank. I found this learning environment difficult, as I was not very socially able to cope with some of the older students. A few made it their ambition to make fun of my naivete. This pops up a lot in my journey.

One day after technical school, I was walking home from the bus stop on a busy road late in the afternoon when a very overweight and drunk man walked past me and grabbed my breast. He then laughed as he walked on. I was sixteen. I felt sick, overwhelmed, and in shock. That walk home was frightening. I felt dirty and exposed and like I was a piece of meat. I was shaking all the way and so numb I couldn't cry. Once home, I couldn't really even voice what had happened at first. I sat there disoriented and trembling. My brother and mother kept asking me what happened. I shakily told them, and immediately my elder brother, twenty at the time, got in his car and went searching for him; he was so angry. I'm actually really grateful, for his sake, that he didn't find him. My mother rang the police, who came and said that in order for them to investigate, I would have to make a formal complaint. I was really scared that if I did this, the man would find me and hurt me even more; and because of this, I didn't file a complaint, but thankfully I never saw that man again.

Around the same time, I was employed at a department store that sold homeware. I was working with a lady who said she was a Christian, and we got on well. She said she had some horses in the country and that she could take me and my friend (who was a horse lover) up there to ride them. We arranged one Saturday to do this. It was very remote, but the horses were beautiful. One of the horses had a foal, and because I was a little nervous about riding horses, I rode the foal. Everything was going really well until we turned to head back to the stables. The foal saw its mother, and we were off. It bolted, and I was petrified! I saw myself falling in a heap but thankfully managed to hold on for dear life and got back to the stable in one piece. I haven't really wanted to ride a horse since. My friend and I were starting to feel a little anxious around this lady, however. She kept saying and doing things that felt creepy. Finally, when she said to me, "Do you want to come wee-wee with me?," my friend looked at me, and we both realized we needed to leave immediately. Making our excuses, she suddenly became very defensive, and it started getting rather scary. This lady was a pedophile, and we had only just realized it. We somehow got to a phone and rang our parents. I have now forgotten how we got home, but once we did, we filed a complaint with the police, and she lost her job.

These traumatic incidents affected me deeply. I already felt stuck in my theological space, and now I was frozen in my identity. My boundaries had been crossed in the most public and degrading way. I didn't even have a chance in either of these situations to escape the person's abusive intentions.

I wouldn't let anyone touch me, hug me, or even sit too close to me. If they did, I would physically recoil. I didn't want to go out. I didn't want to see any of my friends. I didn't trust anyone. I turned inward and found it hard to cope. I somehow walked through that trauma, but it left me with a crevice in my trust toward others. What followed was a couple of months of sexual disorientation. I had just had a man grope me on a main road, and now a lady who claimed to be a Christian had tried to seduce my friend and me.

After this time, I was fortunate enough to start attending a youth group at an Anglican church. The link between this season of healing and my previous season of abuse is important. God's grace brought me into a safe space with safe friends. As I look over my story, over and over, God was stepping into our dance with his grace.

My friends and I had great times together listening to music, traveling, and having adventures. This group was very safe and healthy for me. We all loved Jesus and were all getting our car licenses and enjoying the freedom of independence. I remember one day we all went boating. My friend and I got out to the middle of the lake, and our boat capsized. We were laughing so much we couldn't coordinate ourselves to right the boat. Our friends on the other boats had to come out and rescue us, and we all were in such a state of pleasurable chaos that it took hours to all get back to shore. It was a beautiful, hot summer's day, so no one really cared that it took us so long.

During this year, the climate of my home life became increasingly toxic. Dad had learned how to make his own beer and would store it below the house, under my room. One very hot Australian evening, I was in bed when there was an almighty bang, followed by many other explosions. The beer had over-fermented in the heat. We got up, and all I could hear was Dad swearing that his beer had exploded! Poor Dad had lost it all.

There were other repercussions to Dad's new hobby. Dad's home brew had a high alcohol content and was rather potent. I would get home from college and, before dinner, Dad would be drunk. He would then fondle his private parts as he watched television while I was in the room. This was highly shameful and indelibly built on his previous actions when he was drunk at the campsite a couple of years earlier, which had changed my relationship with him. He had been a safe, fun person before these incidents. It wasn't until I studied psychology that I was able to identify this type of behavior as, in fact, sexually abusive. It had affected my perception of myself and my sense of emerging womanhood.

My mother found this very hard. She had come back to faith only a couple of years before, and now her husband was behaving like this. I am sure this contributed to the disunity and disharmony now protruding into our home. Dad changed a lot when Mum became a Christian. I watched him slowly relinquish his self to my mother. I suspect this was to avoid her rage, as he hated confrontation. He had all these hopes and dreams that her religious fervor had now quashed, as he was not a believer. Some of it was also due to Mum's anger toward his smoking and drinking, particularly when Dad would have coughing fits. I decided to try smoking when I was fifteen and would steal Dad's smokes out of his car, assuming he had no idea I was taking packets at a time. I would go to my room and smoke, thinking I was so cool. One afternoon, Dad caught me smoking, and all he said to me was, "Caught ya!" I spent the rest of the day freaking out that I was going to be in so much trouble. The fact he never talked about it again made me even more scared. I never smoked again from that day forward!

I remember getting ready to go out to the movies with my friends after Mum and Dad had just had a volatile fight, which included crockery and other objects being thrown around the lounge and kitchen and off the balcony. It was close to my seventeenth birthday. I was waiting for the time to leave; Mum was telling Dad to leave, and Dad was refusing. This standoff had lasted several hours, and I left not knowing if Dad was going to be there when I got home. I spent my time at the movies worried about what would happen. When I got home, my father was still there, but now I was put in a position where I felt I had to choose between my father and mother, and either choice would be seen as betrayal by one of them. Because of recent events with my father, and my mother's growing spiritual influence over me in my chronic confusion, I chose Mum. This, I know, hurt my father deeply.

Dad stayed and tried desperately to get things back to the way they were, but the crippling toxicity was now deeply ingrained in our way of being a family.

As events got more precarious, my mother's way of coping was to seek control in her stressful circumstances, using her theology about God to smother my desire to disengage from her. These circumstances led to intensified religious activity on my part, which in turn led me further into deeper levels of control from my mother. For instance, I would obsessively read the Scriptures and would share with Mum what I was learning. She would often point out, out of her own fear, where she believed I was wrong or off track. She became obsessed with the "truth." It is hard to describe what I mean here. It was really unhealthy and bordered on mental illness. It was like she was using Scripture to find a center point because she was spiraling. I kind of get this. We often come back to the Scriptures in an acute way if we are going through a difficult time. But this was different. She was also fearful I would head into what, for her, was dangerous spiritual territory. Yet, through her obsession, she was leading me into deepening canyons, where I was trapped from being able to hear from God for myself.

Now I understand, having researched spiritual abuse, this resembled cult theology. Most cults will have a point of divergence that is obsessive to that cult. It defines what makes that particular cult's line of "truth" unique and "right." There is a term in psychology called "theistic triangulation." It's where a person controls another, or others, through partnership with God. Not literally of course, because our Father doesn't control anyone. But a person who leads a cult or is cult-like or spiritually abusive will often use lines such as, "If you don't agree with me about what God says in his Word, then you don't agree with God, and therefore you are deceived and will be cut off from God." I hear you thinking—"That is a bit extreme. Was your mum really that bad?" In a couple of chapters, you will see that, yes, she really was. I am deeply saddened by this now. I watched as fear took my mother, a beautiful, strong, and free, vibrant woman, and turn her into a narrow version of who I knew her to be.

Her acute disintegration into cult-like behavior meant I felt I was being strangled—not just spiritually, but also physically, emotionally, and mentally. I became preoccupied with Mum's emotional status. We all were. This is all part of the mix of me going deeper into a whirlpool of fear and identity confusion in my relationship with God. I had such a strong sense of who God was all these years—the only truly secure relationship I had up until I was about twelve. Now I felt not only that I didn't know anything, but that what I did know was so obviously wrong, and if I didn't learn the "truth," I was in constant danger of going to hell. During these years, I betrayed the young, confident girl I longed to become, and it would take years for me to find her again.

After technical school, I got a job with a bank as a teller/processor. This was my first foray into full-time work. It was also my first experience of the adult world where bills and responsibilities increased. I enjoyed my job but found it stressful to be a teller in a really busy branch in the heart of the city with everything going on at home. I got my driver's license that year and bought my first car. Getting my license was a major juncture into independence.

I started dating a young man from church. He was the leader of the youth group and very respected. I wish I had listened to the caution in my spirit not to go on that first date, but he was very handsome and was so "spiritual." Oh dear. It was two months of pure hell. It was a very toxic relationship. I remember going to the mall with him one day and feeling hungry. I wanted to buy some food, but he said to me that no girlfriend of his was going to be fat and prevented me from purchasing anything. I only weighed 105 pounds (48 kilograms) at the time. He would often joke with his mates, "I wonder how long this one will last?" They would all laugh and make bets. Well, it lasted two months. The day he decided to break it off was the day that I found out he was dating the lead singer in the church.

I spent the next year recovering from my first relationship and the inevitable fallout from it. I decided I wanted to go on an adventure, so I booked a four-day white-water rafting expedition. I went on my own and drove four hours to where the rafting would begin. It had been raining quite heavily, and we would raft downriver for a couple of hours, stop and eat, then raft again until we stopped to set up camp for the evening. On the fourth day, on the last leg of the journey, we were going to be on the roughest part of the river, where the rapids were extremely fast. There was one part of the morning raft that would take us over a section called "Devil's Cauldron." Yes, the name says it all. The guides in charge of the expedition said it was a grade-5 rapid, which is the highest and most dangerous and is never normally rafted. Usually, they would take the boats out, walk around this section, and enter again further downstream. This time, the guides decided it had rained so much that the water level had risen sufficiently to raft this particular section.

I will just explain why this particular section was a grade 5 before I tell you what happened next. There was a huge boulder that suddenly gave way to a deep and very large crevice underneath. This meant that when the water cascaded over this boulder, it dropped right down and was then sucked back in and up and over again, like a washing machine. Here we were rafting down, and I was on the back, paddling left. The guide had communicated to us that when we got to this section, we were to paddle hard while holding on tight. I was having the time of my life as we jettisoned around the bend, but then the raft hit something, and I went flying into the water. The guide looked like she was about to lose her mind as she screamed for everyone to mobilize quickly and get me back in the raft. I had fallen out at the very top of Devil's Cauldron. They got me back in, and we went over the rapids and headed to an eddy. The guide collapsed in the boat. I did not know until we got to the base at the end of the rafting trip just how close I was to going into the washing machine. I was then told that once someone had fallen in at the same place when the river was not as high; they stayed in the washing machine for twenty-four hours before their body could be retrieved. I do love an adventure!

Can you see a pattern here? There are pockets of shame-laden events, and then here I am participating in courageous activities. It seems like I was two different people; one who was shame-laden—and one who was confident.

By this stage in my life and circumstances, I could not wait to not only leave home but also leave the trauma I had experienced. There were so many grief-laden memories now stored in me that I felt like I was suffocating from the inside out. I wanted desperately to leave the torment of my circumstances and find a new life. Traveling for work to different locations, hours from my upbringing, was an important time as I started to process my faith independently from secure locations and away from my mother.

Digging Deeper

My recollection of events of this season had been quite selective and self-centered. I was obsessed with trying to protect myself. In recent years, I have come to see this more clearly. I felt so guilty when the Lord started healing me and I started seeing the self-protective ways I had behaved. Instead of berating me for this, as I expected God to do, he gently told me to never hate myself for the constructs I had built to ensure my survival. I encourage you with the same wisdom. Be thankful for the constructs that got you through that period of time until you had the emotional and psychological space and resources to step into maturity and build more healthy ways of living. When it's time to let go of your constructs, let them go. When I refer to "constructs," I am meaning those psychological ways of reacting to life's circumstances that we develop to cope with our wounds. For instance, if we have been let down in a relationship with a significant caregiver, we may block any significant person in the future from getting too close.

I would readily take on a scapegoat role in relational difficulties. The scapegoat role is where an emotional, relational event happens, and to diffuse the negative energy in the circumstances, one person will take on the role of the scapegoat, taking the negative energy and carrying it in themselves. Negative energy, in this situation, includes the blame, responsibility, and abuse of the relational breakdown. This happens in order to bring peace to the chaos and confusion about who is right and wrong. Usually, the scapegoat has no idea they are the scapegoat, and they usually have no idea of what is right and wrong or where the fault lies.

Psychological Justice

The events of these years led to the establishment of psychological constructs in me (or the development of dysfunctional ways of surviving) that would enable my mother to gain increasing dominance in our relationship. Where is God's *psychological justice* in this? I see it in the way my Father had established within me a core place where he dwelt. Even though my childhood faith was being smothered, it was deep, and it was real. His presence within me gave me the courage to keep going.

What's Your Story?

What was your role within your family dynamics? What constructs or ways of being did you develop that you would like to revisit?

Season 2

Establishing Independence

This year you will eat what grows by itself, and the second year what springs from that. But in the third year, sow and reap, plant vineyards and eat their fruit. (Isa 37:30)

JUST BEFORE MY TWENTY-FIRST birthday, I was offered a position within the bank that would require me to transfer to Sydney and to undertake legal training to become a lending manager for the Northern Region. I did not know anyone. I was so desperate to start again that none of that mattered. I had to leave. However, I took with me all the labels I had accumulated over the years. I also took the vessel of abuse hidden deep within, which was now full and spilling over. Abuse shuts you down. In his grace and wisdom, my Father knew this. He knew that I would have to move physically to escape systemic abuse. God had been preparing this escape plan for a while. Now I see it so clearly, but back then I was just thankful that I could leave what had become so incredibly suffocating and go to a place where I might just be able to breathe again.

Little did I know when I left home what an adventure awaited me.

I arrived in Sydney broken. I often catch myself thinking that I'm not sure where I would be if I had stayed in Newcastle. I cannot imagine, to be honest. I wasn't escaping as part of a normal psychological progression into independence. I really believe moving to Sydney saved my life. Escaping abuse cannot be minimized to a decision to not be abused anymore. God knew I needed to be physically drawn away. I didn't even know how trapped I was. God had been protecting, loving, and holding me all this time. I am constantly overwhelmed by my Father's intimate knowledge of me and his desire to rescue me.

Sydney became a transitional space. Transitional spaces can be life-giving in times of great change. During my time in Sydney, my Father provided a stable environment that enabled me to feel safe again in his presence. I was flourishing in my work and life. I was the youngest lending manager for the region at the time.

One Sunday, I was walking around Sydney Botanical Gardens and kept having a deep desire to be on a boat. It was the weirdest experience. Operation Mobilization (OM) came to my Anglian church that night to talk about their boat ministry, and particularly the *Logos II*, which was about to be fitted out in Holland. I knew that I knew this was God's direction for me. However, I felt scared at the prospect of entering the mission field. I was afraid I would not measure up and was telling Jesus how I couldn't go to OM, listing all the people and circumstances I knew that proved I was right. Clear as a bell, the Lord gave me the verse Mark 8:29: "'But what about you?' he asked. 'Who do you say I am?'" Oh, that was a hard question. What was I going to do about Jesus?

As I investigated what it would mean to join OM, to board the *Logos II* for two years, I was advised that a sister ship, the *Doulos*, would be in Australia. It was suggested that I take up the offer to undertake a two-month discipleship program to see if it was something I wanted to continue to do. The *Doulos* traveled from Brisbane to Sydney. This was a really formative time. I met some other crazy Jesus-freak believers and felt like I had found my tribe. Everything I had felt and loved on my own with Jesus was now exponentially magnified on a traveling mission ship with four hundred other people. After my eight weeks were finished, I went back to work and told the manager in charge of my traveling schedule that I was resigning from my position as lending manager to join OM for two years. The management tried everything to keep me. They offered me more money. Then they offered me whatever position I wanted. My mind was made up, however, and I could only answer them that Jesus was more important.

I was a little concerned with how leaving my family would affect my parents, and Jesus gave me this word that has been a life principle: "I will deal with the consequences of your obedience to me." This was such a comfort to me then, and has been a very deep comfort for all the hard decisions I have needed to make throughout my journey with Jesus.

As I prepared for the mission field, the Lord gave me this Scripture: "This year you will eat what grows by itself, and the second year what springs from that. But in the third year, sow and reap, plant vineyards and eat their fruit" (Isa 37:30). I was not sure what this meant at the time, but later I would understand that my Father was going to bring about a shift that would mark a delineation line between my past and my future.

The Great Escape

On January 18, 1990, at the age of twenty-three, I boarded an airplane with two Australian guys bound for OM Germany via Rome. This date marks probably the most momentous day for so many pivotal shifts in my life. I left Australia on this day, and as you read, you will see how many other significant events would occur on this date. That tells me something about the character of my Father right there. I had never been on an airplane before, so I was very excited.

This would be a season of great friendships, fun and adventure, and knowing and being held in the hands of grace. When my new friends and I landed in Rome, we had four hours before our next flight to Germany. One of the guys I was with said, "Let's hire a taxi and go see some sights." My dad had instilled in me a love for travel and adventure, so I was all in! That taxi ride into Rome was the most hilarious and scariest of my life. The driver was dodging and weaving through the traffic, screeching tires like a crazed maniac! He took us to all the main sites in the city of Rome. This was my first taste of another country. Coming from Australia, I had never seen anything over two hundred years old. Entering the Colosseum was breathtaking. Walking around these ancient ruins in the middle of a bustling city exploded my sense of being in the world. These ruins are over two thousand years old, and I was walking around looking at the stadium in awe. We then went to St. Peter's Basilica; I'd never seen anything like it. (As an aside, in years to come, I would become passionate about researching first-century Rome.) The driver then sped us back to the airport. It was like a scene in the television show *The Amazing Race*. We arrived in time to hear our names over the loudspeakers, saying the airplane was waiting for us. We ran like mad people to the boarding area and just made it. So much fun!

We flew into Frankfurt and then were driven to Mosbach. My mind and senses were overwhelmed with joy at the architecture and history I saw as we drove to our destination. I slept for a long time once I got to our accommodation, and woke up quite disoriented. I stayed in Mosbach for orientation for two weeks. I got to know some of the locals and enjoyed many walks through cobblestone streets lined with beautiful Tudor houses. It was magical. I did get quite a sore stomach, though, as I was not used to the dense German bread!

God had a surprise for me in Mosbach. I had traveled all this way believing I was heading for two years on the ship *Logos II*. However, the leadership came to me and asked if I would go to Zaventem, Belgium, instead, as they needed a bookkeeper in their head office. I said goodbye to the new friends I had made and left for Belgium. I had been dreaming of going to Spain as much as I had going to Africa. It felt like such a loss at the time.

The head office in Zaventem, Belgium, was close to the Brussels airport. The base was filled with mainly office staff and mechanics, as they serviced all the transit vans for the "Love Europe" outreaches that were huge back in the early nineties. We had at least fifteen different nationalities on base, and we had people traveling through all the time. I was in charge of booking accommodation for guests. I organized their travel and did the bookkeeping for the base. This year in Europe was the first year my Father said I would eat "what grows by itself" (Isa 37:30).

I traveled home on my own for a brief hiatus, returning to Germany via Brussels to join another group heading to *Logos II*, which was now in Sierra Leone, Africa. Again, I cannot believe now how I traveled to so many places on my own. I often think of the duality of believing my label as weak and immature alongside with my actions, which seemed to defy those labels. We boarded an airplane and traveled for what seemed like forever, and then I saw the plains of Africa beneath me. My poor new friends on that airplane—I shrieked and yelled as I was so excited to finally be there. It was beautiful. My friend Louis, sitting next to me, had a sore arm for a while as I kept hitting him in my excitement.

We landed at what was not an airport but a crude runway. Our luggage was literally thrown out of the airplane. Somehow one of the team managed to catch a friend's musical instrument midflight and saved it from being destroyed. I was not ready for what awaited me in Sierra Leone. It is one of the poorest nations in Africa, and at the time a devastating civil war was an ongoing crisis. We got on a bus to go to the port, and the entire way there, little children would crowd the bus as it moved, begging for food. In all my travels until then, I had never felt fear. But I was frightened. I was completely caught off guard. I had no framework or past experience to place this cultural tragedy.

Once we got to the boat, the crew had to protect us and our luggage to get us on board safely. All these beautiful, hungry eyes, desperately shouting for help, was heartbreaking. Many of us were traumatized, and I found I couldn't leave the boat for the first week as I was in profound cultural shock. One of the female leaders came and helped me talk through the theological angst and the extreme guilt I had of being rich, i.e., from the West and white. She was very helpful, and I was able to continue on by accepting that I was in my Father's hands and I could make a difference by being there, even if it was just to a handful of people. The cultural divide was immense, but I started getting more involved.

I had seen pictures of poverty; however, looking directly into the eyes of suffering is another thing. I can never forget the smell of sewage running down the streets and children washing and playing in it. I cannot forget. I was working in the little café at the end of the ship, and one night had two grown men fight over the rubbish bag I was trying to take to the rubbish collection. Thankfully, one of the deck crew on watch came to my aid. I couldn't understand why they were fighting over this bag. I was told later it was because they could sell not only the bag for money but also the used cups inside. This was beyond comprehension to me. How do I go from signing off million-dollar loans in the bank for my job to looking into the eyes of a desperate little child?

Slowly I adapted, and I made some lovely friends in Sierra Leone. I enjoyed the full-on Pentecostal church I was privileged to attend. "Africa time" is real. We were ready on the boat to leave for this church service at ten o'clock in the morning and waited and waited, until finally someone arrived at one o'clock in the afternoon or so to take us.

After years of dreaming in Sydney, we were setting sail. It was with an incredible sense of joy that I had waited, and now here I was. Our itinerary would include traveling along the West African coastline, then crossing the Atlantic to travel along the South American coast.

Life on board the *Logos II* was always busy, with loads of opportunities to have fun while ministering. I was introduced to a card game called Dutch Blitz. This game is fast and furious, and we were addicted to it. A group of us would gather in the dining area most nights to enjoy a stressful but always fun game.

I was lucky enough to go deep into the bush with a team in Equatorial Guinea. The area we were going to had not seen people from another culture for four hundred years. We were deep in the heart of the bush, and it was beautiful. I had an amazing experience and loved the people there. I had been taking anti-malaria tablets, but they were ineffective in this area and once back on ship, I developed cerebral malaria. I and a few others on board started hallucinating our worst fears, and had very high temperatures and extremely severe headaches. I was very sick for quite a while and could not leave my cabin.

After six months in Africa, we set sail for South America. We sailed into Recife, Brazil, and I fell in love. I felt I had found home. The people were so like me—lots of talking and hand movements and so excitable!

We spent six months traveling the coast of Brazil, then Argentina, where we left to sail through the Straits of Magellan to Chile. The voyage took us through some of the most violent seas as we entered the Straits. The ship rolled from side to side and up and down, and many of the crew became very sick. They had tied all the chairs and anything moveable down as much as possible, especially in the dining room, but it was so bad that most of them toppled over and slid with the movement of the boat. I was working in the laundry at the very front of the ship at the time, which is the worst place you want to be if you are not on the deck. I was lucky enough to never get seasick, but it was rough. I loved standing on the front of the bow and took sheer delight in the adventure of a lifetime. The Straits of Magellan were majestic. The ship route was very narrow at some points, and the ship had to slow right down to navigate some of the sections. The sheer mountains were covered in snow and were very close to the edges of the Straits. It was a magical adventure. The memories are seared in my heart.

We arrived in Chile in summer but it was bitterly cold. I had Christmas in Porte Monte. This was my last port, so it was a very sad time, leaving my new "family." I had made some incredibly close friendships with the group that I had joined with, and a lot of us are still very close to this day. This year on *Logos II* was the second year the Father said I would eat "what springs" from my first year (Isa 37:30).

After a culturally mind-blowing year, I flew back to Australia in January 1992. My journey took twenty-six hours, as I had to take a very long bus ride to Santiago before flying to Australia via a short stopover in New Zealand.

Once home, I wondered what I should do next. I knew I could not stay in Australia, as it no longer felt like home. The Lord spoke to me to wait a week and I would know what the next step would be. A week later, as the Lord had said would happen, I got a call from the New Zealand manager of OM, asking if I would like to move to New Zealand to work with them. "New Zealand?" I thought. I wanted to go to the streets of South America and be a "real" missionary. Anyway, the long and short of it was: I recognized this was the Lord's leading.

So, my next stage would be to move to New Zealand. This was a very difficult year for me and for those I lived with. I was experiencing re-entry culture shock and felt I had no escape route. The New Zealand office was different to the ship ministry. I had lost all my new friends and the buzz of the constant energy on the ship. I was very lonely. Thankfully, some of my *Logos II* friends lived in New Zealand and I was able to begin forming what have proved to be lifelong, stable relationships.

The Lord was so clear in his direction in many of these junctures, considering how fractured I was psychologically at the time. His faithfulness astounds me. Transition times are very painful, however, and leaving OM after my placement was finished was difficult. I felt strongly that I wanted stay in New Zealand, but I was twenty-six and had nowhere to live, no money, and no plans. I decided it was time to go back to Australia. That same day, out of the blue, a past teacher at the Bible College of New Zealand (BCNZ would later be named Laidlaw) told me of a job. It was a temporary secretarial position for three months to cover for someone on vacation. I applied and got the job and, well, that was it really. I didn't know at the time that moving to the Bible college would solidify New Zealand as my home for over twenty years. This move signified the completion of the promise from the Lord that in three years I would be sowing and reaping in a new place (Isa 37:30). Time to plant and settle down.

After temping at BCNZ/Laidlaw and then temping in the corporate world, I was offered the position of receptionist at the Bible college. A few weeks into living on campus, a friend organized a party, and there I met a group of people who would become my lifelong friends. Many of us were ex-missionaries or in ministry. One, in particular, was my friend Jacqui. She had just come back from Youth with a Mission (YWAM) in London. I had just finished OM, and we were both trying to settle and create a new life in New Zealand. We both needed to find a place to live, so we decided to flat together and found a nice home. To this day, she is still one of my closest friends. I met another man in this time, who would become my husband. John and I had met on the *Logos II* in Africa, but we never really talked on the ship. All this happened because my friend Ruth decided to have a party. Ruth would also become a close friend. She was working for an evangelistic youth ministry at the time. We have woven in and out of each other's lives over the past twenty-six years. As you will see in my continuing story, my new friends and I would experience many challenges and heartaches together.

Digging Deeper

Leaving Australia and traveling the world was a very important time for me. As I have already said, OM became a critical transitional space as I left my network of the familiar in Australia. Our Father knows there are times when we need to physically move from environments, places, or people that will keep us lodged in time. For me, leaving Australia marked the beginning of finding my voice and my relationship with God again, and ultimately finding healing. I spent two years with OM overseas and one year with OM in New Zealand. In psychological terms, transitional spaces, people, and places are important in the processing of deep wounding.

God also gave me transitional mothers during these years, who precipitated a shift away from the controlling dominance I had felt from my own mother. I grew in confidence as I traveled and navigated new cultures and situations. I found that the places my feet could walk were broader and more life-giving than those I had known and left behind. I hadn't realized until I left Australia how imprisoned and trapped within my circumstances I had been.

On the *Logos II*, we lived and worked together in close proximity, and inevitably people's past would come up in conflicts or cultural values. However, the deep friendships we were all able to foster are still strong today. There were many tears and much laughter together. Experiencing the world on a ship was the most life-infilling experience of my life.

It was important for me to visit other cultures, for my eyes to be opened to see the world that Jesus died for. Traveling so extensively was an explosion of sights, smells and history that changed me. To experience so much in such a limited time marked me. I had to face other ways of thinking and seeing the world and experiences that transported me from a young girl living nescient in my cultural space to finding my place in the world.

The world has become increasingly global in the last thirty years. When I left for OM, there were no cell phones or computers to keep in touch with family or friends when we were away. Once we left our country of origin, we only had communication through letters—real mail. When the bags of mail were delivered to the ship, everyone would congregate to wait for their mail. It was devastating for some who did not get much or any mail. Not having contact and traveling extensively meant I was really free to experience life on my own.

The next transition was to build a new life in New Zealand. This would prove very difficult for the first year, but moving to Bible college was another crucial shift in my psychological processing. God surrounded me with a huge new family, with friends who were also learning how to come home from mission, and with wonderful spiritual mothers and fathers who helped instigate the massive shift that needed to take place in myself in order for me to truly be set free. These relationships, like those from being on mission, are still as strong and valuable today as when they were forged.

Psychological Justice

Coming to New Zealand after being overseas was very hard in the beginning. I did not know many people and had just been through such an exhilarating couple of years overseas. I was faced again with my disabled experience of my identity in Christ and was suffering with an acute sense of cultural displacement. There is a mixed cultural response given to Australians living in New Zealand, and I found this very confronting after being in such an accepting multicultural environment. I have still not found a way to deal with this beyond how I dealt with it then, which was to try and stifle as much of my cultural identity as possible. I changed the way I said certain phrases, as these would cause many conflicts and humiliating moments for me. I tried to tone down how loud I was, which sometimes made things worse. All these adaptations had a significant effect on my psychological self. However, once I moved to West Auckland, my confidence began to increase. Being at Bible college significantly affected my apprehension of my identity in Christ, as I was now in a more stable environment where my theological studies started to solidify my identity in God to an increasingly secure place. *Psychological justice* can be seen in the way my Father was starting to cultivate a confidence within me to interpret the Scriptures for myself, beyond my mother's theological framework.

The significant relationships that were being formed also meant I was able to start processing some of the control and trauma of my past. Being so far away from my homeland enabled me to have the psychological space I needed to explore my developmental dysfunctions. My relationship with John gave me the security to face my family, as I now belonged to someone significantly able to help me do so. *Psychological justice* recognizes the need to have secure places where a person can deconstruct those ways of being that are rooted in wounded imprints from our past.

A common pattern is emerging as we navigate my journey. I thrive wherever I am valued and loved for who I am. Where I feel I am labeled, which induces shame, I digress to the labels of my teenage years and the ones I am presently given.

What's Your Story?

When has God brought you into transitional spaces or given you transitional people? What labels do you think you may have accumulated in your journey? Have a think about how they developed, so that you may be able to process these.

A New Family Is Forged

In 1994, at age twenty-seven, I visited Australia with John. Our time together in Australia was amazing, but the time with my family was tense. My mother did not seem to like John from the outset.

John and I love processing life deeply. We spent time in our courtship beginning to explore our past and preparing for marriage. It was very exciting but at times deeply confronting. The trauma we had both encountered growing up resulted in many fiery exchanges and difficulty in communicating. We were the best of friends, and our friendship deepened as we had found in each other a soulmate who understood what it was like to grow up in a dysfunctional family. Because of this, we had then and still have a deep need for Jesus. Our courtship was a fun-filled, fiery, and spirited adventure.

John and I could have rigorous debates over almost any topic, and I found these really interesting. This would prove helpful as it meant he wasn't afraid to help me deal with the huge complexities I would have to process with my birth family. God knew I needed someone strong and resilient like John to get through what we have gone through. I am amazed that with all we have had to endure, we celebrated twenty-six years of marriage this year. It also solidifies why the Lord led me to stay in New Zealand in 1993 when I had no job, no money, and no place to stay. He knew I would still be here thirty years later.

After dating for four years, John and I married on January 18, 1997. I was thirty and he was thirty-four. We had a beautiful wedding. After our honeymoon, I started studying full-time at BCNZ/Laidlaw toward a Bachelor of Ministries degree, after doing a few courses before getting married. However, three months into our marriage, I discovered I was pregnant. I was so stunned. The pregnancy went well, and I continued to enjoy my studies.

Jessica was born in the early months of the following year. I found my rhythm and really enjoyed Jessica. Three months after Jessica was born, I found out I was pregnant again. I rang John at work to tell him, and his receptionist said he just went white! I must admit, I was a bit taken aback myself. I was studying part-time again at Bible college, and it was a great place both to have a child and to be with child.

However, I started having some major problems during my pregnancy. I had placenta previa, where the placenta lies very low in the uterus and can rupture and terminate the pregnancy. I was bleeding on and off and was ordered by the doctor to have bed rest for two months. I did not have family in New Zealand, but the people in the church we attended were amazing. Community is so very important. They made rosters for dinners and cleaning. Another friend did my laundry and ironing, and another the vacuuming. I was really anxious and would go to the bathroom incessantly to see if I had bled anymore. Each time I would cry and think about what I had done that day that may have made it worse. I would go to the scans on my own, not really sure how to process what I was told. I don't think I really understood much of what was said, as all I kept hearing was that there was a significant risk I could lose my baby. Resting is really hard for me when I am going through something difficult. My first response to stress is to clean. To not be able to physically process my pain and stress was really, really hard. Sitting or lying down with a heap of time to think, while also trying to look after Jessica, was intense. However, I think Jessica and I bonded over this time as well. Not being busy meant I spent a lot of time with her. She would need that for what was to come.

During this time, I kept getting Scriptures similar to this one saying, "The firstborn belongs to the Lord" (Exod 13:2; 34:19). I was clueless as to what God was saying through these Scriptures. I concluded it meant that I was having a boy and that he belonged to the Lord. I really had no idea what this meant.

I also had a dream where I was on the high cliffs above a popular West Auckland beach called Piha. In the dream, I peered through a hole in the sky from what seemed like another dimension and watched below as Jessica was running along the beach with a bright blonde-haired little boy following her. From this dream, I was convinced I was seeing the baby I was carrying, so I chose the name Michael, after the archangel Michael, who watches over and protects God's sons and daughters in the book of Daniel. When I gave birth, we were so surprised the baby was a girl that we didn't have a name for her for six weeks. We finally settled on Kristiana, meaning "daughter of Christ." Little did I know how prophetic that would turn out to be. The little bright blonde-haired boy—well, I was seeing into the future at my little boy Joseph. This dream came true one day when Joseph was about two years old, and I shuddered when I witnessed it. The Lord gives me prophetic dreams of the future because they are signs and symbols of his active involvement in my life and the lives of my children. They are always declaring the reality of what is to come, so I can have assurance that somehow, in the midst of chaos, he is in control, and he sees what I cannot. He has trained me to know and listen and sit with these dreams and the prophetic, and increasingly, I would see them for others.

Digging Deeper

Years later, I would come across the verse Mark 1:10, "Just as Jesus was coming up out of the water, he saw heaven being torn open and the Spirit descending on him like a dove." That is what I felt I had seen; that heaven had been torn open as I looked into the future. The same idea is in Acts 7:56, "'Look,' he said, 'I see heaven open and the Son of Man standing at the right hand of God,'" and Ezekiel 1:1, "In my thirtieth year, in the fourth month on the fifth day, while I was among the exiles by the Kebar River, the heavens were opened and I saw visions of God." These verses comforted me that my Father had opened the heavens for me to witness the future, so that I could have assurance that he knew what was coming and would be with me.

What was the Father saying about the firstborn belonging to him? Sometimes, it seems, the Father talks in riddles. It can be years sometimes before I see what he is saying in the present. I have learned to wait on him and hide these impressions or Scriptures in my heart. He always reveals himself eventually. This phrase will make sense in the next chapter.

What this means for my walk with my Father is that I can trace his hand. Our Father's thoughts and actions toward us are not random. They are meaningful, a sign that he is fully invested. Whenever things feel out of control and the word he gives sometimes makes it more confusing, I know that it will only strengthen our connection. The Trinity is so actively involved in my life, and I do not take that for granted. His riddles are incredibly meaningful.

Psychological Justice

After coming to faith, marrying John was probably the most significant shift in my theological and psychological development. John is strong enough in his own person to handle all the processing my psychological past would require. He helped me start recognizing some of the abuse associated with my mother.

Another significant event was forming solid and enduring friendships during this time, relationships that would survive all that was about to happen in our lives. These friends have been loyal and faithful through all our trials, have helped shape in me a deeper, more secure identity in Christ, and have given me the courage to see my Father's *psychological justice* wrought deeply in our circumstances.

What's Your Story?

What prophetic dreams are you holding? Don't let go of them just because they seem like riddles right now. Like Mary, learn to hide them in your heart and let them strengthen your present. See them as deposits of hope.

Season 3

The Prolonged War

"Many waters cannot quench love; rivers cannot sweep it away. If one were to give all the wealth of one's house for love, it would be utterly scorned."
(Song 8:7)

As THE TITLE SUGGESTS, my Father began to increase dreams and visions in my walk. Patterns started emerging as he started training me to hear his voice. These dreams and visions were often pre-empting what was coming, but not specifically. They were deposits that, when brought together, would make sense of really difficult circumstances, clues almost to understand that he was manifestly involved in my world and cared deeply for me.

After such a joyful year with Jessica and a successful resting period to carry my baby to full term, there was much excitement and anticipation over her birth. We felt we had been given a miracle in that her growth and health were strong.

However, I was about to enter a prolonged period of darkness. My faith and heart would be wrenched in ways that I can't believe I endured. I sank to the deepest depths that I had ever been to. All that I had gone through in my childhood would, in this season, reveal the broken and fractured images of God I had accumulated. God's faithfulness held me. There are glimpses of his intervention and intimate revelations that would enable me to see his hand. However, there were many, many nights and days that darkness was my closest friend and companion. My dark night of the soul, my Gethsemane, was just around the corner.

The Great Sadness

I gave birth to Kristiana on March 31, 1999, at the age of thirty-two. Frighteningly, the umbilical cord was wrapped around her neck twice. Jacqui told me years later that Kristiana was blue and took a while to breathe. I was so relieved at the time that Kristiana was born on March 31 because I was fearful she would be born on April 1—April Fool's Day.

Krissy was born with really thick jet-black hair. There was so much of it. She had the deepest blue eyes that would melt your heart. She loved being social and spending time with Jessica. I have some beautiful photos of Jessica and Krissy together playing on a mat. She had a few ingrown toenails that would give her a lot of pain. I remember she loved making lots of noises, so I thought to myself that she was going to be a real talker and in the center of any social gathering. She reminded me a lot of myself. When I saw pictures of her and myself as babies, side by side, the resemblance was astounding. John remembers that she loved drinking from her bottle and would guzzle the milk really quickly. We had to change the teats on the bottle to try and help slow down the flow of milk.

After Krissy was born, I was not coping as well as I had done with Jessica. Jessica was only thirteen months old, and I was concerned I had postnatal depression. John decided that I might just need a weekend away at a retreat, but I didn't feel any better when I got home.

As the weeks went on, I started feeling worse. I was getting intense pain down my right side. It felt like the pain was radiating from my womb. I went to and from doctors for weeks as I had kidney infections, but they wouldn't resolve. Eventually, I ended up at the hospital in agony. The doctors who assessed me were focused on my womb because I had just given birth, but the tests they performed came back normal.

The doctor wanted to send me home with antidepressants after nothing abnormal showed up in the X-rays they had taken. I was in so much pain, and again felt like my ability to voice what I was going through was not being heard. As I went to bed that night, alone in the hospital without my baby girl, I cried out to my Father to please show me what was wrong. He answered me, "It's your kidneys. Get them to check your kidneys when they do the ultrasound in the morning." I had never had a problem with my kidneys, so I was not sure why the Lord would say this. However, the next morning, as the sonographer did the ultrasound, I asked her to check them. Sonographers are normally not allowed to do anything other than what the doctor has requested, but I insisted, and thank goodness she did. The next minute, there was a flurry of doctors looking at the screen. My right kidney was more than twice its size; given a couple of more weeks, it would have burst and could have resulted in loss of kidney function, sepsis, or death if not picked up in time. God, in his faithfulness to me, intervened in a personal and direct way by telling me specifically what was wrong, and this saved my life.

The doctors organized an urgent contrast X-ray and saw the magnitude of the problem. They said to me, "You must be in agony." I said I was, but because I wasn't screaming in pain, they had previously believed I had been exaggerating. The problem with my right kidney was significant, as there was a complete blockage in my urinary tract (which links the kidney to the bladder). It was like a kink that twists a hose, and the official diagnosis I was given was a PUJ (pelvic ureteric junction) obstruction that needed an operation called a pyeloplasty. If I had gone home from that hospital without this diagnosis and without further intervention, I would have been in dire trouble.

I was transferred to Auckland Hospital and, while waiting in the emergency ward, my friends Ruth and Nicky came in. Nicky had been looking after Krissy and brought her to the hospital for me. Krissy was hungry and wanted me to feed her, but I couldn't as my breast milk had dried up. My friend Ruth said she could breastfeed Krissy as she had a baby at the time, but I recoiled at the suggestion because I wanted to be providing for my daughter. It was chaotic, painful, and debilitating on so many levels. As a mother, I felt like an absolute failure. I felt helpless and unable to care for her when she was taken from me as I underwent yet another test. I didn't know who was caring for Jessica and Krissy at any given time, as John was still trying to keep up with work. I can't imagine what Jessica and Krissy must have felt. The people looking after them were so beautiful and motherly, but I am sure that not knowing where I was or what was happening must have been disorientating and painful for them. The faithfulness of my friends Ruth and Nicky at this point amazes me. They both had young babies of their own, and here they were, traveling all over Auckland with my babies to help me.

After finally getting a diagnosis, I was discharged. When I got home, I rang my mother and father to ask if they could travel over from Australia to help us. Jessica was only fourteen months old, and I couldn't look after both the children and have surgery. Thankfully, they said they would and came within a couple of days. This was a massive thing for my parents, as they were getting older and did not have a lot of money saved. John had a rental house across the road, and a friend and I prepared it for their arrival. I went into hospital a couple of days later. John dropped me off and went to work. I sat there alone, feeling very nervous about the surgery.

The surgery took six hours. It took some time to come out of the anesthetic, and when I did, I was extremely cold and shaking. The ureter going from my kidney to my bladder was completely kinked, and the surgeons had to remove that section and insert a stent. Recovery was really, really traumatic. I had a tube draining the surgical site and an epidural portal in my spine. I was in constant pain and very nauseous for many days. Mum and Dad would bring Kristiana and Jessica in to see me, but I was too disoriented to hug or even acknowledge them most times.

About four days after my kidney surgery, I was complaining to the nurses about how sore the epidural site was. They said it was normal for it to be a bit sore, but I started vomiting profusely. They tried all sorts of anti-nausea medications, but none of them helped. I started getting some seriously strange and problematic neurological symptoms. John came in with the girls, and I was in and out of consciousness and feeling completely out of my body. I overheard the leading doctor tell the nurses to watch me for any further decline in my neurological symptoms. It transpired that I had bacterial spinal meningitis. This was a very serious situation, and my life was in real danger. I felt so much fear and knew I was in serious trouble. John left me, feeling extremely worried, and went straight to our church. He found the elders and a few others at an engagement party and pulled them aside to pray for me. At the exact time they prayed, my symptoms suddenly ceased, and I started feeling more in control. There was palpable relief at the hospital amongst the nurses and doctors.

I got home after day seven, but I was still very sick and recovering. My kidney site became infected and I needed a nurse to come every day to wash and dress it. Around day nine, I started feeling better and said to myself, "I feel like I am ready to enjoy looking after Krissy." I remember standing at the changing table changing Krissy and her cooing at me. This would become a really special memory. My mum said to me, "She remembers you."

We moved the furniture around a bit so I could get more comfortable. During the course of the day, the Lord kept saying to me that I needed to do what the Scriptures instructed and leave my mother and father. I shared this with my mum, as I really had no clue what the Lord was trying to say and wondered if my mum may have some insight.

The next day, Krissy was not well. She was having terrible coughing fits and sometimes would stop breathing. She had done this a few times after she was born, and the midwife was concerned enough at one point to arrange for Krissy to see a medical specialist. He monitored her for a short time but surmised it was not serious enough to warrant more attention, and Krissy was discharged from the hospital system.

At dinner, I fed her with a bottle, but she was not settling. My dad tried to walk around with her to try and comfort her and see if she needed burping, but she continued to cry. I tried holding her for a while, and then

John tried. We all decided maybe it was better to put her down and see if she was just overtired and needed to sleep. After a brief period of crying, she stopped. We all believed she had finally got worn out and fallen asleep. Mum and Dad walked back to their dwelling across the road. John went in to check on her ten minutes later and screamed in terror, "She is not breathing! Ring an ambulance!"

In my limited capacity to function, I rang the ambulance—heart pounding, fear throbbing every part of my being. I was shaking uncontrollably and found it difficult to dial the numbers for an ambulance. The operator on the end of the phone tried to assure me that the ambulance was on the way. I kept shouting into the phone that Krissy was not breathing and screaming, "Why are you taking so long!" I went in to see John, and he was desperately trying to resuscitate her. He yelled out to me, "Ring people to pray!" I phoned my friend Ruth and asked her to phone others. She arrived not long after I rang her.

I waited at the end of our very long driveway, trembling, walking up and down helplessly, and desperately looking for the ambulance to arrive. Minutes felt like hours as John tried to resuscitate Krissy in the house. The ambulance arrived, and I screamed to the paramedics, "Krissy is not breathing! Please hurry!" They tried to assure me she would be okay and calmly collected their medical supplies from the back of the ambulance. I was really agitated by their seemingly slow pace.

The paramedics came in, and we watched as they tried for ten minutes to resuscitate Krissy. As this was happening, I felt the Lord ask me to let her go. Just as the Lord said this, I could see she was gone, and I released her to Jesus. As I did, the paramedics handed her to me and said, "There is nothing more we can do. We are so sorry." Out of my spirit sprang forth the hymn, "The steadfast love of the Lord never ceases; his mercies never come to an end. They are new every morning, new every morning; great is thy faithfulness, O Lord, great is thy faithfulness."[1] I am not sure why that song, and why then, but it cascaded out of me like a river. It was like my Father, Jesus, and the Holy Spirit were enveloping her and me in that moment of holy exchange. In the song was the promise of my Father's mercy and faithfulness. This is a strong and enduring theme in my walk and dance with my Father; that no matter what I have faced, the beautiful Trinity has been enduringly faithful to me.

In the time it took for the ambulance to come, the elders of our church had arrived and were sitting in the lounge. My friend Ruth came into Krissy's bedroom, and as I sang of the Lord's faithfulness through violent tears,

1. "The Steadfast Love of the Lord Never Ceases," written by Edith McNeill.

Ruth joined me. The ambulance officers indicated to me that a funeral home would need to take Krissy from me and would arrive soon. My first thought was that I wanted to change her nappy and put my favorite clothes on her before they came. My faithful friend helped me do that. I was still in that moment clinging to being her mum. I needed to love her and care for her even though she was no longer with me.

I then took her into our lounge room. John had gone over to get my mum and dad. We handed Krissy around the room so everyone could say goodbye in their own way. The police arrived as we did this. They had come to make sure there was no foul play. When they were satisfied that it was a terrible accident, they left us to it.

The person from the funeral home arrived and laid Krissy in a black bag and zipped it up with her inside. I am finding it hard to describe in words what this moment was like. Inside my head, I was screaming, "She is not going to be able to breathe! She will suffocate!" They then silently left and took her away to be autopsied.

Shock. Silence.

Emptiness filled the room.

We then had to tell our sixteen-month-old daughter, Jessica, that her sister had died and was now with Jesus. She had only just played with her a couple of hours before. My poor parents were in deep shock. They had spent so much time caring for Krissy and loving her while I was in hospital and once I was home recovering. John and I just wept, our minds scrambling to process the reality and trauma we had just experienced. Krissy was gone, taken away in a zipped-up black bag like a piece of luggage. The room was filled with shock and deep grief. One by one, people left, and Mum and Dad went back to the house across the road. I am not sure how we slept that night, or if we even did. Over and over our minds replayed the evening's events. There are no words that can describe such a wide range of emotions that bellowed and tumbled over and over us, like a tornado that keeps whipping up the debris and funneling it toward another rotation of an alternate reality. We wanted the tornado to cease and all to be calm again. Normal no longer existed, as it had been swallowed up into a vortex of chaos. How does one go to bed like normal when one has just witnessed their baby die? What did she die from? Why are we even going to bed? Could I ever go to bed and sleep again? My house had one room empty. There would be no getting up during the night to feed Krissy, or to settle her, or to cuddle her ever again. How does one do normal when it is everything but? Questions swirled in and out like a violent storm.

The next day came, and with it cards and flowers. Many visitors. Many tears. We tried to figure out Krissy's funeral arrangements and what songs we wanted and what order; it was so overwhelming, but necessary. Little Jessica was walking around in the flurry of activity, hearing and witnessing all the tears and wondering where her sister was. I remember hating the flowers as they reminded me of beauty and happiness, and this definitely was not a beautiful or happy time. I wanted to throw them out, but I knew people had given them out of love.

On the days leading up to the funeral, the district nurse would come to the house to dress my kidney wound. I remember, on the day of the funeral, the nurse came to clean the surgical site in the morning, and I told her that I was burying my daughter in a couple of hours. It was so surreal. I suddenly had a desperate need to get photos printed and a memory book. I was trying to clasp on to anything I could from the little time I had spent with her because of my illness. I didn't have many as I had been in and out of hospital. Thankfully, friends had taken some photos of her, and these photos became precious to me.

I remember feeling so traumatized and vulnerable as I went shopping for things and wished in those early days that I could wear black so that people in public would know I was grieving and be kind and compassionate to me. I reflected later that someone should market little black bands or something simple around the wrist to signify to others that this person is in grief. Trying to do normal things in those first few weeks was extremely difficult.

The worst feeling was that I still had a mother's instinct to look after Krissy, but she wasn't there to mother. Jessica was so small, and there was so much grief surrounding her. I hate to say I am not even sure I noticed her sometimes in the blur. I know grief was filling my soul, and I know, in hindsight, it was what it was, but it has left its scars on us both, even though the Lord's healing is present and continual.

I went to see Krissy at the funeral home with my mother, Jessica, and John. My mum tried to warn me she wouldn't feel like she did the last time I held her, but I had never faced the cold, stark reality of death, as no one I loved had ever died before. I picked Krissy up and almost dropped her because she was so cold, stiff, and hard. This experience deeply impacted me. If it wasn't for my mother's calm words that night, I don't think I would have been able to move on and release myself from that moment. We wanted Jessica to be able to say goodbye. Jessica gave Krissy her favorite toy and kissed her on the forehead. It was so hard as parents to watch her do that. Jessica had to leave her sister behind. I can't even begin to think of how confusing that was for her. We left the funeral home feeling empty, and I desperately wanted to go back in there and take her with me. One of the most difficult experiences of my life was to leave Krissy behind alone in a cold, dark room in a box.

On the day of her funeral, the shock was evident not just in us but also in all who came. A friend of mine had brought her young child to the funeral. She was crying a little, as children do. But I couldn't handle it. I asked her to take her child out. I think I just couldn't handle the sound of a baby crying at a time when mine was silent. I shared my testimony of how Jesus had met with me in this process.

We had chosen a Celtic rendition of the song "We Rest on Thee, Our Shield and Our Defender,"[2] and as it played, people were offered the opportunity to come and look at Krissy one last time. We were not prepared for the whole gathering to get up and pass by her. Many had not even met her yet. The music was eerie but deep, and allowed many tears and a shared grief to be experienced. Many thoughts, notes, and toys were placed in her coffin. She looked so beautiful.

When they closed the coffin—I suddenly screamed silently. It got caught in my chest and then throat as I struggled to breathe. As they took her out to the waiting funeral car, I was again overwhelmed at the coldness of death. She was gone.

People mingled, having cups of tea and food. I couldn't mingle and was not hungry. I sat behind, trying to compose myself.

There was a section for children at the cemetery, filled with flowers and children's toys. It felt comforting, in a strange way, that she was going to be surrounded by other children, and also because other parents had experienced what we were going through right then.

As they placed Krissy in this deep hole in the ground, I suddenly realized there was nothing more I could do. I couldn't organize her photos or write another eulogy. I couldn't open her coffin and see her one more time. I was burying my daughter and would never see her face again. My brother was the first to place dirt on her coffin, and it was such a shock to me to see dirt being thrown down on top of her. My heart twisted in agony as I watched more soil being shoveled on top of her. I was panicking inside that they were suffocating her, and it was more than overwhelming for my mind, soul, and body. I desperately wanted to jump in there and rescue her. Horror screamed out that this was just one big awful dream.

The love of family and friends kept me from tunneling into disintegration. My sister had bought balloons, and as we released them to the sky, I was reminded of where Krissy now was as I looked up. This was an incredibly

---

2. Written by Edith G. Cherry, 1895.

important moment for me as I was shifted back into the faithfulness of God, where I was centered and safe.

My heavenly Father gave me such strength and dignity that day. I don't know how I managed to speak at the funeral or even get dressed that morning. I can only say my Faithful Friend enabled me to endure the grief no mother should have, that of burying her daughter. Yet I knew my Father had done that with his Son, and this comforted me because he understood.

We went home to try and gather ourselves together. It was not easy as the silence was deafening. The crowds had dispersed, and John and I and our family all sat around trying to collectively come to terms with what had just transpired. Five days before, we had been moving furniture and I was enjoying being a mother again and getting back to normal; here I was now where everything was anything but normal, and it was doubtful it ever would be again.

Those first days and weeks were incredibly hard. As the days went on, the shock and numbness would wain and intense pain would explode in my chest and entire being. Grief isn't just an emotional response; your whole body, psyche, and intellect are all under severe strain. The simplest of tasks become loaded and all your energy is given to just surviving. Jessica was a delight. Her gorgeous personality and strength gave stability. I don't actually know how I responded to her in those days and weeks after Krissy's death. I don't know how she felt about her sister not being there anymore. She was so little. I know it impacted her.

People tried to help, but what can you do and what can you say? One poor woman tried to console me with the theological premise of sovereignty, saying, "Well, God is sovereign, so he must know." I screamed at her, "Well, he must hate my guts then!"

I can't really encapsulate the horror or the pain of this journey in writing. I wish I could play you the song we had at the funeral. It captures the eerie, beautiful, yet soul-filled elements. After the funeral, I went to check on my mother, only to be greeted with a barrage of her pain that I wasn't being there for her. Looking back, it was partly grief on her part. However, it was also a startling revelation of where my relationship with my mother really stood. She was angry at all the church people coming, whom she believed were not genuine. I started seeing that my relationship with my mum wasn't what I had envisioned it was.

I wrote screeds in my journals, filled with much wrestling and deep pain. There were cries of "Where are you, God?" and then comfort would come, and I would rest deep in my Father. In all honesty, though, I was deeply conflicted. I was holding huge fear and anxiety and doubted that my Father was really with me. I oscillated between believing God was full of grace and mercy toward me and, in my next breath, perceiving him as fickle and one who would punish me by withdrawing from me. In the middle of all this, the central tenets of the cross would become increasingly important. I could not get enough of the Scriptures that talked about God's grace covering my sin, and especially those that talked about Jesus' paying my debt (see 1 John 1:7). My belief was simple: Krissy died; therefore, I am responsible. I just needed to figure out what I had done to be punished in this way.

I was really struggling with how I could live life without her. In church one day, I even surmised that Jesus had lived thirty years away from his heavenly Father, so I just needed to do that. I was grasping for anything that would help me sustain the journey ahead. The deep wrestling questions that twist my soul in torment, such as "Why?" and "What if?," swirled in and out like destructive waves of the sea during these early weeks. I struggled so much with God's sovereignty versus my responsibility versus life just happens. "Was it my fault?" "I shouldn't have moved the furniture." "What if I just didn't put her down that night?" There were so many agonizing questions and no answers.

My friends Robyn and Leonora, who were phoned on the night Krissy died, were separately crying out to God for Krissy's life to be spared when they both received the same Scripture from the Father, John 12:24: "Very truly I tell you, unless a kernel of wheat falls to the ground and dies, it remains only a single seed. But if it dies, it produces many seeds." Robyn shared with me recently that she fought the Lord over this Scripture, as she was so shocked to think he was not going to heal Krissy. I now see that Krissy's death is producing much seed and much fruit.

I remember visiting Robyn, and I disclosed to her how I was over people saying this was God's will and trying to comfort me with the reality that Krissy was in heaven. I was so angry because I did not want Krissy to be in heaven; I wanted her with me. Robyn was so very kind during this time. She also had several miscarriages during my grieving period with Krissy. She was such a comfort to me even though she was grieving herself. We walked our grief journey together for many years.

My friend Jacqui came over, and I revealed to her my agonizing, deep-felt reality that Krissy died because I had sinned somehow and as a result God was punishing me. She was so wonderful in trying to help me see God wasn't like that. These deep conflicts showed me where I was holding incongruence between what I deemed I believed and the theology my gut was living from. My gut in these months was winning. I cried out over and over to God, asking, "Why?" One day he replied, asking, "Would knowing why help?" I then realized knowing why would not bring her back and maybe open more questions than I could handle. My Father said to me, "I can't tell you why, but I will give you myself instead." I do not believe our Father sends things like this into our lives. Life happens and we suffer, and he comes and gives us the grace to process. He definitely does not send suffering so we may be purified and fit for his purposes. This would resemble an abusive Father. My Father stands with me in all the seasons of my life and works them together for my good and the good of those who have suffered with me.

I can't underestimate the pain my family and friends were also going through at this time. Those closest to us were also struggling with why and how this had happened. They had spent a lot of time with Krissy when I was in and out of hospital. They had traveled the journey of healing with us, and it could not have been easy for them as they also had busy lives and some had children. To them, I publicly thank each of you. This is my scriptural promise for you from Proverbs 19:17: "Whoever is kind to the poor lends to the Lord, and he will reward them for what they have done."

John and I had been gifted a marriage weekend retreat in Taupo before Krissy died. It was the week after the funeral, and even though we were in deep grief, friends and family encouraged us to attend. As we arrived, the Celtic hymn that we had played at Krissy's funeral, "We Rest on Thee, Our Shield and Our Defender," was playing at the precise day and time, exactly a week later. It felt unbelievably surreal. The people who were running the retreat found out what had happened to us the previous week and about our connection to the song and went out of their way to ensure this wasn't playing again for the rest of the weekend.

A couple of weeks later, the autopsy report came back and described Krissy as having "perfectly healthy" organs. The pathologist's conclusion was that Krissy died of sudden infant death syndrome, i.e., "cot death." "Perfectly healthy" resounded in my being, shattering all sense of reality. My perfectly healthy baby died crying in her cot. It was such a profound sense of disbelief, as I had hoped there would be some sort of reason given for this hideous event, some sort of defect or problem that would place the horror of what had happened at the feet of some other door. But no, there were no doors.

John and I coped very differently with Krissy's death. John needed to go straight back to work. I wanted to talk and cry and weed the garden. My mother left a week after the funeral to get back to Australia to recover and grieve, while Dad stayed to help us. I didn't find out until I talked with my brother years later that my father had stopped smoking cold turkey after having been a smoker for over forty years, because he assumed he contributed to Krissy's death. I can't imagine what my father must have been going through during this time, thinking he had some hand in what had happened. I never got to talk to him about this. I am grateful he stopped smoking for his health, but I hope he did not carry the weight of Krissy's death in himself after this. I will never know.

A serious virus called Type A influenza came through Auckland, and we were all very, very sick. My mother rang, upset that I was not looking after Dad. The church we were part of then were incredibly supportive. We were inundated with food and people cleaning the house and loving on us. It was very beautiful to be loved like this. There was one particular lady named Hazel who was so kind. She would bring cookies and drop letters and cards off to me every week. She did this for over six months. She was unfailing in her love and support. Her husband was not well, and later she would need to go into a home herself. She was a beautiful, godly warrior. I still have all her cards and correspondence from this time. Never underestimate cards and cookies when someone is grieving. They were precious for me, and we looked forward to her regular visits filled with love and our Father's compassion. Our neighbor, Bev, was also a godsend through this period. She would often come over for a coffee, or I would walk over to talk with her. She was so kind and would just sit and talk and play with Jessica while I did the housework—a precious person to have in my life in such a difficult time.

Digging Deeper

As John and I talked about the memories of Krissy we had so that we could share them with you in this book, we felt heartbroken that there weren't more to share. We only got time to just glimpse who she was and we felt robbed even of that time as there were so many deeply traumatic events surrounding her few weeks with us. We could not have shared these stories with you had we not known the depth of love and faithfulness of our Father to enable us to get through these years. The memories of others' interactions with Krissy are like rare jewels that help us gain a more rounded sense of who she was and the impact she had on others. Her life was not in vain. She impacted many then, and she still impacts us today. We honor you and your story, Kristiana, and now many others know who you are. Many know the impact you had and continue to have in our lives and others' lives for good. You were born for such a time as this.

Kristiana Michelle Ruth McSweeney, 31.3.99—2.6.99

Psychological Justice

I see *psychological justice* in the way my Father revealed to me, when I cried out to him alone and scared in hospital, that my kidneys were causing my illness. The beauty of my Father coming to me in this way shows his intimate involvement in my life. I might have died had my Father not intervened. He also gave me the courage to ask the sonographer to check my kidneys. My Father, through this experience, was gifting to me more than an answer to my problem. He was also countering the faulty image I had of him as distant and removed. My image of him underwent so many crucial changes through my experience of Krissy's death and during the aftermath of grief.

Being able to speak at Krissy's funeral was due to the reality that my Father brought psychological and spiritual strength to enable me to do so. I read what I wrote now, and I can see my Father's love to me within that speech. To this day, I am not sure how I was able to sing of my Father's faithfulness in the moment Krissy died. I can only assume that the Holy Spirit was manifesting the truth of who my Father was and would be as I processed her death. *Psychological justice* rests on the core aspects of the Father's being, such as justice, faithfulness, mercy, goodness, and so much more. These are foundational characteristics of our Father, and for many of us, these are the very aspects that are challenged when we face painful trials. Part of *psychological justice* is being able to pinpoint where and why we have faulty images of our Father, so we can deal with these.

There were so many times in the aftermath of Krissy's death that I look back on and know only my Father could have given me what I needed. I did not have the psychological resources at this time to have survived psychologically as I did. My Father was so very present with me in all aspects of this process.

The start of my journey out of toxic abuse into an intimate dance of justice with Jesus still amazes me. How my Father could take something as tragic as my daughter's death and turn it toward my good is not just a nice scriptural hope; it is a very life-altering truth that impacted my lived reality. The Father, in his faithfulness, is able to work in us in such a thoroughly psychological and theological capacity that we can come out with more freedom than when we entered our season of grief. I don't know how he does it, but he does. This is *psychological justice*. I am so grateful it wasn't up to me to figure out for myself what was going on with my mother and me. I am grateful my Father knew, and had a plan.

What's Your Story?

Where have you seen, or do you need to see, God encountering faulty images you have of him amidst your journey with tragedy or grief? Where is pain hiding his face from you? Invite him into those spaces if you can.

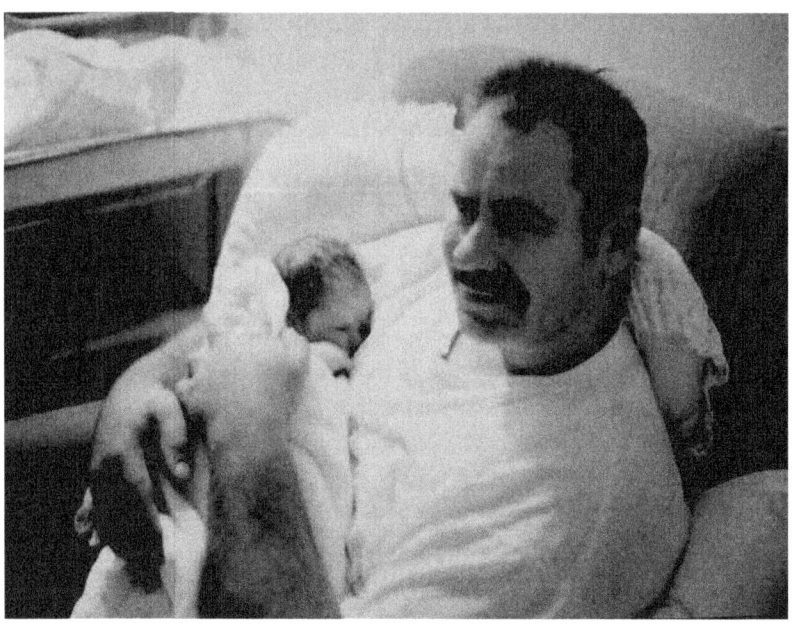

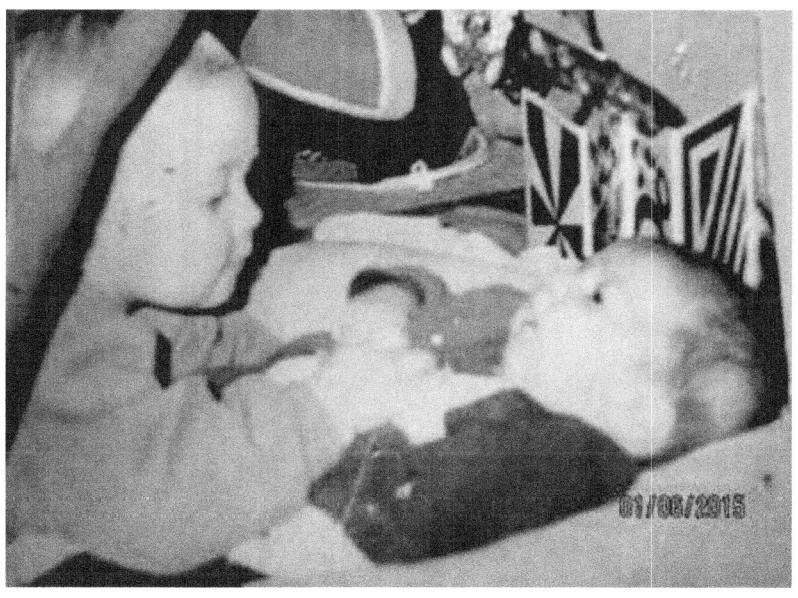

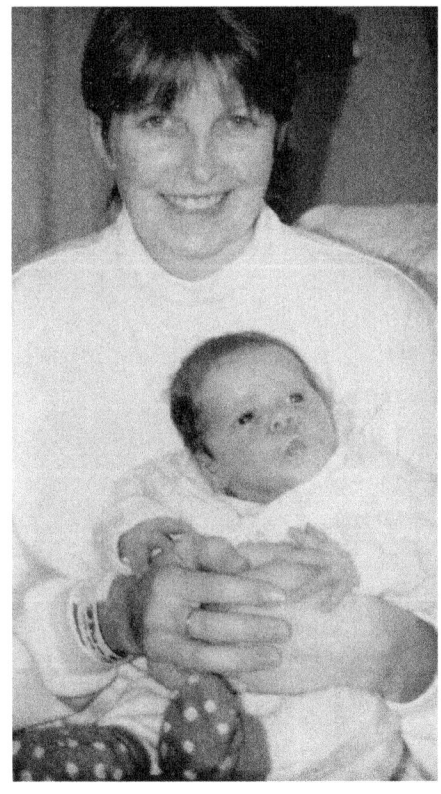

The Pit of Despair

This chapter explores the themes of suicide and self-harm, which some readers may find distressing.

The pit. It is a real place. It is very deep. It is suffocating. It is dark, so very dark. Yet, the darkness is welcoming. Comforting. It promises to embrace you with its heavy presence. Once you are there, you know that evil exists. Those who have been there know the trauma of this experience. The pit is not a place you want to visit, let alone live in. It is a place, however, that invites new tenants of grief to sojourn.

Krissy's death brought all sorts of unresolved grief to the surface, and I felt myself entering into a dark pit of despair. It didn't help that the day after Krissy died, my mum admonished me that it was all right to grieve as long as I grieved "biblically." Mum had taken me to the local Christian bookstore and asked the lady at the counter for books on how to grieve "biblically." The lady looked at us like, "What even is that?" Looking back, this was an indicator of the severe spiritual disorder in my relationship with my mum. My confidence as a wife and mum was rocked. I would eventually come to the realization that being biblical doesn't mean what my mum judged it meant. I shouldn't have been trying to be "biblical" as my mother had directed me to. The underlying theological premise to Mum's understanding of biblical grief was that the only way to be close to the Lord is to suffer. In this theological framework, once I completed this time of suffering, I would be closer to him.

I was always petrified of not having it together. My shame had led to performance. Jesus was the heartbeat of my walk, but false spirituality was always nipping at my heels. My inner and outer worlds were not congruent. All these factors made the grief process and my ability to feel safe in my Father so difficult.

Life was no longer predictable. The spiritual abuse I had experienced in the past kept me from dealing with my misconceptions of God—rather, they enforced their deadly stronghold. The time after Krissy's death was a real struggle for survival. I had to find places to be safe and people who could help me keep sane. Practical things like eating well and sleeping to help with the exhaustion I was experiencing were all playing a part in getting better. I had to forgive the church from my youth for their abuse of power and twisting the Scriptures. I was starting to understand that my Father valued my pain.

About the six-week mark, after Mum went back home to Australia, I hit an emotional wall. Thankfully, I had a good doctor who was able to give me mild antidepressants. A good friend who taught pastoral care at BCNZ/

Laidlaw encouraged me not to be afraid to take them. He showed me that if I had a medical problem, I would take the medication. He said, "Your mind needs some help right now, and your physical body is exhausted from surgery."

As medication kicked in, I started to get physically shaky, distraught, and trembling with anger. I felt completely out of control. I was spiraling rapidly and was afraid I was having a nervous breakdown. My heart was full of pain, and my mind finally succumbed. I started seeing knives and wanting to hurt myself. It would come and go at first, but as the week went on, it got more insistent and I started becoming scared of myself. I knew these were not my thoughts because they really frightened me. I did not consciously want to plan to hurt myself. I told my father, who told me to ring my mum. She told me to ring someone in the church. I did so. Honestly though, I wish I hadn't. His response was for me to just think better, advising me that if I could get my mind to agree with God, then these feelings would go.

Yes, let's just stop and think about that, shall we? What on earth? If I just got my mind to agree with God? Hmm, so that's how one deals with deep grief and trauma. Just think your way out of it. Think. I wished I could at the time. I had a railway track of terrifying thoughts screaming through my brain, and this pastor wanted me to stop each one and just think better.

What utter nonsense. It is a treason of sound theological methodology to appropriate verses, particularly in a pastoral capacity, in this way. This practice leaves many who are suffering with tragedy psychologically disorientated and spiritually bereft. Using the Scriptures inappropriately as Band-Aid's is why some walk away from God, thinking that somehow they were not strong enough to be a Christian. He was echoing spiritual adults in my past who had abandoned me to a spiritual void.

All that this pastor did was seal my fate to damnation. I was in serious trouble. I was so lost. So very broken. In so much pain. I was now in the pit.

This is an extremely dangerous way to speak to someone who is in the process of losing control of their mind. When someone is in deep grief, telling them to simply change their mindset is not only a significant betrayal of pastoral practice, but a serious misrepresentation of our Lord. In Gethsemane, our Lord was so distressed that he sweat drops of blood. I am glad this pastor was not there for that moment. He may have told Jesus to just think better.

When I think of this moment now, I consider Jesus' anger at the Pharisees in the temple—so upright and together, exacting from the poor money and taxes they did not have. I am so glad Jesus gets enraged by oppressors.

One day, I was in the supermarket. I felt surrounded by mums and their babies and, even though I tried desperately not to, jealousy and pain consumed me. I constantly asked God to forgive me. It was like my external reality wanted to be strong, but my internal reality was broken and cascading in a whirlwind of sorrow. On this day, it was so overwhelming that I had to leave the supermarket as I felt I couldn't bear the pain. As I walked to my car, there was a van with the words "He has borne our grief" written on the side door. I sobbed and realized I didn't want to die. False belief had kept me from a simple faith of rest. In desperation, I cried out, "Will you save me, Father? Truly save me?"

My friend Ruth looked after Jessica while I took refuge in a room in her home. I was petrified I would get a knife and hurt myself. Jesus' blood became everything to me: the cross, grace, mercy, forgiveness. But the blood, oh my—I cried out for the blood and quoted the Scripture over and over, "the blood of Jesus, his son, purifies us from all sin" (1 John 1:7). The enemy would try and torment me with my sins or omissions, telling me it was my fault that Krissy had died and that I deserved her death because of my sins. The enemy could do this because I was psychologically broken, and my past had formed in me an image of an unstable God that was unable and/or unwilling to fight for me. Satan's agenda is set out in John 10:10: "The thief comes only to steal and kill and destroy; I have come that they may have life, and have it to the full." The mental anguish of this warfare was the most extreme I have ever encountered. It went on for days, unrelenting. I felt the hoard of hell was hovering over me, seeking my blood, seeking vengeance.

At this time, I had a terrifying dream of a train. To this day, I still feel the haunting and the being driven while having the dream. I was running downstairs to catch a train with the words "It's too late!" ringing in my head, over and over. The train, I realized later, symbolized escaping life—i.e., suicide. Jesus showed me that he had experienced extreme mental anguish in Gethsemane, and I saw myself with him and felt it was a privilege to suffer with Jesus. Although I knew his anguish was even more severe, he allowed me to feel welcome in this experience of his, and I felt he saw it as a privilege to be with me.

Psalm 139:8–10 echoed deep within: "If I go up to the heavens, you are there; if I make my bed in the depths, you are there. If I rise on the wings of the dawn, if I settle on the far side of the sea, even there your hand will guide me, your right hand will hold me fast." Such a precious gift. I knew I had made my bed in the depths. Made my bed—you only have a bed if you are going to sleep there and make it your home. "In the depths, even there." What comfort this brought. God would guide me—with his hand. God's hand close enough to hold mine in this pit. When I read that verse, I knew he had come to camp out with me. I had a real sense of being held in my pit, even though I couldn't exactly feel God. God was not in a rush to get me out of the pit either. It's hard to describe this, but I think God cared more about why I was in there than getting me out quickly, if that makes sense. It's like, sometimes you just want someone to sit with you. My Father just sat with me.

God could see me, and God was with me, and God was camping out with me in this pit. I read Charles Spurgeon's book *Power in the Blood* over and over. It was what music must have been like to Saul's ears when David played for him when the evil spirit would torment him. I can't express how much the power of the blood saved my sanity during this time.

After waking from the above dream about the train, terrified, my Father gave me a vision. I saw his blood covering the opening to the deep pit I was now dwelling in. I saw how much I had been punishing myself regarding the pathologist's report. If Krissy was healthy, her death must have been my fault, and I believed I was the door at which her death lay. I felt I didn't deserve to live because it was my sickness that had caused her to die. It was so hard to grieve when there was no reason given for why she died. "How do I live without her?" my heart cried out. This huge void filled my entire being. Everything hurt. I could hardly breathe. I could hardly think. I was consumed with darkness. I physically felt like my heart was going to rupture. I couldn't imagine a life without her. A life where she is in a grave. A life beyond her grave. "Why is she not here with me? Why, why, why?" Over and over and over. Nothing made sense; everything was being filtered through this one mantra, "Why?"

I wanted so badly to redirect my grief, and I understand why people self-harm. There's an emotional need for a physical marker to show the extreme internal pain you are in. I realized how much inner pain a person can experience to lead them to self-harm or suicide. If you are reading this book and feel like this, please talk to someone. Follow my lead and find people to watch over you; use medication and seek help to find healing for those deep pits we find ourselves in. You don't have to live alone in this pain, although the pain is yours and maybe you feel no one will understand. But even if no one can, they do care. I am here to assure you that as you process, you will find peace again.

A turning point for me was when God gave me a picture of myself in a large pit where Krissy lay in her coffin, and I was huddled over her, refusing to let go. The pit resembled a large underground clay house. Friends were up at the top of the stairs outside the pit, calling out for me to come, but I was getting angry at their calling, and I clung even more tightly to Krissy's coffin. I was not going to leave her. Then Kristiana walked in. She was no longer a baby, but a beautiful young adult with long black hair and deep blue eyes, and she had on the most beautiful deep blue flowing satin dress. She asked me to let her go. She told me she had chosen to be with Jesus, and she wanted me to walk on with my own life. After I experienced this encounter—whether it was real or not I do not know—there came a peace and deep acceptance over my life. Krissy was no longer this little baby that I had to protect and mother at all costs. She was a beautiful, fully mature human being in the presence of her Father, our Father. This meant I could grieve my loss of her, knowing she was not lost and abandoned but safe and deeply loved.

My arms were empty, but she was embraced—fully. She was more alive than I could ever imagine anyone being. Her presence emanated an eternal disposition. There was something incredible about meeting her in this way, outside of time. With me, but not of me. I still sense how it felt to this day. It was all-consuming. The compassion in her toward me was beyond earthly empathy. I am grateful beyond words that my Father would let me have this very real encounter with her. I can't explain it. I feel like Paul when I talk about it. When he had visions, he would say, "Whether in the body or apart from the body I do not know" (2 Cor 12:3). It forever changed how I see my earthly life. It forever changed my perception of death, of grief, of my grieving processes since. My grief had purpose from that moment on. It was still deep, raw, and debilitating, but I was no longer deeply anxious about Krissy and her well-being.

It took a while to slowly ascend out of my pit, but after a couple of weeks, I was able to function with some sort of normality—as normal as one can in those circumstances. I was able to embrace Jessica and focus on the everyday functions of housework and cooking. I took antidepressants for about nine months, and they were very important in my process of working through grief. I thank God that my friend gave me the advice he did.

Krissy's death triggered an explosion in seeing the reality of the spiritual abuse, neglect, or trap I had been in with my mother for a very long time. It also made me more aware of the crumbling foundations in my walk with God. I had all these fractures deep in my being that were inconsistent with what my head believed. The Father began building more solid foundations. I remember driving to a follow-up kidney appointment and crying out to God about what was happening in my life, and he spoke to me very clearly. It was so clear that, to this day, I can remember where I was and what I was feeling as if it was yesterday. He said to me that my foundations were rooted in fear and abandonment, and instead, he was going to root me in his love and goodness. My concepts of life, of suffering, and of God needed to be reconstrued to more sure foundations. I was afraid of evil and suffering and had a belief that God had a part in punishing me with these things in life, but the opposite was true: my Father wanted to protect me, not *from* life, but *in* life.

Up until this point, I felt smothered by my mother, whom I felt was trying to micro-manage me. I was not free, and I was not being loved. Spiritual abuse is where another person assumes the place the Lord should have in your life. This can be in small ways or, as in my case, big ways. It all came from a place in her that was broken and desperate to protect me because she had a deep fear that I couldn't cope with life.

I was struggling so much with feeling weak. I inwardly groaned that if I were a better Christian, I would be stronger. The Lord said to me, "Stop being so spiritual about grief. I want you to be fully human."

I had a vision one day not long after this. In it, I was really anxious about being alone with God. I wanted others to walk with me. I saw myself turning around, and the Lord took my hand and encouraged me to walk ahead. After a few steps, I walked into brilliant light; I fell to my knees and wept uncontrollably and deeply for a long time. I got up, walked a few more paces, then fell for a shorter period of time. After the second time, which was more reflective grief, I picked myself up and walked much more strongly. I dusted off my clothes and walked on, straightened out my hair, laid things to rest, and walked on with dignity and confidence with the Lord's support. I understand now that in this vision, the Lord was showing me how my grief process would unfold, and that the grief would get less and with greater distance between each wave, and that I would finally be able to walk straight and with dignity.

Three months after Krissy's death, I finally had some courage to sit and be with her belongings. Every outfit neatly folded, clean, and in order. Her little singlets and jumpsuits. Her beanies and socks. Everything smelled of her. I cried and cried as I touched her clothes. The realization that she would never wear these was unbearable. Six-month-old clothes that I was dreaming of putting on her when I bought them now lay new and unused. Nappies still sitting in their place. I had time to do this. This time I wished I had been able to spend with her. Clothes I desperately wanted to be able to dress her with. Time taken from me and her through my illness. "Did my absence from her cause her to die from a broken heart? Did she feel abandoned?" She did, I am sure.

The loss of time with her while she was alive was deafening in its excess. Books and toys gathered for her future now lay unused. "Where do I start? How do I start?" I knew I couldn't leave it as it was, like a shrine. I knew it was time. I needed to gather all that pain and make time. I needed to do it for me, but also for Jessica. She needed me.

"How do I preserve Krissy's legacy without keeping everything?" I packed most things away, but placed my favorite outfits and blankets in a special box. I still have them. I asked the Lord if he could take my time of sorting out her things and gift it to her. I prayed as I grieved for my Father to let her know how sorry I was that I hadn't been there for her. How it wrenched my heart in two to be faced with all this time and healing, and she bore the brunt of the lack of both from me.

Although the stages of grief are not static and weave in and out like a violent storm, cleaning Krissy's room started releasing deep anger. It was a scary time as the anger felt like destructive rage. I remember going out and pulling weeds out of the garden as it felt a safe way to dispel the ferocity of dark emotion I was feeling. It was a deep maternal fury that I was scared I might not be able to reign in. For some reason, I was so afraid of people's response to me in my grief. The more I tried to stop grieving, thinking the people around me were over me grieving, or I wasn't grieving in a mature way, or I should just be over it already, the Lord would speak louder to me to stop resisting the grief process. Grief is a gift. I had to choose to let Jesus comfort me because he was not ashamed of my grief or of me in my grief. Grief is a natural and beautiful way of saying goodbye to someone you love.

The date August 20 would prove to be a special day in this process. I was asking God how Krissy died, and specifically if she suffered as she died. He said to me, "I called her by name and it took her breath away." The deep peace that enveloped me was supernatural. A shift came with it, a shift into another dimension that doesn't see time and purpose as we do here. Eternal time and purpose are completely different. He showed me that she was given a choice in that moment, and she chose him. Not long after this, I visited her grave; after initially wanting to dig her up and hold her, a deep acceptance came over me.

It's no surprise to me now that soon after this transition occurred, another transition began, in my relationship with my mother. I had a conversation with her, fueled by her grief, in which she strongly criticized John and the church I was involved with at the time. I felt like I had to make a choice between her "truth" and "discernment" about my surroundings, and my reality. I felt like my allegiance to her was being challenged. I couldn't agree or support my mother's rage and attack on these people I loved, whom she was claiming were not really Christians at all—any of them. She had said stuff like this before, but this time I actually heard what she was saying. I was slowly realizing my mum wasn't the spiritual giant I had idolized her to be, but actually she was quite bitter at the church and life in general. The fact that this conversation happened in the early weeks of Krissy's passing was also significant.

You see, when you have been in a long-term abusive relationship, you think it is normal. I was starting to understand how abnormal it was. I remember when dating John that he would notice certain ways I responded to my mother and would tell me he didn't think my relationship with her was healthy. I would reply that he just didn't know what a normal family looked like. However, I was starting to see there was a gaping hole in what I had assumed was normal, and suddenly everything was anything but. Jesus started showing me what resurrection life looks like. This was not just a different priority, but was my very life. He wanted to be, and was, my life. This was important because I had positioned Mum in God's place up to this point and would soon need the assurance that my Father wanted to take his rightful place.

I felt stuck at one point, and a friend suggested I go to a grief counselor she knew. In my first meeting with her, she identified where I was at. I did not know at this point that there are stages to grief. I had come to the end of stage 4, where I felt I was emotionally ready to move forward from grief, but felt like I would be leaving Krissy behind. I felt that I wanted her permission to move on as I did not want her feeling that, by me moving forward, I did not care about her or would forget her.

The counselor asked me what I needed to be able to move forward, and we prayed about my deep desire to have Krissy's permission. I felt strongly encouraged by the Holy Spirit to lay down my will for Krissy and accept her decision to be with Jesus. In this prayer time, I felt her remind me she wanted me to be glad for her. I felt her appeal to me, "Mum, go on with your life and be happy for me." I realized in that moment that I was not leaving her behind—she had gone on ahead of me. She was safe. I could move forward into acceptance.

I found that working during this time was healing because I could function as an academic and a secretary. I felt I had value and dignity for who I was, not as solely a mother in grief. As I studied spiritual formation, these values of authenticity and intimacy with God were fanned into flame, and others in church started valuing these priorities as well. I formed deep friendships in what became a holding environment at Bible college. A holding environment is a place that is safe while you are transitioning from one season to another, or from one state of being to another in the healing process.

John and I took Jessica on some adventures. The midwife who had delivered Krissy had a timeshare in Queenstown in the South Island and gave us a week of her allotted time. We drove to the South Island and visited some dear friends on the way. Our good friends Patrick and Rosie were living in Christchurch at this point, and we spent a lovely couple of days with them. I have beautiful memories of Jessica being loved and held during this time, and it was lovely seeing her so happy. Patrick has become a brother to me, and I am very grateful for his and Rosie's faithful love for us in our journey. We also visited Heather and Andrew in Gore. They too had lost two beautiful babies in a short space of time. It was lovely to spend time sharing our grief experiences together. Heather and I were able to share photos and cry together as we remembered our children. I am so grateful that our Father brought us together so our hearts could share our precious memories of our babies. This was such an important time, not only for John and myself, but also for Jessica. Heather and Andrew's eldest daughter was also, like Jessica, dealing with the grief that her parents were processing. Seeing the girls have fun together was wonderful. Sitting and allowing each other to voice our journey was a very special time for all of us.

Dealing with shame would become a theme that would keep being highlighted during the grief process, along with fear of how people viewed me. Fear seemed to have been the basis of my relationship with God all along. Added to this was the increasing evidence that my relationship with my mum had to change.

Digging Deeper

I found that Krissy's death not only affected my psychological processing, but also impacted my physiological and spatial responses. Shock creates a sense of numbness, and I felt suspended in a void. Physically, I was walking around dazed and disorientated. My senses were heightened, yet I could not focus. Krissy's death jettisoned me into a place I had never experienced before: the trial of bereavement, where death led me to hunger for deeper purpose and eternal significance. Is there a place where reality is different from here? When faced with an acute phase of grief, all the rules that seem to govern this life are questioned.

There are different types of grief. There is grief that is linked to natural events, such as an elderly parent dying, and there is an acute grief due to shock from a death that has intercepted a life before it has been fully lived. Shock can embed sensory memories deep within our psyche. I remember a couple of years after Krissy's death, I was hanging out the laundry in the garden of our new home. The temperature was cooling and there was a different vibe as fall approached. I started feeling a deep sadness come over me from nowhere, but I thought to myself, "Oh, it's late March. Krissy's birthday must be soon." I was picking up the sensory memory I had lodged in my deepest being during the accumulative shock and grief in the reverberation of Krissy's death.

Part of my being is connected to eternity with Krissy through memory imprints from my experience with her in time. God enables this time exchange so we can continue living in the present, knowing there is more to life than this present reality.

When helping people process acute grief, simplistic prayers that minimize a person's suffering can significantly retraumatize them. There are often multiple sensory residues that can be very complex. For some people, they have already accumulated multiple levels of psychological memory imprints to the point where the loss occurred, and their present grief may further encroach on their already disintegrated self.

This is why two people can go through a similar experience and be affected in different ways. It is so important for people not to judge others based on their situation, as some people have greater psychological resources and psychological space to be able to absorb grief. If you picture a person's soul like a bucket, and the bucket has multiple holes in it, the fullness of grief may drain any healthy resources they may have to cope. Some people are labeled spiritual giants when it may actually be that they have more psychological resources, whereas another person seems to not be coping and yet may have a deeper spirituality because they are aware of their incessant need for God to help process their pain.

Most people I know who have deep spiritual strength have worked very hard in partnership with God to survive. It is important not to judge yourself on another's ability to process. You may find that trauma brings to the surface even deeper trauma that is still unresolved. I remember needing all of heaven's resources to help me just clean the house and cook dinner in those early weeks after Krissy's death. Normality had changed to survival, and my worship became a continual sacrifice. Life became different, as earthly things didn't matter as much because their value had been depleted.

I developed an excessive passion for people and life to be real; I could no longer handle duplicity and felt physically repelled by it. The process of grief was exacerbated as past inner trauma and deep shame began surfacing and choking my ability to handle some relationships because it hurt to be around those who seemed to have it together as mothers. This made the grief process more painful as close relationships were being strained.

Psychological Justice

I am thankful I was encouraged to take medication for my mental health. It is sometimes necessary, in supporting the psychological process of grief, to accept that not all problems can be ministered to solely through the Scriptures. A mental assent of certain Scriptures alone would never have helped my physical body, as weak and broken as it was, to recover sufficiently enough in time to bring peace to my mind. It is simplistic reasoning, I think, to believe that all we need is a spiritual response to life's complexity. *Psychological justice* in this process for me was that my Father intervened to bring holistic support in my darkest hours. His supernatural strength came alongside my need for my body's exhaustion to be acknowledged.

My Father brought *psychological justice* to a very painful and fear-infused psychological memory imprint from my past. When I was deep in my pit, where Satan was seeking to devour my very being, my Father sent help. He came and sat with me in my pit. This was so different than how I had felt as a young woman when I was being prayed for to receive the gift of tongues, but being warned that God couldn't help me and wouldn't help me because I had sinned. Jesus' blood was so powerful during this time. The concept of his blood saving me was no longer theoretical. Jesus' blood became my very life, the very reason as to why the enemy could not take me out. I rested my fractured mind in the deep truth that Jesus' blood could save my sanity.

Underneath my deep grief over Krissy's death was a sea of deep psychological pain from my past that had never been brought to the light. This is where *psychological justice* comes to the fore. Many of us carry on with life, holding unresolved issues in our deepest being, sometimes not even aware our Father sees them and wants to bring his provision of healing to these places. For some of us, it is only when a crisis hits our lives that our psychological ability to function from our developed constructs fails. We are then faced with a double grief. We no longer have the psychological resources we need to continue to bury the deep pain we carry from our past. Our past suddenly erupts like a dangerous volcano into our present. If *psychological justice* became normative in the body of Christ, it could help prevent the enormity of such instances in our lives, if we had the opportunity to deal with our past in a safe and theologically informed way before tragedy hits.

I love that my Father came to me in my pit with a picture showing me why I was burying myself underground and bringing an answer to me as to how I could walk out of this dark place. Picturing myself holding Krissy's coffin and seeing her walk in to let me know what my heart desperately needed to hear—that she was fully thriving in my Father's presence—was

God meeting me where I needed, as I couldn't take myself to him. My faith was broken, yet my Father was faithful.

My Father, through these experiences, was bringing *psychological justice* by dismantling some of my foundations built on fear and abandonment, as he did not abandon me during my darkest moments. When no one could reach me, my Father sat with me. My Father was being to me what others in my past had said he would not be: with me in my darkness. My Father was able to deliver me from the enemy's lies that I would be forsaken if I were not strong enough to keep faith.

I am still amazed to this day to see that the transition from being dominated by my mother into freedom apart from her started with the death of my daughter. The Father has taken what is one of the most tragic experiences anyone can face in life, the death of their child, and brought so much healing and deliverance. This is *psychological justice.* This is not another system of belief, or paradigm of healing. *Psychological justice* is the beautiful gift of a lived reality of the Father's justice available to all believers, no matter what they have done (like Ben) or what has happened to them (like Krissy). It is the Trinity taking all that the enemy and sin have plagued humanity with since the beginning, and turning it on its head and gaining the victory through Christ. Only our Father could turn what the enemy has desperately sought to harm us with, our child's life taken, and turn it into a generational legacy of hope, faithfulness, and healing.

I cannot fully describe my Father's presence in such deep places of grief. Some talk about the presence of God in a church service as though it is a feel-good experience. The presence of God, while definitely a beautiful reality, is far more than this. In a moment of tragedy, the presence of God in a tangible way holds our psychological, physical, and spiritual being in an eternal embrace. *Psychological justice* in this space is a holistic, Christ-centered, lived reality.

What's Your Story?

Where has grief, in its multisensory effects, impacted your physiological and psychological being? Are there places you have spiritualized your grief? Is it time to invite God to come in to heal and shine his light in your places of darkness?

Rebuilding Begins

About eighteen months after Krissy's death, I was asked if I would like to come back to BCNZ/Laidlaw in a part-time position. It meant I could still be at home with Jessica and work while she was at the kindergarten on-site. It was a God-given role, as I found a part of me was able to quickly slip back into work mode. This gave my soul rest as it continued the grieving process. The grief was still there, but it wasn't the raw, debilitating experience it had been in the early days.

The following year, we went on a vacation with John's sister, Rita, and her friend to Queenstown for a week. I felt I was pregnant, so took a pregnancy test, but it came back negative. On the basis of this test, I decided to do a bungy jump off Queenstown Bridge, the first bungy jump location in the world. I found out after returning home that I *was* pregnant.

I experienced an amazing healing during this pregnancy. The scar tissue that had formed in my kidney wound site was not stretching with my stomach as the baby grew, and the pain was unbearable. I went to a Bill Subritzky healing meeting, and he prayed for me. Bill was a prominent teacher in New Zealand at the time in the area of deliverance. After he prayed, the scar tissue no longer bothered me. It was interesting that Bill had asked me, while he was praying for me, whether there had been any trauma or grief that had occurred at the time the scar tissue developed. He felt the scar may be holding grief. I alerted him to the fact that Krissy had died soon after the surgery, and he prayed for the residue of grief to lift. The scar tissue began to stretch from that moment forward. When the doctors at the hospital asked me a couple of weeks later how it was going, I told them the scar tissue was now stretching and not bothering me. The doctors were amazed because, as they said, scar tissue doesn't heal.

Because of my kidney problems with Krissy, I was categorized as a high-risk patient, which meant I was given high priority attention within the hospital system. This came with more focused medical attention and testing. I was so grateful for this.

We were also very grateful for the Cot Death Society. This charity provides support for those who have lost babies to cot death. They came alongside us and gave us a cot death monitor for the crib free of charge. This meant I could put my mind at ease after the birth.

A lot of joy and expectancy surrounded this new baby's birth. It was a healing time, not just for us, but also for a lot of beautiful people who had walked with us. The women of our church gave us a lot of support and organized a wonderful baby shower. I gave birth to a baby boy after being induced, as he was two weeks overdue. My Father gave me the name Joseph, meaning "God will increase." Joseph's birth and his naming signified that our Father was about to increase us and our lives.

About six months after Joseph's birth, the Lord miraculously provided a beautiful new home for us. We had seen this house a year before on the market and believed it was far beyond of our budget, but we could still dream. A year later, it came back on the market. We had a brief look and decided to try and put an offer together. I had a dream that there was a man in pain looking over a contract. The gentleman looked laden with grief and heartbroken that he was selling. He didn't want to sign the contract. There was also a specific monetary amount printed on the contract. The man signed it reluctantly. I woke up and told John the dream and the figure God had given me. That day, the agent rang John and said the owner in question had said to her he was only going to offer the house to us, and we had one night to put an offer together as he would decide the next day. We found out that his wife had left him, and he really didn't want to sell. We put down the figure God had shown me in the dream, which was less than what he wanted, but all we probably could afford at the time. The next day, he signed the contract and told the agent it was because he wanted a young Christian family to own it.

We lived in that home by the sea for fifteen years. It was a third of an acre of stunning grounds. The people who had built the house had used beautiful cypress wood. It had very high solid wood ceilings. After our little two-bedroom house, this felt like a mansion. There was an assortment of lovely fruit trees. We loved harvest time, when the kitchen benches would be filled with green and red apples, persimmons, mandarins, oranges, avocados, lemons, and peaches. We had a large vegetable section that produced great produce. Jessica loved chickens, so she raised them and had a good little business going. It was so lovely having fresh eggs to go with our produce. The property also had winding pathways and a lovely big pond and palm trees. We could see the Auckland Harbor Bridge from our decks. We called it "our paradise."

After we moved there, I had a dream. I was walking along a very wide, dusty road, and every now and then I would stop to have coffee with someone. This went on for quite a while; I would walk, stop, have coffee, and continue on. Then I came to the end of this road, and before me was a valley where thousands of people were standing below, looking up at me. I turned and asked John and my kids, "Are you okay that I do this?" and they all replied, "Yes." So, I turned and started ministering to these people. I had this dream three times in one night; and as you have read thus far, this is a prominent way God speaks to me to ratify that it is him speaking to me. I was not sure what my Father was saying through this dream. However, over the years, this is the dream he has most often reminded me of when I have felt stuck or disheartened in my journey.

We started going to the local church. I had a friend who had prophesied, when I was feeling nervous about moving, that I would have a fruitful ministry there. This word proved true. I undertook a spiritual formation course as part of my studies at Bible college that year, and part of my training was to run retreats. This course showed me I had a gift for helping others pinpoint the incongruity they may have had in their walk with God between their head knowledge and their gut responses to God. My studies helped me to start trusting my spiritual gut as the foundations in my relationship with God were being rebuilt.

John and I ran a family home group at our house once a week. We had so much fun. We all had children the same age, and our house and yard were large, so the children had trees to climb and a playground. We would have a potluck meal, so it was always a treat to have heaps of food and much laughter together.

All these new experiences, such as a new home and developing new relationships, helped to assure us that our Father was indeed making all things new (Isa 43:19) and giving each one of us beauty for ashes (Isa 61:3). He was rebuilding our lives in so many concrete and life-giving ways.

My relationship with my mum during this time, however, was beginning to really strain, as I was gaining more confidence in my own voice. Consequently, her need to gain back control seemed to be getting stronger. I had enabled this terrible dichotomy in our relationship to exist, as I never said what I really felt because she would get angry if I did. God had been helping me to not be so afraid when I talked with her on the phone, and at times I would change the subject just so I didn't have to have those awful conversations with her. One day, I felt the Lord ask me to tell her what I really believed about the gifts of the Spirit. This seems trivial, I know, but it was a massive step for me. Mum, because of having been spiritually abused as a child, hated any of the manifestations of the Spirit, calling them demonic. This is totally understandable when you factor in that she was beaten as a child at bedtime if she did not speak in tongues.

When she phoned on this day, I expressed to her that I believed the gifts of the Spirit are for today. She exploded with rage, declaring that I was a heretic and on my way to hell. I stayed firm; however, after I put the phone down, I physically trembled for hours. I sat on the floor of my kitchen, shaking and crying uncontrollably. It was like years of pent-up torment were being released. In hindsight, I know these were the effects of abusive spirituality. I was still reeling from Krissy dying, and now I realized I may lose my mother.

Thankfully, one of the pastors in the church came around and was able to hold me in my pain. She just sat on the floor with me as I drank in the reality that everything was now different. I felt great guilt that through acknowledging the abuse that was happening, I was also betraying my parents. This causes me great sadness. I could not honor them and continue to lie to them about what I believed and why. My Father said to me at the time, "It is not honoring to your parents to lie to them." Honor, by its nature, requires a person to hold their integrity before another in truth and take cognizance of one's life in light of the truth. To continue to answer my mother's questions concerning my faith with deception would have been dishonoring to her and to the Holy Spirit.

My studies were very important in this process, as they helped me develop autonomy and independent critical thinking about my faith and what I believed. For me, a bachelor's degree was becoming less about accumulating facts and knowledge and increasingly a hungering for spiritual food that would sustain me on my journey away from my mother's faith to my own. Even though this incident left me on the floor in a mess, it also dismantled the stronghold of fear that had been suffocating me and signified a shift as I had now found my voice. My voice was trembling, petrified, isolated, and deeply abandoned, but it was mine and I had spoken. I was proud of myself.

From this moment, I felt empowered to no longer be babied. I admit that the process of leaving my mother necessitated that I also take responsibility for my own actions. Mum, of course, had her issues, but I needed to get to a place where I realized I was enabling this toxic relationship to continue because I still wanted to be mothered. I wanted to leave responsibility for my life at someone else's feet. I started to take more responsibility in my responses to Mum, and this changed my perception of myself from being a victim to taking accountability for my dysfunctions that affected many other areas of my life. Confession was a critical part of this process, as I started to acknowledge and repent of the idolatry I had toward my mother and also the reality of how abusive our relationship was. I was leaving Mum and moving toward a deeper and more stable attachment to God.

Really beautiful things were happening in church for me as I was processing my relationship with my mother. I signed up for a preaching class, as I had never preached before and expected it would be a bit of fun. As I stepped behind the podium, the strangest thing happened; I felt like I belonged there, like I had found what I was born to do. It was the most intense experience of being right where I was meant to be. I preached that night, and the instructor stopped taking notes because he said he was so interested in what I had to say. He said that this was a good sign I should be doing this.

So that's what happened. I was given opportunities to preach in the church on the topics I was studying and from my own experience.

This period of time at Bible college was so encouraging. I made a lot of great friends. We had lots of lovely dinners together on campus, hosted by my lovely friend Sarah. We would sit outside in the beautiful summer evenings and enjoy each other's company, debating theological and social issues.

I continued to study and ran a community-based learning course at Bible college. In hindsight, I began to be filled with pride regarding my performance in my studies. I had been attaining a 3.7/A-grade average in my bachelor's program. Having a huge spiritual vacuum left from having tried to please my mother, I now tried to fill this hole with performance at college. Unfortunately, this was only just the beginning because I still held residues of pride where I contended that my views were right and others' were wrong. It was becoming all about me and not Jesus. I know I hurt so many people during this phase. I would come to see this all when events in my life caused me to face the ugly in myself.

Digging Deeper

Grief comes in waves. There were times I was coping really well, and then out of nowhere another wave would come. The fear in the early days was that the pain would not end or the waves would become permanent. As the second year came around, I knew that the wave of grief would come and it would go and not last as long. Deep pain, deep regrets, deep loss would surface but would not suffocate me. This reflects the vision the Lord had given me of the process my grief journey would take.

I also remember, around this time, the Lord speaking clearly to me about the difference between natural grief and a "spirit of grief." Natural grief is the normal process of grieving a loss. A spirit of grief is when grief turns to self-obsessive indulgence or feeling sorry for oneself. How do you know which one you are processing? For me, it was tied in with whether I would let the Lord comfort me or listen to his promptings to move forward into new things. It is a very personal thing. It is not so much about the length of grief, as that is different for everyone. It is being aware of when it is time to move into the next phase of grief and choosing not to. For me, I knew I was dwelling in self-pity because the Lord told me I was. There were places on my healing journey where I would have to choose to move forward and sacrifice my own desire to stay stranded in bitterness.

Psychological Justice

Being offered the position of executive assistant brought dignity in the midst of processing grief. I am thankful my Father knew I needed to shift into an aspect of my identity that did not necessitate that I utilize psychological resources I needed to recover. I was able to rest in the breadth of the theological research I had already garnered by this stage. It was also very reassuring that my Father had placed me within the safe holding transitional space of BCNZ/Laidlaw.

Having the Cot Death Society recognize our need after Krissy died to be able to put our baby to bed without constant fear ministered strength and confidence to us. Having the cot death monitor meant we were able to enjoy Joseph without constantly fearing he had stopped breathing. This gift offered us dignity and practical help without cost. I love how the Father knows when, in our humanity, we need more than a spiritual salve for our wounds. We needed psychological support with our new baby, and the fact that my Father, in his provision, acknowledged this need is another way *psychological justice* was bringing deeper, foundational psychological and theological security during our grief.

I also see *psychological justice* in my Father leading me to ask Bill Subritzky to pray for my scar tissue while carrying Joseph. Our Father, through this time, continually validated our psychological and physical need for healing of our wounds in all facets of our lives after Krissy's death. My Father showed me through this that there are definitive links sometimes between the physical, psychological, and theological aspects of our lives. *Psychological justice* was affirmed through our lives in the wake of Joseph's birth.

Joseph's birth was also a prophetic demonstration of our Father's increase coming to our lives. We had felt so robbed and forsaken at times that to see our Father's visible present activity within our circumstances gave us hope for our future. In this period of our lives, we were seeing such an increase in so many areas that it felt like we had entered a supernatural season of growth. Moving to such a beautiful, large house and extensive manicured garden was an indication that our physical space had broadened and was symbolic of our family increasing. Moving also saw an increase in life-giving relationships and fun. Our home group and ministry were expanding our tent pegs in so many ways. We felt we had entered a psychologically healthy space that enabled our grief process to be buoyed by joy and laughter. Our Father's intense supply of life-giving moments in all aspects of our lives shows me that *psychological justice* matters to him—that we matter to him.

Having increased in so many ways started to give me the psychological reserves I needed to face my mum and tell her how I really felt about the gifts of the Spirit. In "failing" her, I was able to put boundaries in place. Theologically, I knew I was on solid ground. I needed the Holy Spirit to face the psychological void that would exist after confronting the abuse from my mother. Through my increasing confidence due to new and solid relationships, God was working *psychological justice* in my life in complex and intersecting ways. I hope this garners confidence for you, because our Father wants this for all of us.

What's Your Story?

Can you see God's hand in rebuilding your life either through or after difficult seasons? Take some time to discern ways in which trials have, in time, brought freedom. If you feel stuck, invite the Lord into this space.

Season 4

How Much Longer, Lord?

"Did I ask you for a son, my lord?" she said. "Didn't I tell you, 'Don't raise my hopes'?" (2 Kgs 4:28)

After losing Krissy and having Joseph, I genuinely believed I had had my Job experience. Job lost everything in the space of a couple of days (Job 1:13–22). The journey he went on with his well-meaning but ultimately unwise "friends" is exhausting reading. So here I was, believing—hoping—that we had had ours. Like, you only get one Job-like storm in life and then everything is restored. Right? Man, was I about to find out that just isn't true. My grief as a mother was now finding meaning, and I didn't envisage I would suffer loss of that magnitude again. Just like Job.

Mothering—that word brought hope. I was beginning to be infused with hope again. Soon my hope and faith and confidence as a mother would be tested repeatedly.

A Broken Mother's Heart

In the beginning of 2003, I found out I was pregnant. I was still studying, but I was overjoyed that a new life was growing inside me. I went for a routine scan and was deeply saddened to find out that the baby within me had died. I was devastated. It was all a bit of a blur, really. I was working and studying, and in the busyness, I put losing this bub, whom we had named Jack, down to an anomaly. I grieved in a dazed kind of way. Maybe I couldn't feel it as I didn't know what grief category to really place this in. Unlike with Krissy,

70

there was no illness on my part. I didn't really know how to grieve a baby I never saw, so I think I buried my heart into my studies and kept going. It was strange waiting for my body to miscarry naturally, but I found that as time went on, nothing happened. I soon needed intervention and was booked for a D&C (dilation and curettage). What a horrible experience, going to hospital to have a baby taken out of me and never seeing him for myself. I think that is why it was hard to grieve, as I never held him to say goodbye. After they took Jack from me, I went home. No follow-up, just a regular doctor's visit. But I was empty, and I felt a little lost. Doing normal things felt abnormal. You go to the shops, you fill up your car with petrol, you pick up the kids—all in a daze. I had just lost my baby—and life just carried on.

Six months later, I became pregnant again. I was a little nervous but had put Jack's miscarriage down to a one-off. However, a routine scan showed we had lost this baby too. The Lord gave me the name Mariah, meaning "bitterly wanted." I remember the moment he gave me this name. I was sitting at my desk studying theology. I was trying hard not to go into my ugly space with God, but I couldn't help it. I was so hurt. "Of course," I shouted, "she was bitterly wanted!" Why would he acknowledge my deepest pain with a name? Why could he not just fix the cause? It was so hard to let God comfort me.

Mariah's miscarriage was distressing. The hospital nurse gave me medication to start the process of inducement, then forgot about me, as there were a few emergencies. I started to bleed excessively. I passed out at one point, and a nurse found me. They couldn't stop the bleeding, so I was finally wheeled, almost unconscious, into surgery. Amid substantial blood loss, I watched them take my baby out of me. Poor John had come to see me but had to leave me in the middle of all this because it was very late, and he had to get back to Jessica and Joseph as the babysitter needed to go home. I had lost so much blood that I was given a blood transfusion. It was the most bizarre experience; I was so weak and it was comforting to have blood replenish my body.

Mariah's passing was really difficult for me. After having watched my daughter die of cot death, I expected that experiencing a miscarriage would not be as hard, but it was. The grief did not last as long, but it was just as painful. I remember listening to an Abba song called "The Name of the Game." I sat there yelling at God and asking him, "Why are you playing with me—is this just a game to you?" It didn't make sense to me. I was studying at Bible college, and yet none of my head knowledge could take away the question "Why?" The incongruence in my faith was startling.

Six months later, I was pregnant again, and this time the hospital was more intentional in following the pregnancy. I had an earlier scan, which showed I was carrying twins, but the scan also showed that one of the twins had already died. I sighed that at least there was one remaining baby that had a strong heartbeat. We named the baby twin who died Peter.

I left the hospital thankful and excited that we had a little viable heartbeat. However, not long after this, I was at work and I bled a little. I was trembling and my heart just sank. In trepidation and fear, I walked rather anxiously and tearfully to my friend Jacqui's office, who worked at Bible college as well. I saw her and shakily asked her to take me to the hospital. She saw my face and knew it was not good. She gathered her things and took me to her car. The ride to the hospital was agonizing. I got to a very busy triage area. I waited a while, then was taken to the ward. They ran some tests, and then we waited for what seemed like forever. I sat there going over and over in my head the untold grief of so much loss. I couldn't grasp any thoughts as they just swirled in and through and over and over. I tried to make sense of it all, but the more I tried to make sense of it, the more painful and hopeless I felt. All the past insecurities in my relationship with God and the nonsensical teaching that somehow this *was* my fault were endless. I felt like the most pitiful person on the planet. "My womb is a death trap," I thought. How, as a mother, do you handle that amount of death in your womb or because of your womb? My womb was unable to hold life. I felt so helpless, so hopeless, so ugly and ashamed. I felt like my womanhood was ripped out of my soul and being.

The scan and blood tests revealed that my precious baby had died. This baby that had had a viable and strong heartbeat only weeks before was lying in my womb without life.

I was so grateful for my dear friend Jacqui being with me that day, as the devastation and pain erupted in my being all over again. So much loss over so many years just sat raw in that hospital room. Jacqui is such a faithful and deep friend. She did not offer any platitudes. She did not try and "fix" me or my pain. She sat with me and held my hand tightly. We just sat in silence as I collected my thoughts. The nurses came in, and the doctor explained the results. I didn't hear much of what he said. They gave me my discharge papers. As we got up to leave, I remember feeling so emptied of hope. I left with papers that told me my baby was dead. Notes about the age, size, possible causes? None. What to do? Wait for my baby to miscarry, they said. Wait. Another agonizing wait.

We named this baby David.

The same process happened with David as with the others; I would need intervention, but this time the hospital took him to see if they could figure out what was happening with the development of these babies. We received him back after this process with no clear evidence that anything was wrong, and we buried him with his siblings. We painted stones from our garden pond with the names of all the babies on them and placed them on Krissy's gravesite. Seeing them all collectively telling of our grief and loss is hard, but knowing they are all together is also healing.

Losing David was really difficult for both of us, but it hit John particularly hard. When David died, a big part of John died too. His faith struggled for a couple of years. I rang my mum, hoping for some comfort, and her response to me was that I was a "silly little girl." I was stunned. What on earth? Why would she say this? Such a belittling statement. What mother calls her daughter, at thirty-seven, a "silly—little—girl"?

For miscarrying.

What a moment. I don't think I said anything to her at that point. I changed the subject, got off the phone, and walked around my house stunned by the disdain in her response. Days went on, and the more I pondered her remarks, the more it dawned on me that it was not unusual for Mum to call me this. How many times she had called me a "little girl" or "pet." Yes, "pet." Even writing this makes me wince. I am not sure she even knew that in her mind that is how she perceived me. I was a defenseless little girl or, worse, a helpless creature who could not fend for herself. It felt like it was a label particularly chosen to name me; that I was not robust enough to cope with life.

All I had gone through without her, to this point, made me realize that I hadn't made this stuff up. How she saw me had not changed. My relationship with her was destructive. I now had evidence. I was angry and hurt enough about her reaction that it solidified in my grief a genuine response that I should have had all along. It was time to take significant steps to confront our toxic relationship.

Around Christmas that year, I felt pregnant, but I had not taken a pregnancy test yet. A couple of weeks later, I had an excessive bleed, and God gave me the name Anna. The process of loss was raw.

After losing Krissy, Jack, Peter, Mariah, David, and Anna, I went on a silent retreat for a week. This was very timely. The theme of the retreat was authenticity, intimacy, and vulnerability with God.

I had often been labeled as too emotional and loud growing up. I had suffered so much shame over my sensitive personality and ways of relating. God showed me during this time that I had to let go of not being as strong as I believed others were. I needed to surrender to God my jealousy and fear of not being enough or of being emotional and weak and welcome his love for me in my weakened form. God wanted to come to me with a gentle whisper in my storm.

What was really central in my time with God during this week was the concept of God as mother. This was a huge revelation and not one I was initially eager to embrace. Stepping out of codependency with Mum and other "mothers" into God as mother felt heretical. It felt childish and immature to want God as a mother. To want God to comfort and cherish me, to be gentle with me—all of this seemed foreign.

"I am motherless," I wrote in my journal. I needed a mother, but I was also suffering and grieving deeply as a mother who kept burying her children. Having a mother had been dangerous and destructive, and it was so painful to let her go as I had to cut off all emotional connection. I knew I couldn't lean on my mother like others could for support with their children, their heartaches, or when they are sick, because when I did, I was told I was either silly or not being biblical enough. It was so hard to ask God to be what I needed in a mothering space because it meant acknowledging the need, which was so deep and painful. Although Mum manipulated those needs to meet her needs, my needs were—and still are—valid, as were her needs. This was an important week because in years to come, I would need to know that this God I had been afraid of was the very one who would help me leave the control that had stemmed from such deep fear.

I woke up early one morning during this week with the Lord asking me, "How do you feel as a mother?" The word that came to me was, "No confidence." I didn't feel worthy. The anger and disappointment I held against myself as a mother was deep. The Lord gave me Psalm 23 a little modified:

> The Lord is my mother; I have everything I need. She lets me rest in green meadows. She leads me beside peaceful streams. She renews my strength. She guides me along right paths, bringing honor to her name. Even when I walk through the dark valley of death or the darkest valley, I will not be afraid, for she is close beside me.
>
> Her rod and her staff protect and comfort me. She prepares a feast for me in the presence of my enemies. She welcomes me as an honored guest, anointing my head with oil. My cup overflows with blessings.
>
> Surely her goodness and unfailing love will pursue me all the days of my life and I will live in her house forever. This is your inheritance as a servant of the highest God.[1]

This version from my Father meant so much to me. She lets me rest. I so needed to rest. I so needed to rest in green meadows beside peaceful

---

1. This is my own translation of Psalm 23.

streams. I had walked the longest, loneliest, darkest road. I was longing to rest in the arms of one who would embrace me as a mother—that gentle, all-embracing love. I was desperate for a mother, desperate to be mothered. As a mother, God held me. I was holding all my beautiful babies, and she was holding us in her everlasting arms.

After losing these beautiful babies, I told John I was done. Absolutely done. I had nothing left. I was now thirty-eight, and my mother heart and body felt like it had closed the door and thrown away the key. However, it was just like God to give me another dream. Again, I had the dream three times in one night. In the dream, I had a picture of Jessica and Joseph. I then took two more children, a boy and a girl, and put them in the picture. I stepped back and decided, "Yes, that's good." Then the boy in the picture grew up really tall and strong and filled the room I was in. Each time I woke up, I said to the Lord, "No, I can't go through the grief of losing another child ever again. I can't bury any more children." And I would go back to sleep. The third time, I said, "Okay, Lord, but if one of them dies, we will be over." I was serious.

Not long after, John and I went to Australia for a vacation to visit family. After arriving back to New Zealand, I received a letter from my father containing a torrent of abuse and accusation regarding my loyalty to my family and my lack of respect for what he and Mum had done for me. I was so confused. To my surprise, I heard the Lord audibly say, "Enough!" The Lord came to my aid and told me to leave it with him and not respond. I was finalizing my last papers for my bachelor's degree, and many of my papers on spirituality were so timely. They were helping me get back in touch with the girl I missed from my youth, helping me find her and reattaching her to Jesus so our dance together could start healing. A key factor in breaking the vicious cycle of abuse was growing in my intellectual autonomy. My Father showed me that I no longer had to absorb the anxiety of my family. I no longer had to be the scapegoat. I didn't have the energy to be the scapegoat. I didn't want to be sent out into the wilderness continually because of the inability of others to face their own pain. Abusive people often dump their pain on your shoulders and ask you to carry their inability to function for them.

My hope for a functional family was fading. I had worked so hard to put boundaries in place with my mother. When we talked on the phone, we would not talk about spiritual things, as it never ended well. We would talk about the kids or Dad and her. I tried to talk about anything but God. This was sad in one way, but also freeing. Unfortunately, the track of abuse was too deep. I couldn't pay the high price they wanted to stay connected. That price would have been my soul being aborted.

I attended a course called "Boundaries," written by Drs. Henry Cloud and John Townsend. When I told the pastor about my situation with my family, he gave me the courage to be strong and keep my boundaries in place. A lot of my colleagues from Bible college also went to this church at the time, and it was a very fruitful period of my life. I had a surrogate family to help offset the deep pain I was enduring with my own family. I was flourishing, and my children were healthy and happy.

The pregnancy predicted in my dream happened when I was thirty-nine and, as my Father promised, I was carrying a beautiful little boy, whom we would name Benjamin. The pregnancy went really well. Ben was a little overdue when I went to see my midwife at the hospital in August 2006. As I walked out of this appointment, I saw a pamphlet on cesarean sections in the waiting room, and the Lord asked me to take it. When I got home, I felt led to read it from cover to cover. There was no indication whatsoever from the hospital that I would need this.

The next day, I was induced. Everything was going well until suddenly Ben's umbilical cord came out before him. This problem is called an umbilical cord prolapse. It must be dealt with immediately, as the baby can put pressure on the cord, which cuts off their oxygen supply. A button was pushed, a heap of nurses came rushing in, and the leading midwife said, "We have seven minutes to get him out, and I can do it in five." Thankfully, I had already had a spinal pain relief tap inserted and was whisked into the emergency room across the hall.

Because I had read the cesarean section pamphlet the night before, I was calm. The nurses and doctors could not believe how calm I was. Poor John and my dear friend Cindy were upstairs watching, while I was in theater. The midwife was right; she got him out in five minutes, and he was beautiful! We named him Benjamin because it means "son of my right hand, my strength," and also because in the Scriptures Benjamin is Joseph's brother. The doctor asked why I was so calm, and I was able to share with them that the Lord had told me to read the pamphlet and so I knew at each step what they were doing and why. Isn't our God amazing? Ben was an absolute delight. The pain of the cesarean section was eclipsed by my delight in my beautiful boy.

Digging Deeper

God leads me to help a lot of women who are dealing with the loss of their precious babies or trying to have children. I have found when ministering to women who have had miscarriages that some have not named their babies.

I find profound healing happens for women when we ask the Father to give them a name for their baby/babies. There is a sense for many of deep acceptance and healing. I also love praying for women who cannot seem to fall pregnant. I had one friend who had been trying for a very long time—over ten years—and one day she said to me that when she had turned forty, they had given it over to the Lord, so I didn't need to keep praying. I felt this strong sense in my spirit of the Lord saying that he wanted me to keep praying. I said to my friend, "I am sorry, but I don't feel I have permission from the Lord to stop praying. Are you okay with that?" She said she was. I kid you not, not soon after this, she fell pregnant. She now has a beautiful boy. So many people had been praying for them, and we all felt encouraged by our Father's provision.

The concept of grace was something I had not really grasped, as I was perpetually striving to adhere to the rules of Christianity that my mother kept telling me I needed in order to be safe. One paper I had to write was on the implications for spiritual life of having a foundation of grace rather than guilt. I was starting to see my striving as a performance trap, and grace was my answer to freedom. As I sought to understand what a grace foundation might look like, I started seeing that my inner life hidden in God from others was actually the place I needed to embrace in front of others. The places I hid out of shame and weakness were the very places God wanted me to let him sit with me. My tutor was pivotal in helping me grasp some of these grace concepts.

A quote from a book I was reading for my assignment caught my attention: for some people, "God is the divine equivalent of Ebenezer Scrooge; the God who demands the last ounce of work out of His people and then pays them poorly."[2] That was my attitude to God right there. I felt I was always striving but never really meeting the mark.

I was reading authors who were writing about the dangers of legalism and seeing myself in their reflections. The reality that my striving was a form of grace avoidance was really hitting home. I avoided grace because I felt grace showed I was weak. My mother's influence was still very strong during these years; on top of feeling worthy because I was keeping the rules, I had now added theological academic success to my list of why I could belong in the kingdom. The spiritual formation class was starting to unravel some of this dichotomy.

2. Bridges, *Transforming Grace*, 57.

Psychological Justice

Psychological justice was being manifested in this season as my image of God was being further re-established through God coming to me as a mother. This was broadening and strengthening my understanding of God's character and being. My Father was coming to me as a mother before I knew I would need him to be my mother. He could see the deep void that would be left in me once I faced and lost my mother, and he was preparing to take that role to fill the vacuum. I did not know at this point how much I would need this revelation. The Father is not content that we only know him as a theological expression of the Scriptures. He will come to us in our lived experience in all the ways we need him to—even as a mother (see Hos 11:1–4; Isa 49:15).

The dream I had of Ben and Rachel in the midst of my deep loss, after so many miscarriages, was another visible manifestation of *psychological justice*. My Father was taking a risk with me in the sense that it put his faithfulness on trial in my eyes. My Father had to work enough grace in me to be able to hesitantly trust him in this way. My Father wanted to increase my capacity of trust toward him, and I needed him to prove himself to me. I had been so forsaken by my own father and mother that I psychologically needed my Father to come through for me—especially as I had endured so much deep loss.

My broken mother heart was given *psychological justice* through the events of this season. I had been traumatized through so much loss that the way my Father provided in psychological, spiritual, and physical ways shows me that he is interested in more than a technical, theoretical, transactional relationship. My Father made his presence felt in all aspects of my life, and his heart was to heal deep trauma. My Father wanted me to thrive again, not just survive.

What's Your Story?

Where is your striving a form of grace avoidance? Is the concept of God as mother disturbing or inviting? What do you think your response may be telling you?

The Promise Tested

Here is where we pick up and continue the rest of the story I introduced to you in the opening chapter. I was homeschooling Jess when the incident by the pond happened; events that would happen in the June of Ben's second year would impact all of us.

My friend Ruth and I decided to go to Auckland Domain Pond for lunch on the nine-year anniversary of Kristiana's burial, June 5, 2008. It was a beautiful, sunny, cold winter's day. The Auckland Domain is a gorgeous big park in the heart of Auckland, with very beautiful old trees and some ponds that are over one hundred years old.

We decided to get takeaway coffee and hot chips and sit with Ben and Jess near the ponds. Ruth was chatting with me and watching them, and unfortunately I said to Ruth, "Oh, Jess is fine watching Ben. Let's go grab our coffee," as the coffee shop was only fifteen meters from the ponds. This was one of the most ill-informed decisions of my life. Jessica was only nine years old, and Ben only twenty-two months old. My job was to look after Ben, especially around water, not hand that responsibility over to a nine-year-old girl. A lady got to chatting with Jess about feeding the ducks, and then Jess lost sight of Ben. Jessica did the absolute right thing when she could not find Ben; she ran to tell me he was missing. I thought we would just trot down and he would be there, but we couldn't see him anywhere. A mild concern immediately turned into a harrowing nightmare and sheer terror as we scrambled to find him.

There were contractors doing roadworks close by, so I hoped desperately that Ben might have wandered to look at the diggers, but the more we looked, the more the panic set in and cries turned to shrieks as we yelled out his name, looking for him. People who had now gathered around the ponds also started getting involved in the search with us. At least ten minutes had passed by this point.

Suddenly, I heard a terrified, high-pitched scream from my friend Ruth. The way Ruth screamed alerted me that it was very serious. Ruth had felt God tell her to wait at the edge of the pond and keep looking. She couldn't see anything representing a child, just ducks and a lump of something that looked like a potato chip bag. Suddenly, she saw two little white markings and realized they were the heels of shoes; what she thought was a potato chip packet was Ben's bottom and the checked trousers he was wearing. Ruth jumped in, screaming, and trudged to the middle of the pond, where she found Ben submerged. She grabbed him, walked the terrifying minutes it took her to get out of the pond, and brought him to me.

He was pure white.

He was not breathing.

He was limp, frozen, and lifeless.

I held his soaking-wet, unresponsive little body, but all I could do was drop to my knees and scream. I screamed, "God, have mercy on me! God, have mercy on me!" Over and over and over, I cried out for God to have mercy on me. Ben looked just like Krissy when I had held her lifeless body in my arms this same date nine years earlier.

I handed Ben to Ruth in panic and fear and my eyes pierced hers with the message, "Save my son!" I just didn't know what to do, and I knew I could not do CPR as I was in complete panic. I almost threw Ben at Ruth, and she started CPR on him. The reality of Ben's lifeless body swirled around me like a tornado about to rip my life out of me. I kept looking at Ruth trying to resuscitate Ben, and "horror" doesn't even come close to expressing what I was experiencing. It was deeper and more consuming than I could ever have imagined. I was spiraling in and out of reality. I kept crying out deep groans of fear mixed with intense pain that came from a place in me I did not know existed, a primal scream that was full of certainty that my son was dead. I will never forget the distress of not being able to master my reactions in the situation. I felt intensely powerless.

Someone called an ambulance, while a midwife who worked on premature babies at Starship Children's Hospital, adjacent to the park, just "happened" to be walking past and sprinted over to take over for Ruth doing CPR on Ben, but Ben was not responding. Time seemed to be suspended.

I was still screaming when Ruth suddenly shouted out, "I command this boy to come back to life in Jesus' name!"

At that moment, Ben coughed up water, but he was in a really, really bad way. His breathing was seriously labored and sounded excruciating. There was so much water in his lungs that you could physically hear it, and there was terror in his eyes as he gasped for each breath. I was trembling and could not process what I was seeing. I was not coping. All I know is that if Ruth had not been there and taken control for me, I am not sure how this story may have ended.

An ambulance also just "happened" to be passing by the entrance to the pond when they got the call that they were needed in the Domain. They were with us within two minutes. A special man stood with Jessica in the turmoil and comforted her and kept her safe. To this day, I have no idea who he was, but he was very kind and calm.

Nick, the paramedic onboard the ambulance, was one of the leading paramedics in the Auckland region. He got scissors, cut Ben's shirt in two, and ripped it off him. It was a very cold winter's day, and Ben was lying on a concrete surface with only his nappy on. They got him oxygenated and into the ambulance. His breathing continued to heavily crackle and gurgle, and I was deeply shaken as I listened to him. I could not help him, and it was excruciating seeing him terrified with each breath he strained to take.

I couldn't hold him or cuddle him, as they needed to get him hooked up to medical machinery. I was completely helpless.

I was completely at fault.

The ambulance driver asked me to sit in the front as they needed to attend to Ben. When the ambulance arrived at the hospital minutes later, a host of doctors and nurses all rushed to Ben's aid. The registrar who received Ben from the ambulance that afternoon was very quick to respond and was in complete control. I watched, powerless, as they hooked up numerous tubes and monitors to Ben, while I sat with Nick, the paramedic, nearby. I felt like a spectator as they took my son and didn't ask me to do anything or even talk to me. They were completely focused on my little desperately and gravely ill baby boy. I had just played with him an hour before. I was in deep shock and couldn't comprehend what I was witnessing. "How could I have let this happen?" This question hovered over me like a dark haze. I just sat there as Nick asked me all sorts of random questions to help me focus on something other than what I was looking at. I couldn't really think at all. I just remember that Nick was so calm and so compassionate, and I will never forget his kindness.

Ruth, meanwhile, was back at the pond with Jessica. I can't imagine how my precious nine-year-old girl coped in these moments. Ruth made sure she was okay and secured our cars, and people who worked at the café made sure that security people knew what was going on. Ruth walked with Jessica to the hospital, completely soaked, having jumped into the pond to grab Ben. Jessica asked Ruth as they walked if Ben was going to die, and Ruth said, "No, no, Ben is not going to die." I am so grateful for Ruth imparting her faith that day to Jessica, as she must have been so distraught.

The doctors immediately put Ben into an induced coma. Friends Mark, Sue, and Jacqui arrived at the hospital within twenty minutes of me ringing them. Ruth had rung John to tell him what had happened and also asked that he get some clothes for her from her home as she was soaking wet. John arrived around the time my other friends arrived, and we were all taken to a small room away from intensive care so the doctors could talk to us about what was at stake for Ben. These were incredibly difficult conversations. Mark's friend was the registrar on this day, and she explained that Ben was in a grave condition. She said they would do all they could, but there was real danger that Ben could die from secondary drowning from the extensive water in his lungs. Benjamin's core temperature was 80.6 degrees Fahrenheit (27 degrees Celsius). Another highly possible serious complication was extensive brain damage. We surmised that Ben had been unaccounted for over ten minutes. Ruth rescued him from the middle of the pond with only the heel of his shoe visible. We think Ben had followed the ducks into the pond, then fell, sunk, and floated to the middle. Once Benjamin was out of the pond, it would be another five to ten minutes before he was resuscitated. In all, we estimated that Ben was without oxygen for a minimum of ten minutes and a maximum of twenty. For a little boy twenty-two months old—or for anyone, for that matter—this was a long time for his brain to be starved of oxygen.

Ben was placed in intensive care, where he was monitored twenty-four hours a day by absolutely outstanding nurses and doctors. One of these nurses was Kirsty, and I cannot overestimate her part in Ben's recovery. She sat at the end of Ben's bed on many of her eight-hour shifts during Ben's ten days in intensive care. During our collective meeting, the registrar asked John and I to come and meet with someone who asked if we wanted Ben to be part of an international study on whether it is beneficial for drowning victims or those whose brains may have been starved of oxygen to be kept cold to protect the brain from further damage.

John and I went into a room to discuss this pilot study. During our conversation, I suddenly started feeling very unwell and vacant. I felt like I was going to faint and quite unable to communicate. But I was able to stay focused as John and I agreed to be part of this study. Doing so meant Benjamin would have more tracking and more tightly regulated care. We walked out of the room, and I suddenly couldn't answer simple questions. The enormity of what we were facing with Ben and the surreal nature of all the conversations I was having, on the same day I had started out remembering his sister dying, was beyond comprehension.

My dear friends were at pains to remind me that we still had Joseph to pick up from school very soon, and I just couldn't get my head around this. I was looking at my Ben, who was strapped down with so many tubes that I don't think I could have counted them. There was a huge accessory strapped to Ben's mouth, and he was lying there in a coma, and I had to think about how to pick up my other son, Joseph. I couldn't leave Ben, but I also knew Joseph needed us.

It was decided that John would go and get Joseph, take him and Jessica home, get them dinner, and settle them. We had no extended family to come and be with them, and Jessica had gone through so much that day that we felt it was better she be with John away from the horror of seeing her brother Ben like this.

The nurses were so kind. Someone took me up to the second level of intensive care, where Ronald McDonald House had several rooms attached to a huge lounge and dining area. They gave me keys to my own single room with a bed and phone in it. The phone had a direct line to the intensive care nurses, so they could contact me in any emergency. There were communal bathrooms, and the lounge and dining area had a huge kitchen, where generous people in the public made meals and baked to help support those staying in this house. These meals were available twenty-four hours a day, seven days a week. The lounge area was decorated in such a way that it enabled those who needed to have hard conversations or to meet with family to grieve to do so. It had the semblance of a beautiful motel, but it also had the feel of a place to cope with the horrors of what may be happening for people on the level below. The elevator to intensive care was directly across from the bedrooms. We would spend many hours in this lounge and kitchen, catching up with the children or sitting with friends when there were important decisions to be made. We got to know some of the other parents and what their children were in hospital for. It was a safe communal space to escape to when needed.

After John and everyone else left, I had a small bite to eat and a shower, as I was significantly broken and exhausted. I needed a shower to feel some normality, and I remember how calming brushing my hair felt.

It was about two o'clock in the morning, and I was crawling into bed after talking to John to tell him Ben was stable. I lay down and could feel my body just sink into its own coma. As I did so, I heard the Lord say to me, "Wake up. Ben needs you." This happened a couple of times as I drifted in and out of exhaustion. I got up, dressed, and went downstairs, even though the nurses had encouraged me to get some sleep as it had been, and would continue to be, a long haul.

I arrived at his bedside, and the nurses notified me that protocol did not allow me to sleep next to Ben in intensive care. I replied that I didn't mind, as I just wanted to sit with him because I couldn't leave my son. The nurses were beautiful as they said to me that they wouldn't be able to leave their child either. They went and found a recliner chair and dragged it into the room for me. I sat on the chair and read my Bible as the eerie silence was intermittently broken by the beeping of a monitor or another medication was given.

Suddenly, the monitor measuring Ben's blood pressure plummeted, and an alarm interrupted my silent reading. I looked up and saw the nurse and the registrar making sudden injections into one of Ben's numerous portals. Ben's blood pressure started rising, but as I have noted in the beginning chapter, this would happen a few times before they asked me to get John to the hospital, as Ben was in the process of dying of secondary drowning. (This happens when water gets into the lungs, where it can irritate the lung lining and fluid can build up, causing a condition called pulmonary edema.)

As we prayed with the chaplain, we agreed with our Father with the promises in the Scriptures God had given us in 2 Chronicles 20 and Psalm

18 concerning Ben's future. As we did this, I would find out later there were many others God was waking at four o'clock in the morning to ask them to urgently pray for Ben. Many of our friends who had seen us process Krissy's death and the miscarriages would tell us later they had found themselves responding in prayer, fiercely demanding that it was enough, that we had gone through enough already as a family.

Ben's blood pressure stabilized, and to say we were grateful would be an understatement. We had just witnessed Ben coming back to us for a second time in twenty-four hours. I underestimated just what a long and painful journey was still ahead, and I am not sure whether I ever got back to bed that night. There were so many doctors and decisions to be made in that first twenty-four hours that, apart from food and bathroom breaks, I pretty much dwelt by Ben's bedside.

I spent time stroking Ben's hair and praying. I got in the habit of washing his hair every day, brushing his teeth, patting him down with a soapy wet cloth, and changing his nappy. I still wanted to mother him, and even though he wasn't awake to talk to, I still did, as well as reading him stories and holding his hand.

I remember at one point on the second day asking my friend Jacqui whether she thought Ben would survive and her saying to me that whatever happened, we would walk that road together. That was such a comfort to me in the days ahead.

Every day when someone would visit, the doctors would come and say to us, "You must understand that Ben may not make it. Even though he has stabilized, we are keeping him alive in an induced coma because we don't know what his brain function is." This was all very true, as Ben still had a lot of fluid in his lungs; it was so bad that they called a physiotherapist to come and shift it. This was seriously horrific to watch. They would beat his back so hard that you could hear the sound of the fluid move. I just felt like I wanted to scream and tell them to stop as it looked like they were beating him up, but it was necessary, and it did make a difference.

The constant threat of imminent death or long-term brain damage was intense. I felt like I was in a horror movie that was never going to end. It seemed like Ben was in constant danger, and every time I felt God's peace or hope, I would be reminded of the reality that Ben still could die again in this hospital at any moment. How does a person live in that place?

Three days after his admission, Ben was taken for a highly specialized and equipped MRI to look at his brain function; he would be taken to the Auckland University Medical Research Centre for this. This was part of the detailed research they were doing about saving brain function of drowning victims. My friend Sue came in and offered to take me out while this was happening. I had not left the hospital since arriving with Ben, so it felt really strange to leave, get in a car, and go to the shops. I wanted to get Ben an *Iggle Piggle* toy as this was his favorite show on television. I was able to find one, but it felt so surreal to be walking around outside among lots of other people. I am so thankful Sue took me out that day.

We arrived back to the good news that Ben's brain function looked normal. I was elated until I was then warned, "This doesn't mean he doesn't have brain damage; it just means we can't see any." "What does that even mean?" I struggled to comprehend how this could even be. The great news didn't mean all that I thought it meant. This was a constant battle for me during this time. There were encouraging signs that didn't necessarily indicate anything positive. I just didn't know how to respond anymore. I felt like I was in a washing machine, and just when I hoped the cycle was over and I could get out, another cycle would begin.

Ben had some very special visitors one day. The English rugby team were in Auckland for a rugby match with the All Blacks. Many from both teams came to Ronald McDonald House and into intensive care to visit the children. The nurses informed me the All Blacks were over at the house and that I should go and meet them. I hesitated, but they said, "Get something signed for Ben." Well, that motivated me, so John and I headed over and, sure enough, many All Black heroes were there. I didn't have anything for them to sign on, so I got them to sign a shirt that my friend had brought in for me the night Ben drowned as I did not have a change of clothes. We got lots of photos with them all, and it was really special that they were genuinely concerned for our children. Later that day, the English rugby captain and a few others came to see Ben. They gave me a signed picture and cap for him that they signed. I still have these put aside for Ben, along with the papers from the Vineyard church service that you will hear about later, as well as other cards and memorabilia from the time.

How John coped with continuing to try and work and look after the kids, I don't know. He was responsible for getting them dressed and out the door each morning and figuring out who was taking them where and when. Apart from when Ben went for his MRI, I hardly left the hospital unless it was for a wander with John. John's workmates were amazing. His secretary has been a very faithful friend to our children, and she looked after them several times.

The nurses went beyond their duty for John one night when John had come in to relieve my post by the bed so I could have a shower and a rest. The nurses knew John was missing watching the rugby game, so they procured a television for him so he could watch the clash between England and New Zealand while he took vigil with Ben. It was awesome that we had met a lot of these players during the week and now felt a connection to them as we watched the game.

We were very fortunate that, even though we didn't have family around us, we had many beautiful friends who helped us by looking after Jessica and Joseph. As I was homeschooling Jessica at this time, some of my friends who also homeschooled their children took Jessica under their wings. I knew Jessica was well looked after, but poor Joseph was only five and in his first year of school. He had one boy come up to him at school and say he heard that his brother had died. I wish, in hindsight, I had made the decision to take him out of school until Ben had come out of hospital, and he could have joined his sister in safer emotional environments.

When my friend Jacqui came in on the second day, she said prayer chains had been established in multiple places. Jacqui's mother was praying with some of her friends and, as they were Catholics, someone notified the Carmelite nuns and they were also being regularly updated. There was another prayer group being run from the Bible college where I worked, which was being sent all over the world. There was yet another established at my home church, the Vineyard. Another was being run with the homeschooling group. Even the doctor's surgery department was praying for Ben every day. There were so many people texting and wanting to find out information that we finally decided one person in each group would be responsible for sending the information to everyone in that group. I know my friends Ellen, Kaylene, and Jacqui would get together every night to pray for Ben. What amazing groups of faithful people to surrender their time for us.

It became such a habit after every doctor's visit to send an updated prayer list out that the nurses and doctors noticed a pattern. They saw such a difference in Ben's condition after every meeting that they would actually say to me, "Here are your prayer points for the day" when they listed what improvements they needed to see in Ben's condition. These would inevitably be answered by their next visit with Ben. It became our standard morning routine and lightened the mood a little.

Our home church astounded us when they spent the entire service that following Sunday praying for Ben. They had large squares of butcher's paper, and they had one piece named for each of us. People would go from paper to paper, writing prayers or prophetic words or pictures for us. They had a particularly large one for Ben, and some of their prayers were incredible. I have kept all these, and they are in a box marked for Ben to give to him when he is older. Kevin, our assistant pastor, brought these papers in after the service for us, and we placed them all behind Ben's bed in the intensive care unit as a wall of testimony and prayer. He anointed Ben with oil and released the Father's blessing for healing upon him.

When our pastors were contacted overseas, they rang us, distraught. We poured out our hearts and prayed together. It was incredibly special to hear from them and know we were so well supported. Kevin's wife, Kaylene, packed lunches for Jessica and Joseph for the entire time Ben was in hospital. Others gave money to Jacqui and Miriam for parking and petrol as they traveled to and from the hospital on a daily basis. Another friend, Talita, brought gift packs for Jessica and Joseph and helped out numerous times taking Jessica for homeschooling, as did my friend Kathryn.

Another dear lady from church, Beverley, felt the Lord impress on her heart to purchase a Christian worship lullaby CD to play in Ben's hospital room. We were so touched by this because we knew she did not have a lot of money and this would have been sacrificial for her. We were able to acquire a CD player, and this CD played continually in his room. It made such a difference to the atmosphere, especially as Ben's precarious situation continued.

Our previous home churches were also praying and offering practical help. My friends Bernie and Debbie, from the Bible Chapel, bought three hundred dollars' worth of shopping and delivered it to John. This church also supplied meals and flowers.

The ambulance crew that had arrived first on the scene would visit Ben twice while he was in intensive care. Nick, particularly, had been affected by Ben's accident. These gentlemen would come and visit Ben for his birthday and give him a small ambulance after Ben came home. It was such a special gesture and it meant a lot to us. The premature baby nurse who had resuscitated Ben by the pond also visited. She was so thankful Ben had made it to intensive care. Neither she nor the paramedics expected he would still be here alive days later.

The staff also referred Jessica to be able to see a play specialist at the hospital after she had witnessed and experienced such a horrific thing happen to her little brother. She went a couple of times, and they let her paint how she felt about Ben. On one occasion, Jessica painted a picture of Ben lying on the back of a lion being safely taken care of. The lion represented God, who was looking after Ben.

We were grateful that we were not inundated with visitors. Our closest friends kept constant vigil with us, but we were very grateful there was not an influx. The respect of others to understand the situation and help from afar meant a lot to us. It is hard to keep on talking to new people all the time about a situation that is so devastating. Having mainly close friends come in meant our emotional and psychological resources were going where they needed to go, to our children.

On Sunday, the doctors were not satisfied Ben would make it on his own, so they planned to take him off life support. At seven o'clock that morning, Sue, Mark, Miriam, and Jacqui all walked in. Their constant support throughout this trial touched John and I deeply. I didn't know quite how I was going to face this. They sat and waited with us as the life support was taken off. Thankfully, Ben was able to hold his own. However, we were still not out of the woods.

One evening, on day ten in intensive care, my friend Cindy had come in to see us. I was sitting by Ben's bed, and it seemed that whenever a friend came in, the doctors would make a point of telling us again that Ben's condition was serious and not to expect a good outcome. Even if he woke from the coma, he could still be seriously brain-damaged to the point of being a vegetable. They kept reiterating that we had to stop believing everything was going to be all right.

That night, the incessant stress of constant hypervigilance was taking its toll. I was exhausted. I had lived in the hospital for ten days at this point and had not been home in that entire time. The heaviness of not knowing whether Ben would make it or not screamed inside me, and I could not get away from it. I was pouring out my heart to Cindy, saying how God kept telling me to trust him, but the doctors kept telling me to stop being so calm and trusting because all was not well. I said to Cindy that I just needed God to tell me one way or the other because I didn't know how much longer I could do this. As I was saying this to her, I was in the middle of brushing Ben's teeth. I was holding the toothbrush in my hand as I cried deeply for help, saying to God he needed to give me a sign answering whether to keep believing him or to let Ben go. Cindy whispered to me, "Ben is watching the toothbrush." She had to tell me a couple of times; then I looked up with swollen, red eyes to see Ben tracking the toothbrush. I looked at Cindy and, I kid you not, Ben took the toothbrush out of my hand and started brushing his teeth!

Well, there was my sign because the nurse saw all this unfold too. She hit her buzzer, which brought the registrar in, and he said something along the lines that it takes a fair bit of brain function to be able to do that! The next day, Ben was taken out of intensive care and transferred to a high-dependency unit (HDU). They still did not know the extent of brain function, but they knew there was enough to warrant moving him. They removed all the tubes and slowly brought him fully out of his drug-induced coma.

One of the nurses encouraged me to get into bed with Ben and just hold him. Without all the copious tubes attached to him, I hopped in and it felt like heaven. To hold him after ten days was . . . there were too many emotions to put them in words. I held him tight. All the pent-up trepidation that I had been carrying began to release as I held him. I just lay there for hours in his bed in intensive care. The nurses took some photos, and they cried with me. Ben was really groggy, but his face—every mumma wants to see that face on their child, one of being completely loved, enveloped, and safe. My tears ran down his face and I stroked his hair. I think I even slept with him that night, with the nurse at the end of the bed. No one cared. Everyone understood, even the doctors at this point.

The sense of relief that entered the room was palpable. We, as a family, were not the only ones to have undergone this treacherous journey. The nurses had sat at the end of Ben's bed for eight hours each per day and all through the night watches. If they needed to go for a break, another would take their place. There was never someone not at the end of that bed. They created such a sense of stability and steadfastness. My son's life was in their hands, and they knew this. They loved Ben. They watched and cared for him when I would, through exhaustion, head for bed at twelve o'clock most nights. They would say to me that I was only a phone call away, and told me not to worry because they would watch him for me.

As a mother, I couldn't express my deep love for these women like I wanted to. How on earth do you say thank you to nurses like this? They said that seeing Ben leave intensive care was one of the greatest gifts for them.

Ben was moved the next morning but was not coping with the noise in the HDU as there were several children in one room. He would scream for hours, and any noise would really unsettle him. He was transferred to a sound-resistant room, where he was still closely monitored. Once in there, Ben stopped crying. He was very weak but a lot calmer.

The doctors explained that as the brain reboots, it is not able to handle overstimulation. Ben's brain had to basically get turned back on, and that would take some time. Over the next several days, Ben started coming back to me. He wasn't able to handle food the first few days, but one day Jacqui and I were chatting next to Ben, and he picked up a biscuit and started nibbling at it. Jacqui's eyes were glued to him, and the excitement she was trying to contain was contagious. We didn't want to jeopardize this moment by making a lot of noise, so we silently kept looking at each other with happy panic. He ate his biscuit and asked for more. "Yes!" we both yelped. It was such a special moment.

Ben's doctor visited one day and told me the medical practice had been praying for Ben and that she had had a vision after finding out Ben had been taken to intensive care. She saw a pair of golden hands holding Ben's brain. Wow! How blessed was Ben to have a doctor like her?

Ben started moving more and giggling. An occupational therapist tested his mobility and brain function by watching how he was able to do certain activities. They decided that although he was very weak, his functionality was intact. This meant that on day twenty Ben was given the all-clear, and we were discharged to go home.

There were so many times, as Ben and I wandered the ward, when nurses and doctors would stop us and say, "So this is the miracle child?" Ben had become known as the "miracle boy" who had miraculously survived a drowning. We went and visited the nurses in intensive care to say goodbye, and Kirsty, the nurse who had been stationed by Ben's bedside in intensive care, was very moved that Ben had survived and was now going home without any further diagnosis. Ben and I would visit her again a couple of months later to say thank you, and she said Ben's photo was posted on the nurses' lunchroom as a reminder that miracles can happen. They had asked for a photo of Ben when he first came to the ICU as a reminder of who he was when well. Ben saved more than my life in that ward; through his miraculous healing, he touched many others.

I can't tell you how surreal walking through the front door of our home was. It had been three weeks since I had left one morning to go have a fun day with the kids and a friend. After we got home, Ben would sleep in his cot next to my bed. It was winter, and when it rained, he would scream. We are not sure whether it was because the sound reminded him of drowning or because the noise was too much for his brain as he healed. Either way, it went on for quite a while and was so distressing to see him so distraught. I spent nights just holding his hand through the rails of his cot, so he would know I was there with him.

I found it hard, once I was home, that everyone was so overjoyed—not because I was not grateful, but because deep down I was still back at the pond, traumatized. It was like I found it hard to accept Ben was going to be all right. I wanted to speak of the miracle of his healing, but I couldn't. Mentally, I was still stuck in hospital, waiting for the doctors to tell me of some other problem I had not yet thought of that would silently creep up and take his life. It was like I was under a death sentence for Ben, like I had to keep on top of it before something would happen to take him from me again.

Later, I would come to see that some of this was post-traumatic stress disorder (PTSD), and some of it was due to my need to forgive myself for being the reason it had happened at all. How could I be excited about a healing that was brought about because of my poor mothering? It was very complex, and I found it hard to explain to people. The fact that this had happened on the date I had buried my daughter nine years earlier was unfathomable to me. "What kind of cosmic curse are we dealing with here?" I thought. "Why is death always stalking us?" "What sin am I carrying that is causing these things to happen?" "Surely this many tragedies are not just 'life happens'?"

These and many other questions would haunt me for the next two years. Ben, in his death and resurrection, had saved me in my death to self and ignited my resurrection. This was just the beginning though, and events were about to transpire in my birth family that would bring this emerging Christ-centered self to a whole other level.

Digging Deeper

Through Ben's journey, a very powerful truth was being seared into my soul, that my Father keeps his promises. The promise he gave me of Ben growing up was kept alive when Ben was resurrected and then left hospital. This gave me a deeper awareness of how the prophetic dreams I often got were not so much about giving me an ideal view of what my Father may want; they were declaring into the future the reality of my Father's design. I am not exactly sure how to view this. It does show God's sovereignty, but it is not without partnership with him; yet in Ben's case, we could do nothing to partner with God but stand in our grief and invite him in. I just know that when my Father gives me these dreams or visions, he is being a Father to me and letting me know he has my back and will always be faithful to his promises to me in all the seasons of my life.

My story with Ben is very similar to the story in 2 Kings 4:18–37, where Elisha promises the Shunammite woman a son from the Lord for hosting him in her home. She begs him not to toy with her, but a year later she gives birth to a son. Years later, her son is out in the field; he suddenly develops an excruciating headache and returns to the house. His mother holds him until noon, when he dies. She then rides on horseback to where Elisha is staying at Mount Carmel and takes hold of Elisha's feet, saying to him, "Did I ask you for a son, my lord? Didn't I tell you, 'Don't raise my hopes'?" Elisha goes to where her son lay dead on his bed, stretches himself out on the boy, and the boy awakens. I felt like that for a while with Ben in hospital. I felt I had expressed to my Father that I couldn't watch any more children die, and here I was with my son having died once by the pond and almost again in hospital and in danger of incurring extensive brain damage that would make him a vegetable. I found myself saying what the Shunammite woman said: "Did I ask you for a son, my Lord? Didn't I tell you, 'Don't raise my hopes'?" This was not only a test of God's promise in the dream he gave me; it was also a test of our relationship. Why this test occurred I am not sure to this day, but I know we survived—God and me—and he has shown his faithfulness to heal even the pain I held at my felt abandonment by him at the edge of that pond. This is the embodiment of *psychological justice*. My whole world shattered that afternoon. I was holding a sense of betrayal in my relationship with God. My heart was shattered into millions of pieces on so many levels that it took a long time to heal.

Ben's drowning highlighted that the fight to keep my "self" intact had now entered an acute phase of disintegration. All the attachment systems I had constructed to survive had failed, and I was left feeling completely naked and vulnerable. I remember walking into Bible college and feeling like everyone knew the deep shame I had been trying to hide for most of my life. I was also aware that I was absolutely dependent on a God whom I had never unconsciously really felt safe with.

My Father said to me one day that regret is a form of self-hatred. I needed to forgive and stop hating myself for what had happened. I had to love myself at my worst, as my Father did. This was not a scolding Father ready to send me to hell. He was there holding out his heart for me to lean into and be secure and safe with. This is the place where deep transformation would begin to occur. God was mirroring back to me my mother heart's anguish over Ben. I was beginning to find a new center in Jesus. The false self was in the process of being disarmed, and I was facing my seven-year-old self, who desperately wanted and needed to dance with Jesus again.

Having written this chapter, I have seen a connection between what erupted out of my being as I shouted out for *mercy* by the pond and the song that flowed the moment Krissy died—"The steadfast love of the Lord never ceases; his *mercies* never come to an end." Mercy—I really did not even know what this word actually means in all sincerity. I had been so focused on performing my way into the kingdom that I had not fully grasped that Jesus' mercy is what had opened the veil for me. The Holy Spirit within me knew this and cried out my identity to the Father on the basis of what Jesus had done as a bold declaration of who the Father is. His mercy saved me in Krissy's passing, and his mercy held Ben and me by that pond. Mercy, what a beautiful reality. I long to be known as my Father's daughter, one who embodies the depths of his mercy.

Psychological Justice

Where do I start in detailing all the manifest ways our Father provided *psychological justice* for us during this season? It started with all the people that "happened" to be present around the pond the day we needed intervention. Our Father had in place the ambulance, the paramedics, the nurse walking past, the people looking after Jessica, and even people to look after our cars. The registrars who were on when Ben was admitted. My friends who dropped everything, and continued to do so for three weeks. It can also be seen in the many miracles Ben was given throughout his stay in intensive care through to his coming home. *Psychological justice* can also be seen in the community's response to our devastating circumstances. Everyone involved in Ben's recovery was impacted by our Father's provision. The Father brought *psychological justice* to many during this time.

My Father was not satisfied in giving my son back; he was going to pursue me for complete *psychological justice*. He did not just want to bring Ben a miracle; he wanted to bring multiple miracles to me also. I would need his miraculous help to recover and psychologically heal after such intense and multilayered events. I would need his deep engagement in my psychological processing of Ben's drowning for a long time. My Father's desire for me to know his grace meant that he did not give up on healing me until I knew it in every fiber of my being. *Psychological justice* is so profound in the way it is worked out in our lives. In some ways, the concept is too expansive to fully explain. However, placing the concept within a framework enables us to see the fullness of what the Father wants to breathe into our lived experience. Remembering that *psychological justice* is thoroughly supernatural reminds us that the Father "is able to do immeasurably more than all we ask or imagine, according to his power that is at work within us" (Eph 3:20).

My experience of *psychological justice* regarding my mothering frailty is very personal. My Father was a very real and present help in my troubles. Throughout my experience of PTSD, he kept his promise to bring deep and profound healing. The nakedness I felt through this time was intense, yet I see *psychological justice* here too, as my Father was healing deeper wounds that were lying beneath the trauma of Ben's accident. My deep sense of failure as a mother needed to be touched by grace. Had my Father not shown me this, I probably would still be psychologically stuck by that pond, and I may have never been able to move on from this near-tragedy. I love that my Father was not able to settle with me just receiving my son back; he wanted me to receive the fullness of who the Trinity wanted to be for me. Again, this is more than Jesus dying so that I could get to heaven. This is an example of the intense desire of the Trinity in wanting a deep, enduring, and thoroughly healing relationship with all of his children.

The University of Auckland organized yearly checks with Ben as part of the detailed international research they were doing in saving the brain function of drowning victims. At the end of the trial, they sent us a detailed report of their findings, including their assessment of Ben. He was given complete clearance with no observable effects of drowning on his daily functions. It felt good that our journey had helped medical science conclude that keeping a drowning victim cold is better for retaining brain function from drowning.

In the final edit of this book, I started to become very anxious about recounting my story with Ben, afraid of the accusation (rightly offered), "How could you leave your son unattended? No mother should do that."

I said to my Father, "I cannot answer that question without taking full responsibility."

My Father answered me, "He who is without sin, cast the first stone."

I replied, "But they will cast stones, rightly so."

He answered me, "Then I will catch them."

Mercy. It does not excuse me, but I do not think I will ever plumb the depths of my Father's mercy toward me.

What's Your Story?

Where have you felt disappointed or betrayed by God? Be like the Shunammite woman and go swiftly to God and cry out, "Why did you raise my hopes?" Where do you need psychological justice for the anguish of lost hope? Ask him. There is nothing too hard for the Lord.

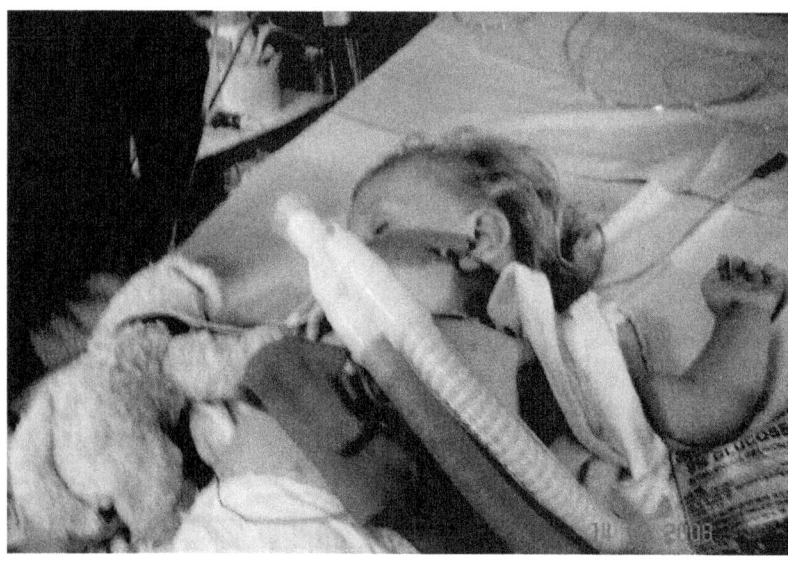

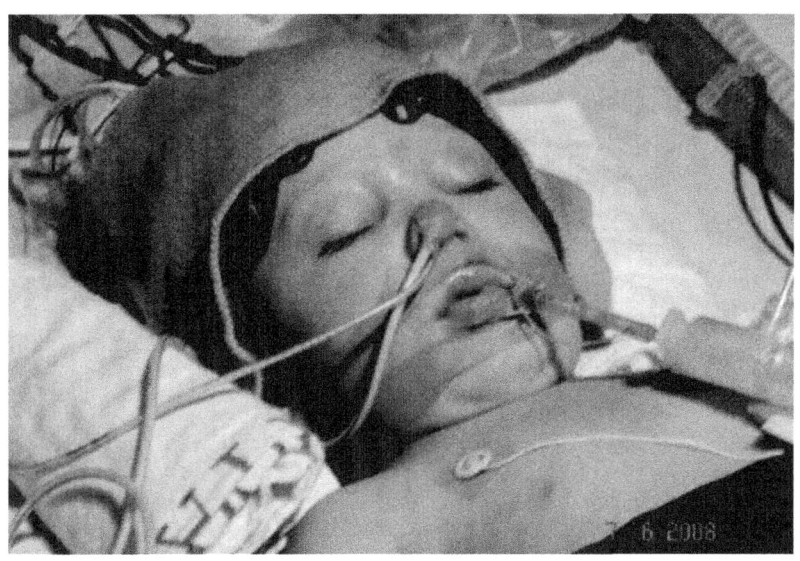

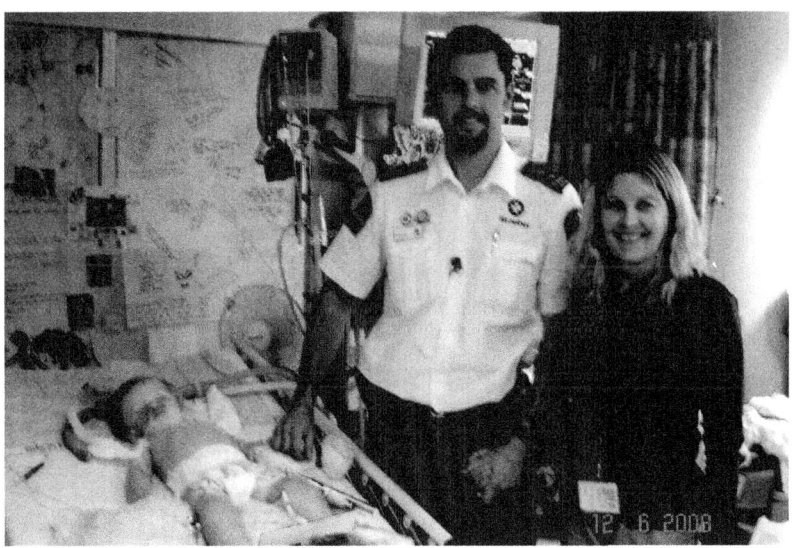

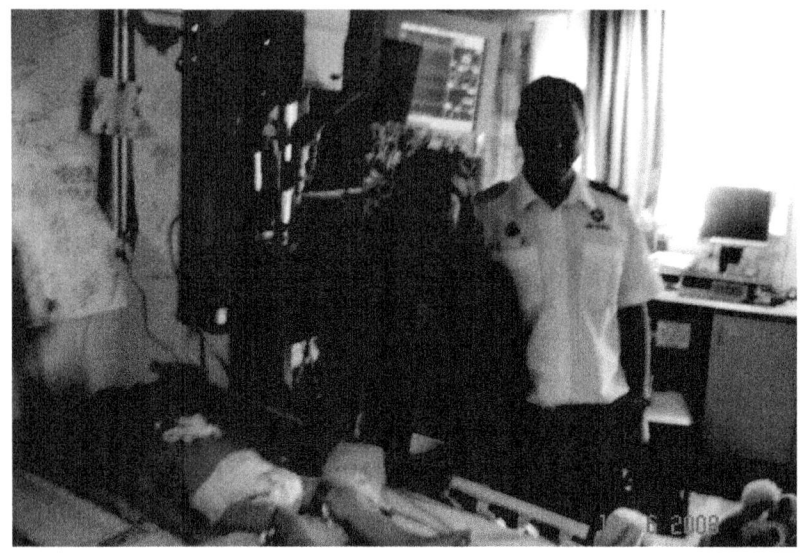

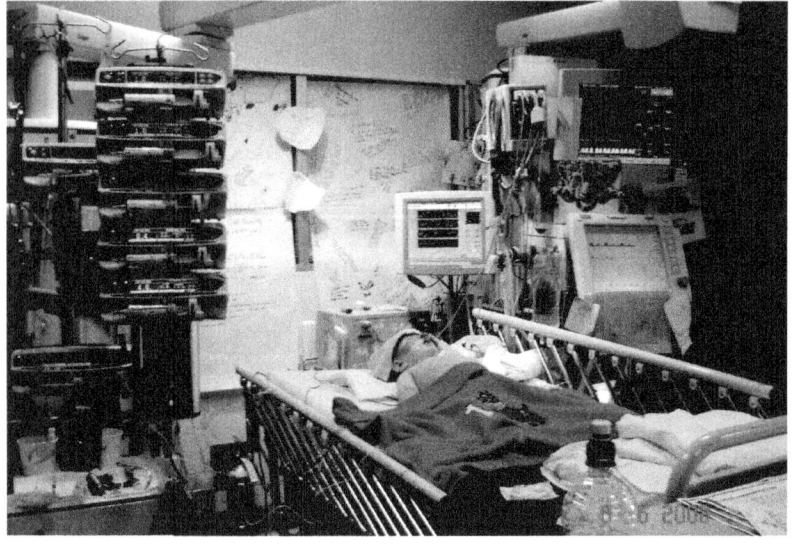

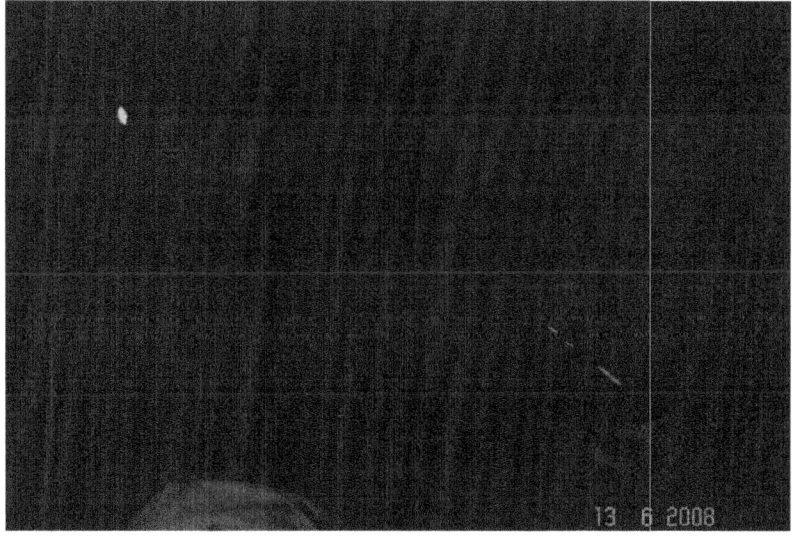

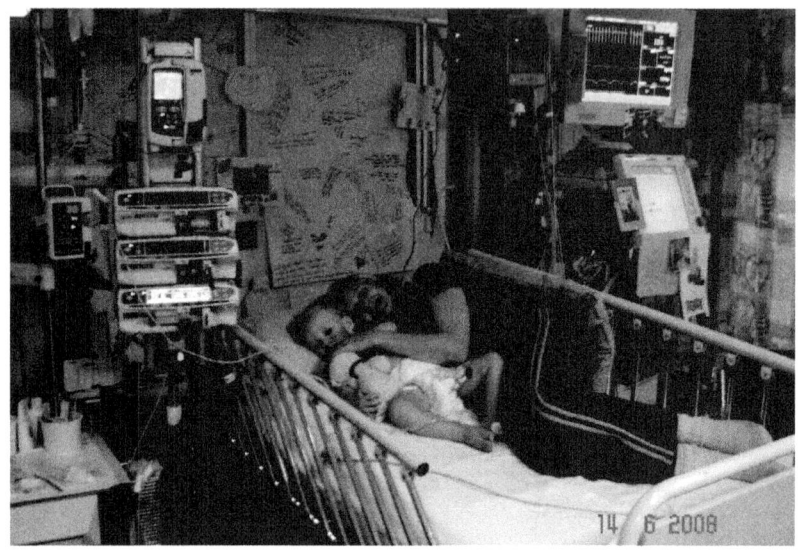

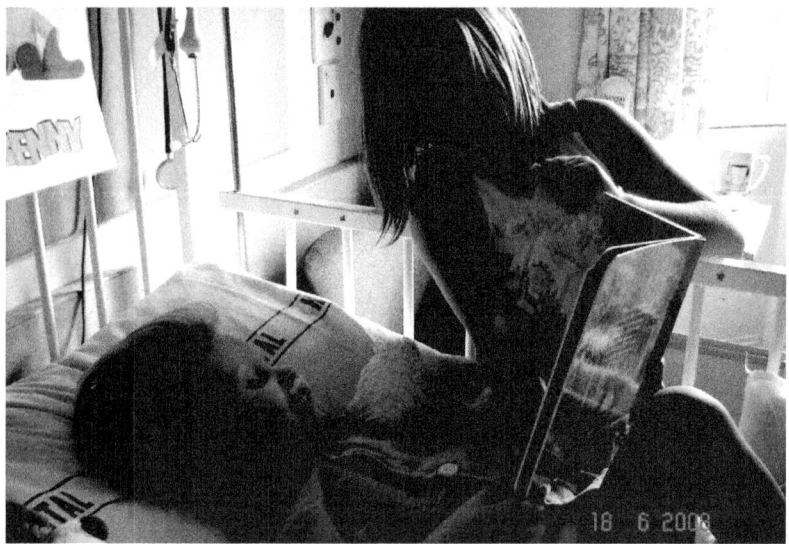

Healing Journey

A wonderful surprise happened on the way home from my farewell from BCNZ/Laidlaw after working and studying there for twenty years. I had been feeling rather nauseous and decided to stop at a chemist to purchase a pregnancy test. To my surprise, I found out I was pregnant with Rachel.

Being pregnant with Rachel was a profound experience as I had forgotten how different carrying a girl is, and this engendered a deeper level of healing in relation to Krissy's death. I hadn't realized that this deep longing for another little girl had been buried with Krissy. Carrying Rachel reminded me of carrying Krissy and the implications of what this meant to me. I felt that with Rachel I was able to capture these months of carrying Krissy again. This was important for rebuilding memories and bringing more healing to my mother heart. I had felt so bereft at not being able to have had more time with Krissy after her birth that to be reminded of her growing in my womb was intensely powerful and healing. It brought some heartache, but it mostly brought depth and substance to my broken experience of motherhood.

I was around six weeks pregnant when I spent a weekend with some of my favorite girlfriends at a remote West Auckland beach. It was such a wonderful weekend. I had a dream that I was carrying a girl, and in the dream she was flourishing and happy in her future. This was so comforting for me.

Rachel's heart rate fell in labor and she was born by emergency cesarean section. I found out at my regular checkup that my water had actually broken a couple of days beforehand. I had sneezed and thought it was bladder leakage. It also transpired that I had liver toxemia, which meant Rachel was born with jaundice. I had a very high blood pressure of 180/120 for quite a few months. My normal blood pressure was 90/60, so this was a marked change and brought a lot of physical symptoms with it. I passed out one morning in the hospital. I was very sick, but I was full of joy over Rachel.

I was forty-two when I had Rachel, and it took me a while to physically recover. I was sick for almost two years. I had symptoms of fibromyalgia, numbness in my legs, and extreme pain down my right-hand side. There were times I could not move. Then in March 2011, I had an acute and very painful case of pancreatitis, and I vomited copiously. I was in hospital for a couple of days, and a scan showed I had a gallstone stuck. This prompted a health warning over the state of my gallbladder.

I kept going for prayer for healing for my gallbladder. I kid you not, at least three different people said, "Beetroot juice is great for gallbladder problems." I got so mad, as I wanted to be healed, not told to do something about it—especially not drink beetroot juice. Why couldn't God just heal me already?

Soon after these episodes and my grumbling, my Father said to me, "I will meet you halfway. You need to change the way you eat, and I will heal you." I didn't want to hear that either, but I said, "Fair enough," and started searching for ways I could improve my health. My Father kept his end of the bargain and helped me do my part. As I was walking through the supermarket one day, I saw a sugar packet with a poison sign on it. We all know sugar packets don't have poison signs on them, so I did a double take, and of course it wasn't on the packet, but I heard clear as a bell the Lord say, "This is poison for you. *Stop* eating it!" I was shocked that I had seen the sign on the packet so clearly and surprised as to why the Lord would say this, but as I researched the inflammatory effects of sugar on the body, I understood completely.

It took time to change habits, but as I began seeing the health results, I have not looked back. And—can you believe it?—I now love beetroot juice, and it is great for the gallbladder and a lot of other things as well.

Along with the physical realities we were dealing with, each of my four children have faced varying levels of educational "disabilities" or been assigned varying "neurodiverse" labels. I won't associate any of these with the names of my children. They have already gone through enough without me then plastering their story in the pages of the public. But I do want to touch on how these supposed disabilities are dealt with by people and the educational system—from a mother's perspective.

As a mother, the process of determining my children's learning issues was very hard, as I found people's perceptions of my children were, at times, not kind. Children on the spectrum can be unfairly targeted with cruel accusations and treated differently. As a mother, I have had to learn to live with the musings of others who say they understand what my children are dealing with, but not many actually do, unless they have neurodiverse children themselves. I am sure I probably did not aid these situations, as I was also struggling with grief and dealing with the complex abuse trauma I was trying to face. I was also trying not to punch people in the face for acting so religious and upright. But that is just the Australian in me talking.

The desire to protect my children versus building resilience has always been a fine line to walk. I remember a time when one of my children was crying one night because they thought being tested meant they were dumb. I would repeatedly tell my children that they are brilliant, but the school system just doesn't know what to do with their brilliance; that the education system is disordered, not them. The labels from professionals are necessary to understand, process, and start implementing strategies for, but ultimately these labels must bow to the name of Jesus and they most certainly do not determine a child's future—only my Father does.

These are silent "disabilities." I put that in quotes because, to me, they are not; they are my Father's gift to a world that desperately needs people like them to think outside the box and provide fresh insights and answers to significant issues the world faces. I celebrate each one of my kids and their varying brilliance. I also stand with others who travel this lonely, often much-maligned journey of acceptance and living out of this brilliance.

The best advice I can give as a mother to others who are struggling with educational hurdles is to not let the world's system of measuring your children be your measuring stick. Love, and a solid belief that your child is innately brilliant within a disordered system, are crucial. These children are intensely loved by God, and my prayer for any parents out there reading this is for our Father to place your child where they can thrive in all their brilliance.

Digging Deeper

I think it would be helpful here to mention the importance of rest when processing trauma or grief. In 1 Kings 19:3–7, Elijah had just defeated the prophets of Baal on Mt. Carmel. Jezebel was not happy and was hunting him down. Elijah was so afraid that he ran for his life. He was so exhausted that it says in 19:4 he came to a broom bush, sat down under it, and prayed that he might die. Each time Elijah woke after having had slept a while, an angel would come and cook some bread for him to eat and leave some water to drink. This went on for a while before the angel told him to get up and travel to the mountain of God. I love this story because it shows the compassion and care of our Father. Sometimes we just need to sleep, eat and drink, and sleep again. Sometimes there are places so deep and painful that we need to spend some time in these places and be okay with not being okay for a while. I think it is important not to betray yourself in the healing process. Take time to let your voice be heard. It can be extremely traumatic for some memories to surface. In these spaces, God is not in a hurry. He will sit with us until we are ready to move on. The healing of our soul and body is meant to be a meaningful and holistic process, not a rush to get to the next level.

I had an experience one evening during these years. I had previously taken my blanket off during the night because I was hot. At some point, I woke up cold. Someone was standing by my bed and put a blanket over me and said, "You are not an illegitimate daughter." I thought it was John and went back to sleep. I thanked him in the morning and he said, "It wasn't me." I realized then that it must have been my Father. I didn't understand at the time that he was confirming to me the opposite of how I felt with my parents. I felt like I was an illegitimate daughter, both to my parents and as a believer in church. I felt that somehow I really did not belong in the kingdom. I had often had dreams where I would be standing either just inside a church meeting or just outside the door. Sometimes I was even on a bench outside the building. I would always feel thankful that at least I was near the door, even if I couldn't get into the building with other believers. This was a constant dream with an attached lived reality. I never felt I belonged anywhere really, but I especially felt I had to do that little bit more to just be a doorkeeper in the house of the Lord. This, as you will see in further chapters, has some of its roots in the attachment filter I had developed in my early years.

As I was writing and unpacking memories from Ben's drowning, my Father prompted me that there was still something unresolved I needed to deal with. My Father showed me I had made a deep inner vow previous to that event, which I was not aware I had made. It was this: "I am not a bad mother, and I am going to prove to others that I am not." After Krissy died, I felt like such a failure as a mother and inferior around many of my friends who were mothers, whom I viewed as more adequately equipped for the role. I had made an inner vow that I would prove others wrong about how I believed they perceived my mothering (which in itself was my perception of their perception). Before Ben's accident, my confidence had grown as a mother, and I had come to feel I was more equal with others. However, inner vows can operate as curses or limitations on our lives, and I still had this as a core place from which I operated as a mother.

Often these inner vows are nonverbal. They emerge from the vacuum that dysfunction creates in the psyche. I had not verbally stated this vow, but I was living from the unconscious reasoning of my thought processes that brought the inner vow into my lived experience.

Along with feeling profound guilt about the events that led to Ben's accident, I had a very deep sense that I was bound to the pond even though I had prayed through the trauma and forgiven myself. As I wrote this chapter, my Father showed me why I still felt bound. The inner vow was that I would prove others wrong, but when Ben died and another mother brought Ben back to life, I felt like I had fallen in on myself. My sense of "That's it; I am a bad mother" became part of my core identity, solidified and confirmed by Ben's death by the pond.

Here I was, eleven years later, writing this chapter, and deep down where the inner vow was made there was a strong residue of extreme anger at myself that I had proved others right—I was a bad mother. This was more profound than the failing I felt after Krissy's death. I was now back to feeling frustrated that I hadn't proved anyone wrong but had actually proved others right (even though they may never have felt like this about me in the first place).

As I walked with my friend Brenda along the beach and processed this, I renounced the inner vow I had made, and the Lord showed me a deeper truth I needed to learn from this experience, to do with justice. My desire in making the inner vow was to bring myself justice for how I felt after Krissy died; that I somehow, through sheer mental and emotional grit and determination, would prove I was not what that experience had made me feel. I was going to get myself justice over an unjust situation.

My Father led me to not only repent of making the inner vow, but also to repent of the motivating action of my heart when I made the vow that I would get myself justice. He asked me to release my desire for human justice to Jesus and repent of wanting to prove myself to others and of taking justice upon myself.

After I had done this, there was another twist to this encounter. I felt a deeper shout come out of my spirit that declared, "I want my son back!" Somehow, after relinquishing the vow and the motivation behind the vow, I found the voice that I had buried at the pond. There has been a marked shift since I processed this, and I have felt much more connected within myself since.

Psychological Justice

Psychological justice is holistic in its effects. We all know that whatever we are experiencing in a psychological realm will touch every area of our present reality. There is substantial research showing how current life events trigger deeper wounds to surface. There is also growing evidence that negative events that impact the psyche can also manifest in the body as illness. When deep wounds of abandonment, rejection, or abuse are able to be processed, many times this results in the body being able to use the resources it was using to suffocate the past, to promote physical healing. In this way, I see the physical ways our Father has provided for us as inclusive of *psychological justice.*

We needed deep friends who could hold us in the journey we were on, and our Father was bringing justice in multifaceted ways. The importance of community cannot be reduced to a church service on a Sunday morning. A prayer time at the end of a service is helpful. However, deep healing of the soul is fostered in safe places that are created within the security of a healthy community. Within these spaces, people can tell their story and begin to unpack the fractures that are limiting their lives.

Repenting of the inner vows I had made prior to Ben's drowning was a very powerful moment that brought a decisive change in how I felt, not only as a mother, but also as a person. My identity had been suffocated by the lies I had believed about myself and who my Father is. It was imperative for my lived experience of my identity in Christ that I deal with these psychological fractures. I am still in awe of how my Father was able to isolate and reveal to me what had happened as it was so complex, but once he unfolded the process to me, it was so clear. The Holy Spirit continued to be a wonderful counselor in this space. *Psychological justice* is a beautiful and healing-infused framework from within which to live.

What's Your Story?

There are always deeper places in our psyche that need healing. Where might your rush to be healed mean that you have avoided deep, holistic healing? Where is shame drowning your cry to be heard?

Season 5

What Is in a Name?

The nations will see your vindication, and all kings your glory; you will be called by a new name that the mouth of the Lord will bestow. (Isa 62:2)

The following season had all the makings of a great book—betrayal, innuendo, illness, villains, triumph, heroes, and knights in shining armor. Oh, but wait. I am writing a book! Great on the pages, great book themes, but not so great in real life. Suffering and glory seemed to mix fluently yet haphazardly together in this season. Deep truths would be seared into my being. Many branches were to be cut off, some at the root—so many that I often felt like a twig! But new shoots were also emerging.

The beauty of hindsight. In the final stages of editing this book, I was amazed when the Lord showed me what he was doing throughout this season. He would name my pride by showing me a reflection of myself in my success-driven mirror. He would then show me how I had been steeped in a shame-based identity. Having named my shame, I was then able to start naming the abuse I had endured in my life in its various forms. The most poignant point was when my Father came to me with a new name from his heart for me. Through this naming and my relationship with him being renamed also came the inevitable renaming of church and its position in my life and my relationship with it.

It was in this season I realized how far from grace I had traveled. I had to face the ugly in myself and how my commitment to shame-avoidant behaviors had hurt some people who were really close to me. My psychological studies were pivotal in locating and naming the deep trauma lodged within me. As I started to take steps to look back on my journey, instead of trying to continue to find ways to excuse or escape my behavior, I needed to fully face my shame-based identity for what it was. After Ben's drowning, I felt a marked vulnerability that caused me to feel psychologically naked before my Father and others. It was a deeply humiliating yet profoundly freeing couple of years.

I tried for years to portray a version of myself to others that seemed like I had grasped with my mind all the knowledge I needed to be non-emotional about my past. Our past, however, if not dealt with, will ultimately shout louder the more we deny its existence. When our fractures are brought into the presence of Jesus, his life and power can heal those wounds, and this enables us to make peace with our past.

Success in my studies led to issues I was dealing with in my birth family being replaced by pride in that I was fostering in my inner being through accruing intellectual knowledge. As I became increasingly confident in my abilities, I became opinionated and less aware of the impact I was having on others. I had to start naming my pride and, more importantly, the abuse I had enacted on others. This was not an easy season. Ouch.

Pride and Prejudice—Naming Pride

I graduated with my Bachelor of Ministries in April 2006. I was pregnant with Ben at the time, and it was such a special season. Unfortunately, during this time I would sometimes hurt others because my knowledge hadn't become wisdom. I had not learned enough to know that sometimes my knowledge was like a sledgehammer in my hand as I laid down my understanding as a burden on the backs of the hurting.

I have written parts of this book from a bed of regret. Deep regret can twist the soul in on itself so that it locks our actions into the fabric of the past. When we hold on to regret, we are putting ourselves on trial indefinitely, locking ourselves into prison because of moments in history and withholding the key of freedom from those actions.

Healing began as I was able to locate and pinpoint some of my issues, and this started to resurrect dreams and longings in me that maybe I could become the mother I wanted so much to be. About a year after Ben's drowning, the Lord gave me a word that created a particularly acute and deep chasm in my soul; the kind that you actually don't want to heal from. I can't remember the exact Scripture I was reading, but the Lord said very clearly to me that I had to stop sacrificing my children on the altar of my success.

Convicted. Deep conviction. The Lord's verdict was poignant and undiluted.

What a lance this was.

It was one of those moments where I felt the deep sword of truth cut through bone and marrow. I was sacrificing my children by elevating my time in my studies above time with them, just so I could impress others with my success. As the tension of motherhood gave way to my studies, I desperately tried to escape the deep shame I carried and became obsessed with worrying about what people thought. Closely related to this was another word my Father gave me: that I was using Jesus to endorse and advance my career.

Yes, read that again.

I was using Jesus—*using*, deliberately—to endorse, give validity to, and advance *my* career.

Jesus had become a tool in my bag of tricks to further my self-deluded ambition.

Oh my. I wept. I wept for days that turned into weeks. I can't describe what it felt like to experience conviction so deeply that I felt I could never look at Jesus again. I was devastated at the depths of the ugly deception I saw in myself. I imagine this is what Peter must have felt when the Lord took him aside and asked him if he loved him. The piercing eyes from the one I had adored all these years now seared my heart, searching for a response of love from me. I couldn't bear the sorrow I felt we were both enduring. I sat for months in his presence, weeping.

It's hard to uncover truth this stark. It's one of those encounters with the Lord that leaves you changed. You can't stay as you are. I was enveloped by a flood of conversations, attitudes, and deep beliefs shouting that my condemnation was deserved. I could see the deep pride and arrogance in myself. I was looking into this big black hole of narcissism, cringeworthy and despicable, even to myself. I had so deceived myself into thinking it was all about Jesus. In fact, this was the worst thing to face. How on earth could I use Jesus like this? How could I make out that it was about him, when all along most of it—not all, but most of it—was about preserving my reputation? Whatever that was.

I still feel overwhelmed when I think of how I was using my dearest friend and Savior to promote myself. I used my intimacy and relationship with him to try and elevate my place in the eyes of others. I wanted to bury the shame of my unconscious reality deeper in order to construct a pseudo-self for others to admire, and I was using my relationship with Jesus and my knowledge about him to do this.

After many, many months, I finally felt my sorrow was spent, and I just threw myself on his mercy. I laid down my ambitions and deception. He would come to me, as Jesus masterfully does, with full forgiveness and acceptance. I really don't deserve all he has wrought in me through this experience. Once seared, the scar remains as a beautiful reminder of how low I sank and how deep Jesus came to release his merciful look of love. This experience changed our walk. Once you have deeply hurt someone, you can never really forget their love in forgiving you. I could not minister or study for a long time after this revelation.

Proverbs 20:10 states, "Differing weights and differing measures, the Lord detests them both." This pretty much sums up my posturing during this season. (The Father impressed this Scripture on my heart years later in a ministry circumstance.) I was weighing myself as upright and honest in my intentions while at the same time measuring others with differing scales. This is one of the reasons why my daughter's painting (see my introduction) has broken scales. My justice was so faulty, so incredibly one-sided.

My Father gave me another verse, just in case one was not enough: "He gave them their request, but sent leanness into their soul" (Ps 106:15, NKJV). I really did not know what my Father was saying to me back then; I just wanted to succeed at all costs. I had to succeed at all costs and it was costing me and others to succeed. I understand this Scripture now. My Father gave me what I wanted—success—but it brought such leanness into my soul. I was not living in the power of the Spirit, and my words and actions looked spiritual but lacked power to affect any real change in me or others. My soul was drinking in the poison of shame, and I was giving this poison, couched as living water, to others. As I have said before, my Father showed me how I had used Jesus in my quest for success, but I was also using and walking over a lot of people who didn't fit my plan or agenda. My life was full of spiritual and visible acts of service that seemed to have upright motives. I was about to learn that the Holy Spirit does not allow us to lay claim to the glory that belongs to the Father and Jesus. Anything we label as ours that is the work of the Trinity, the Holy Spirit will eventually take from us or limit the effectiveness of it if we do not repent.

This is what happened to Moses when he struck the rock in anger to get water for the Israelites. The Lord's response to Moses in Numbers 20:12 is, "Because you did not trust in me enough to honor me as holy in the sight of the Israelites, you will not bring this community into the land I give them." After all Moses went through, at the very point of being able to lead the Israelites out of the wilderness, he had forgotten to honor the Lord. I had labeled my success as my own doing and pursued with vigor my own self-proclaimed agenda. Jesus does not, it seems, like us labeling what he creates as our own. It is like a form of plagiarism. Spiritual counterfeits are not the same as genuine creativity that is born out of intimacy. This type of creativity enmeshed in intimacy was how *psychological justice* was born.

However, during these early stages of my master's program, my success was being born out of a spirit of self-entitlement. I had become a resounding gong and a clanging cymbal (1 Cor 13:1) and a stench in my Lord's nostrils (Isa 65:5).

Digging Deeper

I want to touch on the need for mothers and fathers in the believing community to be bearers of *psychological justice*. I have needed transitional mothers and fathers in my journey. This is one of the reasons we need to go deeper, as there is a widespread need for many believers to be reparented. I have heard it said that we have God as our Father, and is that not enough? My answer is that many of us cannot conceive of a mother or father like God. For me, I knew in my head who the Trinity were from the Scriptures, but many times I could not access that image in my deeper self because in my psychological core, I had embedded images of parental figures from my childhood that were confusing and sometimes frightening. These embedded images are a collection of good and not-so-good attachment moments and are the ones we can often project onto God. We often need deeper work to unravel any faulty parental images, as these embedded memory imprints form the image of God that we carry in our deepest being.[1] I value greatly the transitional mothers and fathers who have helped me to process my unconscious God images, and now I hope I am a transitional mother for others.

Psychological Justice

My process highlights the importance of *psychological justice* in dealing with our heart motivations and what fuels these. Sometimes we are so focused on our behaviors, and we try to change these through a simple adjustment of our mindset. This may work in some cases, but more often than not our behavior stems from deeper places of unresolved psychological wounding. If you have deep wounds that you are not facing, they will be affecting your lived experience, whether you are aware of these or not. *Psychological justice* is so crucial for us to grasp if we want long-term foundational and holistic change.

As believers, we need to appreciate that we are all different. My emotional base felt in the past like it was interpreted as weakness, and sometimes

---

1. Halstead, "Forgiveness Matters Course," 85.

it still feels that way. I had to deal with the root of the label "too emotional," as it was having a very destructive presence within my lived reality. This has always had the effect of shutting down my voice, as I felt less worthy to speak or bring my input to a situation because I was seen as less logical. Those who are logical are sometimes misinterpreted as aloof and uncaring. I think this is where the *psychological justice* framework can make a real difference to our lived communal experience. We are a body who needs to help each other be the most authentic version of ourselves we can be. We need all personality types and our different and varied psychological and spiritual histories to be able to fully grasp together the breadth and depth of the love of God that is in Christ Jesus our Lord. So, next time we are tempted to dismiss another based on their personality, let us bear this in mind: we need that person we want to diminish *because* they are different to us.

What's Your Story?

Have you used Jesus in your quest to be spiritual for him or for others? Where may you have used differing weights or measures? Have you had or could you be a transitional person for someone?

Master's Studies—Naming Shame

Alongside working at Bible college, I had started my master's studies. I was fascinated by the historical setting of first-century Israel. Learning about bandits, people calling themselves "messiah," and the revolutionary gangs that wanted to overthrow Rome in the name of religious fervor was fascinating. Looking at the topography of the land and the economic, political, and religious structures that framed the Gospels was informative. The perspectives I gleaned on some of Jesus' teachings, and his inferences to the sociopolitical leanings of the Pharisees and the different sects, created new levels of meaning about who Jesus was directing his messages to and why. There is so much to be learned from history in our quest to understand Jesus in his setting.

I was then fortunate enough to undertake a leadership paper with Mark Strom. His doctoral research on Paul and the Greco-Roman philosophers and sophists of the first century was influential in directing my thoughts towards my research. The way Mark, in his book *Reframing Paul*, explains the setting of first-century Rome is one of the most significant I have read. Mark details how Paul uses particular words and phrases in his arguments to subvert that which first-century philosophers held in high esteem. This is extremely important for understanding Paul's writings.[2]

I also started doing some preliminary study on inner healing for another paper. I had several minor brain explosions as I began grasping theories such as attachment theory, object relations theory, and psychoanalysis. I then had to learn to engage with these theories on some sort of intelligent level. Meanwhile, Rachel had started to walk and was into everything.

I was required to write my biography from a psychological perspective for a master's course Phil Halstead was teaching on inner healing. It was a turning point in my healing process. In an article he outlined specific points of forgiveness that could aid a person's process of healing. His delineation of sins was insightful, as they helped me to isolate specific areas where I needed to take responsibility for my own actions and where I needed to forgive my parents.[3] Until this point, I had forgiven Mum and Dad over and over, but nothing seemed to shift. I still felt the control and did not know how to make things right. In reading these categories of forgiveness, I felt I had found my voice to not only deeply forgive, but to start naming the dysfunctions I would need to process to change—really change. The most important of these delineations in my process was the category of sins under the heading "exclusion." These include sins where domination and abandonment are prominent. I wrote a letter to my parents asking for their forgiveness for my sins against them and offering forgiveness for their sins against me. Sins of domination and abandonment have the effect of making the victim feel excluded. If you do not toe the line and surrender to the dominant system of belief or emotional regulator, you most definitely know you will be out. I felt like this most of my life.

I was able, through psychological theories, to identify more precisely the systems of abusive toxicity of my upbringing and link the process of healing these to my thesis research. My deep love of the healing and spirituality of God's people would be fanned into flame as my story began to take on new meaning and purpose. I was no longer dealing with my past for my own sake. My research was helping me garner a wider scriptural and psychological base for a more significant purpose. I was also gaining a deeper appreciation of the scope of healing my Father desires for his children—not a slight healing, but deep, passionate, and all-embracing.

The more I focused my research on the theological elucidation of the cross and the psychological dynamics of inner healing, the more I realized the danger inherent in healing the wounds of people slightly. By slightly, I

2. Strom, *Reframing Paul,* 152.

3. Halstead, "Have My Parents Sinned against Me?", 57.

mean that we cannot simply give out Scriptures like they are Band-Aid's. A Band-Aid is a temporary covering for a wound. But if the wound becomes infected, you need to visit a doctor to get antibiotics to treat the infection at a deeper level. A Band-Aid will simply not be enough. When it comes to our wounds, sometimes we need to dig deeper and invite our Father to heal past trauma. Where there is sin, either on the part of the one offending or part of the one who has been wounded through the sins of another, there cannot be genuine healing without the cross and what it has to say about sin. We just can't bypass a true acknowledgment of the role sin has in our wounds.

One morning, I awoke from a dream with a diagram outlining a model for helping people like myself walk out of a shame-based identity. It was a very clear image. The model outlined six steps. Each step had its own heading, with a corresponding question. In the middle was the symbol of the cross, labeled "forgiveness," synchronizing all categories. (This model will be the focus of my next book.)

This *psychological justice model* is for those like me, whose lived experience is bound by a shame-based identity, but it can be helpful for anyone wanting a more congruent lived experience on their faith journey. The easiest way I can define a shame-based identity is to share a helpful outline that John Bradshaw lists in his book *Healing the Shame that Binds You*:

1. Shame is a healthy human emotion.
2. Shame then becomes a state of being.
3. Shame takes over one's identity.
4. Shame becomes toxic and dehumanizing.[4]

This is a basic process that takes a person in their early attachment years between birth and two years from a human born into a sin-dominated world, where shame is an inherent part of being alive, to where shame becomes the axis or basis of someone's identity.

This was very helpful for me, though ironically I found it extremely shameful to admit I had a shame-based identity. I now had to name the extent of how this identity was impacting my behavior. The very essence of being shame-based is the dehumanization of being alive. I felt forever guilty for everything. I felt shame about who I was and what I could and couldn't do. I was never free from the poison of shame. My psyche was constantly under attack, and this often depleted the stores in my psychological well-being that enabled me to function in everyday situations.

4. Bradshaw, *Healing the Shame That Binds You*, vii.

The more I researched and wrote my argument for the presentation of the *psychological justice model* my Father had given me, the deeper the realization I had of what I needed to do and how crippled I was. I was able, through the object relations theory, to start isolating the "objects" that I needed to process. In simple terms, objects are people or our experiences with people, either good or bad, that we internalize as representations, and these form the basis for the way we will relate in future relationships. I was able to start naming how past abuse was unconsciously affecting my ability to function in healthy ways within my current relationships. Writing this needed to be highly academic, as it was a master's-level paper, but it also involved coming to be known in a very deep and life-defining way. This was no simple paper to be written to pass a course. This was about my true self— who I am in my core, indestructible in God—being found and given a voice. This paper proved to be pivotal in capturing what I knew I was meant to be and do for others. I became obsessed with knowing how to bring healing to myself and my children, but I also felt I was starting to grasp some tools to be able to really help others. God gave me a very clear ability to be able to take what I was learning in my academic studies and apply it to everyday situations and trauma.

I'm almost positive my supervisor had never had a meeting like one of the ones we had during the course of my research for this particular course. Rachel was crying and wanting me to breastfeed her while I tried to focus on the theme of justice in the Old Testament and what it means with my supervisor. Then a packet of chips got dropped on the couch, which Rachel proceeded to stand on. Meanwhile, Ben tried to help, which just made Rachel cry. I tell you, it really tested whether I was up to the challenge of writing this paper. My supervisor, Phil, to his credit, handled it all with grace and dignity. I remember saying at the time that I knew why there were not many women in higher education—because they were too busy cleaning.

It was an article written by Daniel M. Bell Jr. that revolutionized my understanding of justice. As soon as I read his phrase, "Jesus is Justice," I knew my understanding of justice had just been torn to shreds.[5] Studying justice in the Old Testament was a start, as I had begun embracing a Hebraic understanding of justice. I was learning that justice in the Hebrew mindset was all-encompassing; it was not a solely individual affair but had a comprehensive community function. The social justice laws in the Old Testament reflect this.

When I came to studying Jesus' understanding of justice, my world really changed. If Jesus is justice, then he becomes the axis of everything

5. Bell, "Jesus, the Jews, and the Politics of God's Justice," 97

we consider needing justice. Jesus' embodying justice means his death on the cross was not only a defining moment in terms of salvation of individuals, i.e., justification; it has implications for defining broader definitions of justice.

If Jesus died for those caught in evil and puts his hands out to bring justice to the perpetrator, then justice takes on another level. We can no longer demand justice without giving it, even and especially to our enemies. Consequences still remain, but we are no longer in charge of that either. I prefaced my research paper with a dedication to Jesus: "I dedicate this paper to the one who, in the face of multiple injustices, silenced his voice, in order to secure justice for me, to give me a voice, a voice of justice."

In October 2011, I wrote in my journal:

> Unforgiveness toward another is a form of self-hatred. To forgive another and release them from their sins against you releases you. So, the question then becomes, "How much do you love yourself, and how much do you love God?" Because Jesus was adamant; you can't do one without the other, and you can't do either and withhold forgiveness. This is justice. The shocking realization is that I can't cry out for justice and not walk in it myself. Ouch.

I became obsessed with this concept of Jesus as Justice. What did this mean for interpreting the New Testament? I had studied the Old Testament concept of justice and felt the Hebraic understanding must undergird the new because the new covenant wasn't replacing the old but was a fulfillment of it.

My next quest was to understand how Paul used the Greek term for justice and righteousness *(dikaiosýnē)* in his letter to the Romans. This felt like a pressing, urgent need; however, I had not yet learned Greek or Hebrew. I was about to study one of the most controversial and fought-over subjects in the New Testament—the justice of God as it is utilized in Romans. Not only was I going to attempt to define justice from Romans with no prior Greek learning; I was also going to cross disciplines by including first-century philosophical worldviews and psychological theories. I wanted to apply the result of these interdisciplinary conversations to the present lived experience of believers. Yes, passion blinded me to the baptism by fire I was about to experience in my academic career, as I would be writing this as a forty-thousand-word paper in a level nine master's thesis.

Not only this, but of bigger concern, I would start learning that God would not let me be restricted to accruing head knowledge; he would require me to live this thesis. I will take you on the tumultuous journey I had to wade through in the following chapters.

Digging Deeper

In this season, through my studies, my Father was providing the psychological, theological, and historical components necessary for developing the framework for *psychological justice*. I was fortunate enough to study first-century philosophy and Greco-Roman culture. It was a massive theological shift to comprehend the historical constituency of Israel in the time of Jesus. Studying attachment theory and object relations theory was vital in building a solid psychological foundation. I was also building a comprehensive understanding of justice from the Scriptures.

In the Old Testament, the nations surrounding Israel would use shame as one of their strategies in war. The oppressive nation would take prisoners hostage, strip them naked, and force them to walk the streets in shame. They would use shame in all sorts of ways to establish domination and therefore strip those they had taken captive of their culture and their ways of being in community. We see this with the Babylonian Empire. Israel was stripped of their temple and their ways of worship, and this affected their way of being in community. Isolated as individuals, they wept for Zion (Ps 137:1). Some of these military tactics are still in force today. One of the purposes of using shame in warfare is to isolate and weaken the opposition. When the enemy can establish shame in a family, a church, or a community, then he can isolate and cause division. The effect of division is to cause the strength of the community to give way to factions that can easily breed deeper shame to be lodged. From this position, we lose our power as a community to bring the changes needed to combat the destructive consequences shame breeds.

Understanding that shame can warp our identity and can give the enemy a stronghold in us through which to control us highlights the importance of dealing with our fractures. We need to step into the lived reality of who we are in Christ and out of what shame has controlled us to be. We need to wage a war against shame and not perpetuate the enemy's agenda. This includes shame-based ways of being a faith community. This starts with recognizing our own shame-based ways of living outside of our position in Christ.

The enemy's tactics have not changed with God's people. If the accuser can breed shame-based ways in our faith communities, then he can infiltrate and destroy the greatest gift the Father has given us in Christ: our dignity in being put right within community.

Psychological Justice

During this stage, I was learning to study while at the same time being intentional about focusing on the presence of God. This was another theological shift for me, as I was starting to understand I didn't need to perform for my Father by finding success in my grades. He wanted me to experience *psychological justice* further in my understanding of who he is, my Father. This would undergo deeper testing and revelation in the years to come.

My Father was passionate about giving me *psychological justice* and gave me the resources to identify, name, and process abuse. Halstead's delineations of sins were pivotal in this process. To be given the *psychological justice model*, to help others like me process and deal with the triggers of a shame-based identity, is a precious gift of my Father's trust in me. The model helps me understand how psychological wounds form and how they inhibit growth in emotional and spiritual functioning.

What's Your Story?

Does the description of shame resonate with you? Halstead's proposal that detailing specific sins to forgive may be helpful in processing unforgiveness. Where in your life are there situations that you may be able to appropriate this type of forgiveness? Where may Band-Aid's, i.e., superficial responses, be hiding shame in you?

Naming Abuse

Do you remember how I talked earlier about the beating I endured in the bush? If you have been through abuse, you will empathize with how difficult it is to name it and call it out. The reasons are manifold, from losing family or friends to the shame it is to understand you are being abused. After naming shame, which was a painful journey for someone addicted to performance, I would now have to name the effects of shame in my life. I had to start naming abuse and the web of control for what it was. This was as difficult as losing all my precious babies as it meant redefining who I was, how I grew up, who my family were, and how I viewed the world—pretty much the most significant loss I would need to face in order to be free.

In January 2010, at the age of forty-three, the Lord began urging me to face the toxic abuse in my relationship with my mother. He instructed me very clearly one day, "Do not protect the abuser." I was going to obey either my Father or my mother. However, whenever I would talk about the severity of the abuse with others, I would almost always get thrown back in my face this phrase: "You need to honor your mother and father." I use the word "thrown" deliberately. As a consequence, I would stay in the abusive relationship and allow myself to believe that somehow it was more Christian of me to allow abuse in the name of honor. My Father, thankfully, would not give up on me. He pursued me over and over with his voice, saying, "Love doesn't control." My relationship with my mother could not be predicated on submitting to her control.

In my thesis research, I came across the concept that one of the greatest contributors in recovering from abuse is the victim finding their voice. I love this sentence Matthew Linn penned: "I do not think we have the right to forgive another until we have honored the voice within ourselves, however long that takes."[6] God was starting to show me that the root of my inability to see the abuse was in my inability to forgive myself for what I allowed my mother to speak into my life.

I remember being in so much anguish over the increasingly volatile relationship with my mother that I wrote this in my journal, as I wrestled with how to love her but not let myself be controlled by her: "That's the pain of the anvil. The furnace of the fire of love. The sacrifice required is in your lack of security in another's control."

That last line was the crux of it. I was astonished to realize that I felt secure being controlled. I was increasingly aware that in order to be free, I would need to face the emptiness that abandonment breeds. This was probably the hardest part of my journey out of abuse. Control is suffocating, but it feels safe. You are conditioned through successive abuse to increasingly relinquish control of more parts of your soul and life. To walk out of deep abuse requires great courage and a large measure of self-forgiveness. It is vital that psychologically healthy people surround those that leave abusive relationships. While in an abusive relationship, a person has been psychologically conditioned to accept the blame or the abuse meted out. It takes time to build healthy internal psychological structures so that the person does not leave one abusive relationship for another.

The psychological resources it takes for someone to leave an abusive relationship cannot be underestimated. Abuse changes the very structure of a person's soul. Do not be quick to ask someone to enter into reconciliation if they are not psychologically equipped with the resources it will take to keep boundaries in place. In my case, I was not in a position to take the stance I needed to take to keep safe with my parents. I had only just named the extent of the toxic abuse that our relationship had been fostering. It

6. Linn et al., *Belonging*, 129.

would take time for me to come to the place where I would be able to offer reconciliation with dignity.

My Father showed me that I was legally bound to leave my parents. I was not able to be fully at rest in my covenant union with John until my agreement with my parents was renounced. My Father said very clearly to me, "I give you permission to leave. You honor them by leaving them. You do not honor them by being bound to them."

On August 5, 2010, I wrote and enacted a list of specific areas where I needed to forgive Mum. I include it here because I have found that naming the specific areas that may need forgiving helps to locate and process your pain.

I forgive you, Mum

1. For isolating me and cutting off relationships and for alienating me from others through your theology or your manipulatio.

2. For pronouncing judgments and curses if I did not agree with yo.

3. For spiritual abuse that denied my free will and usurped the leading of the Holy Spirit in my lif.

4. For controlling my marriage and friendships through the use of God's Word out of contex.

5. For discouraging me from having confidence in my own understanding of the Scripture.

6. For denying that I am an intelligent and mature woman before God and God's daughte.

7. For using me as a scapegoat in order to diffuse your anxiet.

8. For violating my trust and abusing your authority to control and manipulate me with shame-based religious teachin.

9. For shutting the kingdom of God in my face by robbing me of my personal faith and replacing God, my Father, with yoursel.

10. For betraying our special trust.

11. For threatening to throw my father out of my life.

The depths of pain, confusion, and fear were all-consuming. Even in writing this chapter many years later, I found more layers of pain that needed to be voiced. I found that the words "For betraying our special trust" resonated deeply within me. In the core of my soul was a young girl that adored and loved her mum and just wanted their special relationship to never end. We had a very special bond and that young girl still felt a sense of betrayal.

I am not angry or bitter anymore; I am just very sad that it has turned out the way it has. This is not necessarily a place that needs forgiveness; rather, I believe it needs embracing. I know my Father tenderly embraces and loves this young girl, and I know she has been heard.

This process is not the result of a couple of prayer sessions. It becomes a series of continual life decisions. The course of action I undertook to name the abuse and forgive my mother needed to be specific, but the Holy Spirit would not let me stop there. The Holy Spirit convicted me that I had to take responsibility for *my* part in enabling this toxicity to continue. I needed forgiveness in the following specific areas:

1. I have received grace and mercy from my Father, and therefore I need to extend it.

2. I don't have the right to withhold mercy by holding on to anger and bitterness.

3. Jesus was totally abandoned by the Father for my sake, yet in absolute physical, mental, emotional, and spiritual abuse he forgave me.

4. I will not control Mum.

5. My Father calls me to bless her and pray for her heart, her family, her finances, and her ministry, and that my Father will cause her soul to prosper.

6. I cannot take a legalistic stand and demand justice.

7. I will not play the part of the accuser and stand in Satan's shoes for him.

8. Jesus is the sole honor and judge of all.

9. I will not pray prayers that resemble witchcraft, i.e., being driven to control in return, and through anger, cursing.

10. I will no longer remain a victim.

11. I honor you, Mum and Dad, by leaving. I now take full responsibility for my life.

I read a book by Marc Dupont called *Walking Out of Spiritual Abuse*, which was very timely, and I would encourage anyone going through this process to read it. As I read this book, I felt that I had an advocate who was helping me to name and discern the toxicity and whirlpool of trauma I was experiencing. Dupont states what I knew: there would be "consequences for breaking the silence."[7]

7. Dupont, *Walking Out of Spiritual Abuse*, 169.

I also need to note here that just as I was not yet in a position to be able to reconcile with dignity, my mum didn't have the psychological resources to reconcile in a healthy way either. She was also feeling betrayed by me, I am sure, because I was no longer responding to her in the ways I had used to, especially with reference to her relationship with God.

My relationship with Mum was also being paralleled in my relationship with God. As I let go of the false image I held of Mum as a heroine, I was able to let go of the misconceptions I held of God. As I detached from idolizing my perception of Mum's image of God, I was made aware of how the false ways I was imaging God also had to be dismantled. I was forced to face my lack of identity in God. It's like I had to meet God again for the first time, for who he was, not what I had projected him to be. This was humiliating and isolating, but also deeply freeing. I needed to accept responsibility for my own life, choices, beliefs, and decisions, and no longer hide behind blaming my mother's dysfunction. Before this process, I would project all my problems as stemming from Mum's failure to release me. But once my Father set the responsibility on me to detach, I was then faced with the awful truth that parts of my life had, to some extent, been founded on lies.

In this process, I was finding there is responsibility in grace. Did I want to be well? (John 5:6). I am thankful God my Father was my therapist and was going to pursue me for healing despite me. Through Ben's accident, he worked enough courage into my relationship with him to trust him to make the exchange. The tragedy by the pond helped me start dismantling an image of my Father as a punishing God and revealed an abundant, grace- and mercy-filled Father, and this enabled me to make that transition. I also understood why I would choose mother figures for female relationships and then would feel suffocated, controlled, and belittled in them. God started making me aware that I was doing this, but I didn't know why. When honor has been used as a means of control, it will take time to recover and find new ways of being healthy in relationships.

I think the hardest part of walking out of abuse was not only admitting the extent of the abuse but also having people minimize it with clichés that God just wanted me to love my parents. It was such a vulnerable process to name and expose the abuse. I was getting stronger in the process, strong enough to realize that it was okay to say no and to say it decisively and possibly forever. People would say God wanted to heal all involved, which was true, but it did not mean I should carry on being abused while I waited for them to be healed. I could only do what I could take responsibility for. The perpetrators constantly refused to own up and, furthermore, would push the blame back onto me, saying it was my fault. Even worse, they were saying I was going to hell for being such a heretic.

For those who tell those who are being abused to hang in there because God wants to bring reconciliation, please stop and pray before you give this advice. Jesus also said he had come to bring division, to cut off abuse, to bring justice to the oppressed, and to release the captives (Matt 10:35).

In the turmoil that enveloped me, I wrote at the time, "One day I will be able to share the extent of the abuse, but for now it is enough to own it. I have no family now, but I belong to Jesus. He is my peace. He is my family. I am convinced he will bring me and my husband and the kids justice. God is fighting for me to be free. The butterfly will be born."

The next issue I had to deal with, once I had named the abusive cycle with my parents, was interpreting the Scripture "honor your mother and father" (Exod 20:12). I really struggled with this Scripture, as people would offer this verse as a mandatory response to my heart-wrenching dilemma. It is also why I often went back into the abusive triangle. How do you honor parents who use their position to dominate and control you?

I was still struggling with what "honor" meant when one day my Father said to me, "You are not honoring them by enabling their abusive control." I had finally come to a place where I was no longer scared of Mum's threats that God would reject me if I did not toe her theological line.

Mum really believed I would go to hell for believing the gifts of the Spirit were still active, and she was also deeply concerned that I was more committed to the church and my friends than to the "truth." There is no denying my mum's life had been hard, and she had been spiritually abused growing up. I had really hoped we could find middle ground, and I spent years trying to put boundaries in place. My Father often warned me when I was hopeful my boundaries were working that nothing had changed, and in fact it was worse than I could imagine. Unfortunately, I kept getting sidetracked by well-meaning people who would tell me to keep loving her and Dad. Sometimes, however, if people don't want your love and they only know toxic love, the only way to love them is to stop the abuse and leave. The hardest part had been accepting that the sexual, physical, emotional, and spiritual abuse really was as bad as it was, and it was time to move on. In the midst of all this, the Lord was forging in me a new name and a new beginning.

I actually felt the Father say to me, when my brother visited, that by staying in the relationship, the cycle of abuse would continue and they may never see it. My leaving could somehow be the only chance any of us, my siblings included, had for freedom. The abuse was so deep and widespread in all of us that it was like a bomb that needed dismantling. It felt like my parents were fixing the blame for our unhealthy relationship on the fact I did not worship God correctly. I knew that unless I left then, I would never find myself fully, ever. The choice was either to "honor" them, as others were saying, and abandon myself, or to honor my Father's advice to me to leave and live fully alive to him and for him. I chose my Father, even though it meant many would doubt my sincerity or wisdom. I knew it might even cut out any future ministry, but at least I would have a pure heart before God, doing what I knew he wanted me to. Even so, it was extremely difficult to go against the flow and swim upstream.

A professor pointed out when marking my biography for my master's paper that my mother's actions could be considered narcissistic. I initially found the label jarring. However, through the process of naming abuse, I came to understand that this in fact accurately described my experience of her.

I had come to accept the abusive nature of our relationship but never suspected I could be dealing with narcissistic abuse. I had been so convinced I was at fault. Narcissists often depict the victim as the perpetrator. They gaslight others' intentions as evil, which might explain why I was always doubting myself in relationships. I remember going through a stage where I said "sorry" all the time, for everything.

My research noted that narcissists can portray kindness and are endearing, but it is not always for your benefit. It can be a smokescreen to garner more of your soul. Narcissists can act weak and vulnerable and portray that they cannot cope without you. The truth is that they cannot cope unless they have your idolization of them feeding their grandiosity. These were stark truths I was finding very hard to process as they reflected my experiences with my mother.

Another painful realization was that unless narcissists can see their actions are unsafe, there cannot be authentic reconciliation. It was hard to let this shocking truth sink in; my heroine was likely using me as a pawn to keep her lifted up from her bed of shame. In fact, my idolizing her was like fuel feeding her need for significance. Seeing this pattern continue with others has been difficult. I watched my father slowly relinquish himself to my mother. Mum enmeshed herself in my relationship with my siblings to the point we could no longer be connected.

Her sweetness bound me to her poison. I have had to tell myself many times, "She doesn't love you for you. She longs to be indispensable to you. She loves that you admire her. She loves what you were able to be for her. Love would not control me. Love would seek my freedom." I've reconciled in myself that she believes she love me, but does not see that shame has built a nest in her trauma. She no longer has room for me unless I can feed her hunger for significance. Our relationship can never be healthy until she is able to see her actions clearly.

I had now given voice to the narcissistic abuse I had endured. I had named it, taken ownership of its effects, and discharged it of its power to continue to name me. A new name was emerging, a name from God himself, shining ever clearer. What a Savior to save a wretch like me, to give me a name and a future—a name written on a white stone, white for acquittal, for purity and being set apart (Rev 2:17). I felt I was on holy ground; a new day was dawning, and a new name was calling me forth.

Digging Deeper

Here are some of the steps I needed to take to start building better pathways of being and relating to the world around me. I need to clarify, I am not a counselor, and not all people will find my process helpful, but some of it may give insight for your journey as you seek to deepen your own walk with Jesus and others. It may also be of assistance to those who want to offer insights on how to recognize and walk away from abusive relationships to help others you may come in contact with. However, if you find deep abusive stories begin to surface, I would strongly advise you to find a counselor or someone trustworthy to help you walk through that process.

1. Relinquishing Control

   As stated previously, this is a very hard thing to do. Even though everything within you is screaming out for freedom, you are still very much fixated on how to survive within the controlling dynamics in the relationship. These dynamics are so ingrained in your perception of yourself and life that relinquishing control can feel like death. This was the most prominent area I had to work through as I came to understand the whole intent of abuse within my relationship with my mother was that I was hers and only hers. I, as an individual, needed to be cancelled so my mother could feel safe. I really felt that day on the kitchen floor, after I had told my mother I believed in the gifts of the Spirit, that I would just turn to dust psychologically speaking and be no more. Do not underestimate the effects of asking someone to leave abuse. It seems from the outside that it is ludicrous to stay, and it is. But for a victim to leave, they are leaving all they have ever known, and it will take time to reorder and learn how to function without the addiction to being dominated.

2. Discerning Constructs

The next step after naming the abuse was to discern where I had built constructs in order to survive. For me, the most prominent was acknowledging that I had used Jesus to escape the truth of my life. Excessive religious fervor kept me from taking ownership of ways I was acting to try to ensure my safety in relationships. In essence, I was acting like my mother to others. My anxious attachment filter was preoccupied with how I was being perceived, and this led to a stronger than normal fear of what people thought. I was addicted to pleasing people and God. Having a shame-based identity, I never felt at peace in myself unless I was pleasing someone, being controlled by someone, or controlling someone. As I started naming my mother's control, I also had to start naming my own.

3. Deconstruction

This led to the decision to begin to be intentional about deconstructing unhealthy and destructive ways of relating. I needed to forgive my mother to start seeing these ways in myself. I needed to then forgive myself and ask for forgiveness from those I had hurt and controlled. This was quite freeing but also very shameful. I started finding, however, that repenting of my sins toward others began to free up vital psychological space within me, which would enable me to start building healthier constructs and relationships.

4. Facing the Void that Control Leaves

The hardest part in this process is always facing the void the addiction to control leaves. Addiction to being controlled in abusive relationships is very similar to any other addiction. The self relies on these ways of being as though they are necessary for life itself. Feeling isolated is part of facing the deep abandonment that instigated the controlling relationship in the first place. I entered into the abusive relationship with my mother out of a deeply felt necessity for psychological survival. I would need to leave for the same reason.

5. Choosing to Feel Rootless

Part of the isolation was choosing to embrace feeling rootless. I remember feeling like I was suspended in a void. I felt I had lost one of the main connection points in my reality. It scared me to realize just how much control I had given over to my mother. I had surrendered and allowed myself to be almost fully aborted in life. Not even my attachment to God was as strong as my attachment to my mother. I had to learn to sit with this void and find my heartbeat in it. My voice was hidden within me but was deeply traumatized. This part of the process, I think, was the hardest. The self that surrendered to abuse absolutely hated being alone. It would do anything to reattach and to find roots again. I was very thankful my Father kept me from going there, even though I desperately wanted to. Again, I reiterate here that I don't think it is wise to ask someone to go into a mode of reconciliation at this point in the journey. If they do reconcile, it may not actually be reconciliation but another way of bowing down to abusive patterns that will cause them to begin the addiction all over again.

6. Facing and Embracing the Self in God

In this place of being rootless, I started seeing God as my Father and Mother. My Father enabled me to start the process of forgiving myself and helped me to embrace and start reconciling with this self that he had made. It was almost like I needed to be reformed in the womb and reparented. I was so conditioned to the generational form of abuse I had inherited that I needed to almost begin again.

7. Rebuilding Identity

In this phase, I was able to start rebuilding identity, not just within myself but also in relation to God and others. A person like me, with a shame-based identity, will not be able to just transfer into a more secure identity in God. A person cannot go back in time and be reattached. I think a person with a shame-based identity will always be finding places within themselves where they need to confront destructive constructs and reconstruct. I know for me the process is ongoing. There are times when I am doing well and feel like I have resolved so much, and then a situation arises that, for some reason, takes me back to what feels like square one, needing to start all over again. This is seldom the case, however; usually another level of healing is taking place and a deeper, more sure identity in God is being developed.

8. Importance of the Scriptures and the Spirit

The importance of the Scriptures and the Spirit cannot be undervalued. Reconstructing ways of being is not simply a matter of retraining the brain to think differently or mastering one's constructs. It needs a far deeper and more profound work than only a cognitive approach can bring. I believe it can only safely be done in God. Studying at Bible college and researching the Bible in depth has given me anchors within which to solidify this self in God. I read something in my research that

I remember exploded hope in my soul during this time: the true self cannot be destroyed.[8] It is still there, hidden in God. This is not a New Age search for identity; this is God coming in his fullness and helping a person deconstruct ways of abuse through repentance, forgiveness, and mercy-filled grace, to find their center in God and not in the ways of abusive relationships.

9. Community—New Constructs

As I started dismantling old constructs and building new, more permanent structures in God where there was no control, I started being able to be in community in healthier ways. Of course, years of toxicity were not going to be reconstructed instantaneously. I am still in the process of becoming whole. I thank the Lord for his unceasing and merciful patience with me. He is increasingly becoming my center.

Psychological Justice

Unpacking honor was a massive shift in my theological understanding of justice, as I was then able to psychologically stop the abuse in the name of honor. *Psychological justice* also prioritizes naming scriptural misappropriations and dealing with the consequences these have for our Christ-centered lived experience.

It is hard to describe what my research and learning meant for my dance with my Father. They were shaping my Christ-centered lived experience. My research was giving me the strength to deal with the extent of the abuse I was beginning to name, not only theologically but psychologically. In this process, my Father wanted to not only give me *psychological justice*, but also enable me to stop the lineage of control by dealing with the deeper psychological and theological fractures that had affected my generational line for decades. An important part of this process was understanding that the Lord is my inheritance, as this enabled me to renounce the physical inheritance, helping to stop the extent of the legacy of abuse coming to my children and their children.

Having named the abuse I was processing, it was also time to start naming the abuse I had enacted on my children. I had a dear friend during this season who challenged me about my relationship with one of my children. He said to me, "Please stop controlling them." I remember feeling the Lord's conviction acutely pierce my soul. I fell to my knees and sobbed for what felt like forever. My Jesus sat with me and helped me acknowledge

8. Kline, "Merton's True Self," 731.

that I too had fallen into the narcissistic trap that I was beginning to face with my mother. My friend was mirroring my heavenly Father's words to me regarding my mother's parental control. "Enough!" resounded in my being. I saw clearly how I was chillingly continuing the narcissistic generational legacy. I saw myself for the first time reflecting my mother's ways. I started grasping that to truly be free from my mother, I had to repent and face squarely the effects that my mother's narcissistic grandiosity had entrenched within me. Repenting of controlling my children started healing deep wounds in them and me.

I was also starting to face that I had spiritually pressured my children, as my mother had pressured me. I had placed on them ways of being "spiritual" that were not spiritual in the least. They were legalistic measures that I was allowing others to speak over us that resembled spirituality but were just another form of control. I am still walking this road of forgiveness with my children. I long to see them set free from the spiritually abusive ways in which I have acted toward them. I am driven again and again into the arms of the one who has given me *psychological justice* from my mother's heritage and am seeking my Father to release my children from furthering that legacy by imparting *psychological justice* to them also.

What's Your Story?

Does my story highlight any types of abuse that may be operating in your life or in those you love? What steps can you take to start questioning these?

My Father Gifts a New Name

One of my favorite movies is *2012*. It is based on the real fear and hysteria that existed concerning the ending of the Mayan calendar in December 2012. The movie depicts the impending elimination of the Earth by an asteroid. 2012, for our family, felt just like the movie. We thought we'd had our share of tragedy. Little did we know a giant asteroid was heading for us, and we unfortunately did not have any ark built and ready to shelter in.

On April 12, a letter came in the post addressed to John but written to me. I came home from Bible college, and John was in the lounge; he looked at me, deeply troubled, and said, "This came in the post for me today, but what is inside is for you." He handed me the letter and watched as I read it. As I read, I couldn't quite believe what I was reading. Confusion and sorrow, mixed together like a toxic fluid, washed over me like acid rain. It is hard to describe how drinking a cocktail of toxic abuse can make your soul, mind, and body feel. It impacted me on every level all at once. This letter was from my parents, so the effects reached deep down into the soil of being born. I felt like I had been ripped apart by the very ones who had brought me into the world and whose role had been to protect and nurture me. The depth of pain I encountered that day I cannot describe. To be betrayed by your parents, falsely accused and misunderstood, was phenomenal. I sat there in disbelief and in so much raw pain that I wondered if I would ever feel alive again.

The crux of the letter was that if I insisted that the gifts of the Spirit are for today, I was no longer a true believer, I was cut off from God, and I was no longer their daughter. The choice was stark and its effects immediate.

I was no longer their daughter.

My parents had disowned me?

I walked around numb for the rest of the night. John was in so much pain watching me face what he had suspected all along, but the abuse he had witnessed was rooted far deeper than either of us considered remotely possible. My brother had been right; this was a generational legacy of abuse.

I fixed dinner and did the normal things of making lunches and getting the children off to bed. John and I sat and tried to decide what on earth we were going to do now. None of the boundaries had worked, and even trying to give some distance to gain some perspective had not succeeded.

I remember waking up feeling really overwhelmed with the other huge situations we were facing that week. John would be getting some medical results back, and there were a host of meetings about my children's learning "disabilities." My Father gave me this Scripture: "Commit your way to the Lord; trust in him and he will do this: he will make your righteous reward shine like the dawn, your vindication like the noonday sun" (Ps 37:5–6).

What made this whole process much more intense and extremely disorientating were well-meaning believers stating that the Scriptures said I just had to forgive them, reconcile, and then God would heal all involved. I was in deep pain after losing my entire family, and I felt I didn't warrant support from my wider church family until I had reconciled with my parents.

This is when the Holy Spirit just exploded like a volcano in me. It felt like the Trinity came to my aid and, like a violent storm, said, "Enough!" I had a supernatural strength I had never felt before rise up in me that it was time to name and end this abuse now.

Part of my master's research focused on the psychological effects of abuse. One day, I read an article on PTSD in a magazine. I cannot remember the magazine now. I wrote the details on a napkin, as I was so moved by the description of trauma. It was a piece based on an interview with Meryl Streep for her movie *Osage County*. Meryl's friend encouraged her to take the role for all the daughters that needed someone to voice the trauma of having the type of mother Meryl would portray in the movie. Meryl recounted her friend saying, "Trauma violates your belief in yourself, your judgment, your body, other people, even God. It deprives you suddenly and even violently of what you had. It destroys the sense of safety, predictability, and justice you assumed and expected in your life." I found this definition of trauma really hit home for me, regarding why dealing with my past was so difficult.

Trauma had also affected my ability to work on my thesis. I could not access my abilities as the emotional resources that I had been writing with were being diverted to so many other places. I was trying to reason and write from a place of emotional deficit. As this is my primary creative center, this was like trying to draw blood from a stone. I had poured my life out, and there didn't seem to be any space in my being to think from.

Some Christians' responses were fixated on the theological premise of honor, yet they could not even hear me when I would tell them the complexity of the toxic abuse I had lived through. They wanted me to respond to a deeply traumatic situation based on their fixed theological position without listening to how profoundly it was affecting me. I had others, though, who had either been through abuse or were experienced in dealing with people who had, and they all gave me the same advice—leave.

I needed to thrash out the complexity of my response and start the process of having legal documents written. This was necessary because there was a clause in their letter warning that I would be disinherited if I refused to agree with their theological premise. God had already revealed to me in a dream about six weeks previously to legally refuse any inheritance from my parents, which I had considered extremely bizarre at the time. Once I received my parents' letter, it made perfect sense.

John and I wept and waited before the Lord through the night, asking him if there was any other way apart from legally responding. If we bowed down to their stipulations, it would mean denying our Father the foremost honor. One of the most painful things we ever had to do was instruct the lawyer to reply. We said that we felt it important to respect their position and therefore accept being disowned. We would not be honoring God by agreeing with their stipulations. I legally needed to accept disinheritance and no contact. This was extremely painful. It was debilitating and exhausting on so many levels. My Father was so close, but I now understand how people who need to get restraining orders in order to leave abusive relationships feel. Renouncing an inheritance from my parents was difficult, not because of the monetary value, but because of the loss for my children of their grandparents.

Not long after this, I was sitting with John on our cane chairs in our lounge room on a beautiful fall day, and my Father said to me, "Your parents no longer have a right to name you. I will give you a new name." I was puzzled. The name he whispered in my ear was Lydia Rose. I imagined this new name would only be voiced in an intimate place between myself and the Trinity.

I started taking deliberate steps to walk out from underneath my parents' abuse and into learning how to dance again. Somewhere along in my dance, I had forgotten the steps. 2012 is the year I would learn to dance again with my Jesus, whom I was now beginning to know as Justice.

November came, and I was sitting in the same cane chairs on a beautiful summer's day with my friends Tui and Lisa. I disclosed to them what the Father had said to me a couple of months previously. As we talked, I got the distinct impression from my Father that this was not just an intimate name between us; he really wanted me to change my name. I told him I was not going to do this, as I already felt weird enough as it was.

My friend Lisa got wind of my argument with the Lord after I made a passing comment and, well, that was it. She had her phone out and started researching then and there what I would have to do to change my name legally in Australia. Within ten minutes, she found the forms and asked me what I was waiting for.

Oh dear, I really had just voiced this, and now I knew I had to do it.

I was trying to process this quietly, but the Lord's joy over me was so great. One day, over and over, he kept saying to me, "Proclaim it from the rooftops" (Matt 10:27). In our modern world, where do you go to proclaim something from the rooftops?—Facebook. This is what I posted:

> Today I take my first step! Can't wait! Timing is everything. Isa 62:1–5. Today I start the process of changing my name to Lydia Rose. I think I will write a book about it one day. It is really just a culmination of a wonderful love story of an abused little girl being saved and adopted and given a new name by a Daddy who has paid the ultimate price for his daughter! No more performance—just a love affair with the one who created me a noble woman, not a slave.

On November 11, the documents for the name change were all signed and ready to send. I felt overwhelmed at most people's loving, positive affirmation of this next step in my life.

In December, I graduated with my postgraduate diploma in theology. I was graduating from my studies, but I felt I had also graduated on a lot of other more meaningful levels. I had finally graduated from an intense season of abuse into liberation. 2012 had lived up to its name, and I had found my ark—it was the beautiful Trinity that had been safely carrying me from conception. My roots were now deeper than my parents; my source had been unearthed in God, and it was time to enter into a new freedom and learn to live from a surer identity. However, having a sure identity and learning to live in freedom would not be as easy as I anticipated.

Part of what the Father was teaching me was that my name change was not just a name. He said to me, "You are highly favored" (Dan 10:11), then drew links to my name Lydia, meaning "noble from birth"—in opposition to my former name, which means "star/performer." My Father said my new name represented that I no longer had to perform for favor. It was overwhelming to hear my Father say this after having lived a life where, to gain value and favor from those I loved, I felt I had to perform. My Father wanted me to know at a more conscious level that my dignity came from being highly favored by him, not people.

It was a wonderful start to 2013 with receiving the official documentation of my name change from Australia on our wedding anniversary, January 18. Yes, the same day I left Australia. This date now symbolized the day my Father celebrated his naming of me. He was deeply passionate about naming me. I feel the depths of his heart when he calls me by name. I hear the pride reverberate in his voice. I feel his deep sense of justice toward me. The Father is incredibly invested in us. He really does take seriously being a Father (or mother, brother, or sister).

It took a while to process the official name changes required, and it was costly. I started organizing a party to celebrate a new name for a new beginning. My name change highlighted what I was starting to learn; my heavenly Father would never violate my freedom. Being in love with God is much harder than religion, as true love puts the responsibility on oneself to love deeply. This is a much heavier responsibility than obeying some religious rules. Our relationship with God our Father should lead us into intimacy, and intimacy is felt deeply and on multiple levels. I didn't want to settle for anything less; I wanted to lay down my life, not because I had to, but because I was in love with Jesus. I had a revelation one day that I had spent most of my Christian experience trying to prove to God that I was what he already said I was.

Digging Deeper

The struggle John and I experienced lamenting over the dilemma my parents' letter had presented us led to a deep convulsing of our entire being.

Did we need to be this rash, this final? The Lord replied that we did. He also showed me why:

> "Not just for yourself but for your children and your children after you. I will be your inheritance, and your legacy will be that you fought for them and stood firm for their freedom. You are a stalwart in this generation, and you will be the dividing line between what has been and all that I long to be and do for the generations to come. Fight for your children and your grandchildren. This is no longer about you; this is about those who will come after you. Do this for them."

The Father would often take me to the book of Nehemiah during this process, particularly verse 4:14: "After I looked things over, I stood up and said to the nobles, the officials and the rest of the people, 'Don't be afraid of them. Remember the Lord, who is great and awesome, and fight for your families, your sons and your daughters, your wives and your homes."

On June 3, I wrote in my journal:

> I was grieving over all that had been robbed from us and the seeds of painful obedience that we have sown, and God gave me a picture of me taking all that I felt the enemy had stolen through abuse/death and gathering even the crumbs, then he asked me to sow them into the Kingdom, where he could bless them. As soon as I did, before me grew up thousands upon thousands of plants, and the acreage kept going further than my eyes could see, touching generations from now.

"Though my father and mother forsake me, the Lord will receive me" (Ps 27:10).

The most significant shift to happen after taking my Father's name for me was that I no longer felt I had to remain in abusive relationships. I now had a choice. I no longer needed to feel guilty for saying no to people or opportunities. My Father had given me permission to keep myself safe. I could love freely because I now had a *choice*. Any type of abuse takes away a person's choice, and this takes away their voice. Because of my Father's gracious work in my life, I was increasingly living from a place of freedom where my identity was no longer shifting in line with the emotional needs of others. The Father had given me a new name for a new season because our Father hates any form of robbery, and he will move heaven and earth to put things right. This is what he was doing for me. I had been in bondage, as I certainly hadn't had a clear voice. I had felt trapped in religion, and religion is what my Father hates the most. He gave me the gift of a new name because only he has the right to truly name me. You see, abuse names you in so many core ways, but my Father's first words, when my parents disowned me, were that my parents no longer had a right to name me.

Psychological Justice

When I think of 2012, the word that defines this year for me is "dignity." In the midst of John's health deterioration (more on this later) and the process I needed to go through with my family, I see my Father desiring to release me from a lifetime of toxic false identity. It was like I entered a cocoon and had to die, and once through this, I was able to morph into a butterfly that is free. There is no greater example of building resilience and the effects of *psychological justice* than that of a life which had been trapped in dysfunction and is given freedom.

The power of our voice stems from our ability to choose, and this comes when we know we are secure to choose. I had been secure in being controlled. My Father showed me the root of my sin and how it was affecting me. My Father didn't sugarcoat my problem. He also showed me how the solution lay in forgiveness. I needed to forgive myself and my mother and take responsibility for my part. The book by Dupont was so important, as having boundaries when you have been in any form of abuse is crucial but very difficult to put in place. *Psychological justice* was being wrought as I dealt with the toxicity in my relationship with my mother. One of the consequences of this was that, theologically, my image of God was being deepened as I met him as my Father. The letter to my parents brought a measure of breakthrough into freedom, as I was offered a choice in the way I responded. There was great value in recognizing my choice would have significant consequences for myself and my children. The power of my choice led to me gaining a clearer voice. I needed to face head-on the spiritual lies embedded within my psyche, which were affecting my relationship with my Father and others. The letter from my parents and my subsequent letter in return enabled those lies to be faced squarely and honestly.

I could not believe it when my name change became official on the day of my wedding anniversary and the date on which I had left Australia over twenty years previous. I still felt a little nervous at people's responses or expectations of me in respect to my new legal status as Lydia Rose. I had no idea what this would mean for my future, but I knew it was my Father's desire for me. *Psychological justice* is seen in that my Father knew how deeply betrayed I had felt with my parents' decision to disown me. I was an orphan in a way, and my Father took it upon himself to adopt me in more than a transactional way. As Romans 8:15–17 states, "The Spirit you received does not make you slaves, so that you live in fear again; rather, the Spirit you received brought about your adoption to sonship. And by him we cry, 'Abba, Father.' The Spirit himself testifies with our spirit that we are God's children. Now if we are children, then we are heirs—heirs of God and co-heirs with Christ, if indeed we share in his sufferings in order that we may also share in his glory." In naming me, my Father was changing my concept of him as a God removed to a Father involved. This was so different to the way the Father had been theologically presented to me.

The new name my Father gave me represented a lifetime of process to get to this point. It wasn't a light decision, and it was born out of severe pain. I know for some, changing my name came across as rather brash and unnecessary. My Father knew, though, just what I had processed and how much a new name was fitting for what had transpired. My health was significantly affected for the better with my name change. I am so thankful my Father prioritized *psychological justice* in my life above anything I could do *for* him.

As I wrote this chapter, I suddenly saw the narcissistic ties that had bound me to my mother. As I was researching the indicators of narcissism, I saw my experiences in the descriptors. I want to clarify that my intention is not to label my mother with narcissism, or with any other psychological label. My purpose is to demonstrate how when we know our story, we are more likely to see patterns in our relationships and begin asking what they might mean, and how they might aid our process of healing and forgiveness. The goal of naming aspects of our journey is always for the healing of all parties. With that in mind and having read my story thus far, let us trace these threads together:

1. Mum usurped control over my faith and beliefs;

2. Used labels such as "pet" and "silly little girl" to minimize my voice;

3. Scapegoated me several times to diffuse her anxiety;

4. Caused me to second-guess myself repeatedly, i.e., gaslighting;

5. Was often jealous of my other strong connections;

6. Dismissed vital and healthy relationships by belittling their relationship with God and labeling them as "not Christian";

7. Used violence in our arguments, with crockery and other items being thrown, to the escalation of beating me in the bush without any explanation;

8. Being angry and hurt after Krissy died that I was not there for her;

9. Finally, disowning me as her daughter for believing in the gifts of the Spirit.

As a consequence of the deep healing the Holy Spirit has wrought in me since this season, I was delighted when my Father showed me that all the places where my mother's narcissism had left crevices in my soul, my Father has now upended:

1. I now have my voice.
2. I am safe.
3. I am connected deeply with my children, dear friends, and a wonderful wider community.
4. I can say no; I now have a choice.
5. I belong.
6. I am valued.
7. I am free.

What my Father promised after Krissy died has transpired. I was rooted in fear and abandonment, and now I am rooted in his love and goodness.

Having experienced his healing, I am watching my Father provide *psychological justice* for my children. My Father, through my name change, had begun unraveling these threads. With my new name, my Father started creating a fresh tapestry woven with dignity and love.

What's Your Story?

In what areas in your life do you need a new name from the Lord? What names have been placed on you that do not belong to you? For example, negative aspects of your personality, roles within family structures, or a traumatic experience.

Freedom through Betrayal—Renaming Church

After Ben's resurrection, we were struggling with how to live a normal life after witnessing such a supernatural deliverance. Our faith and our world had been stretched, and we didn't know how to incorporate our journey with Ben into our journey with church.

We moved to a new church in 2009 and stayed until we moved north in 2016. We were beginning our healing journey out of the toxic relationship constructs with my family. I cannot fully describe the powerful freedom our family experienced in this church during these years. We felt we belonged and had such fatherly and motherly input and access to creativity we had never thought possible as a family. It was a time to recover, receive, renew, and rest.

In one service, I felt the Holy Spirit nudge me to the front to dance. I resisted at first, but I danced, and something in me came alive. I had not danced like this since my youth. I had put theater productions together and taken them around the North Island of New Zealand at Christmas. I had put on events to raise money for young people going on missions. I had choreographed dances and dramas. But I had not danced freely like this for a long time. I had never danced freely before the Lord with his people like this, ever.

After the service, I was asked if I wanted to join the dance team. "There is a team?" I quizzed. Well, that blew me away. I became part of the team, and I absolutely loved these girls. The more we danced freely in worship together, the stronger our bonds became. It was worship like I had never experienced before. The best part was that the children were always invited to join in this way to worship too. My children got to wave flags and banners and ribbons and enjoy dancing with us. There was color and fun and beauty, and it was a privilege to be part of something so special.

We were learning to treasure the presence of God in a whole new way. As a family, we would, on occasion at home, lie on the floor together, put worship music on, and rest in our Father's love. These were very special times. We were learning to know the Father and Jesus and the Holy Spirit in a very new and freeing way. It was comforting for us as a family, to be in this atmosphere and know that the miracles we experienced with Ben our Father wanted to continue to do for others through us. Our understanding of how great our God is was expanding, and our ability to receive him in this way was also increasing.

The more I danced, the more the Holy Spirit taught me what he was doing in the service. Dance was growing from something I was doing to worship God to something God was doing in me as I was now learning how to hear the Lord when I danced. There were times the Holy Spirit would say to dance a certain way, or different movements meant certain ways he was working. I was also developing a prophetic dance, where movements were tied in with certain expressions that the Father was breathing prophetically over the meeting. I would see the validity of this when people would come up to me after the service and say they felt or saw something when I did a particular movement; it was often a confirmation of what my Father had revealed he was doing. Other times, the sermon would be about what I felt the Holy Spirit was saying. It was an incredible time of learning to dance with the Trinity on a deeper level.

I had a wonderful experience dancing with the flags one Sunday. I had two flags; one flag represented fire and passion, and the other flag restoration. I felt I should dance with both, but they were quite large. I struggled a lot at first, but the more I did it, the more fluid it became until I was able to dance with them as if they were one. It was a prophetic act on two levels. One was for the church, representing that the passion and fire for evangelism and healing unified with the continual restoration the Father wants for his children. The second level was for me in relation to my master's thesis. I was really struggling to integrate the fields of psychology and theology. Halfway through the dance that morning, I felt the Holy Spirit speak to me and say, "See, they are one now. You struggled in the beginning and it was really messy, but now look at you." From that point on, I was able to do things with the flags that I did not think were possible. It felt like an extension of my own self in God. That combination of restoration and passion for justice totally blew me away. I felt honored my Father would encounter me in such a way. I was increasingly aware that my Father, like in the Parable of the Prodigal Son, is continually looking for his children to bring them home and give them justice. I wished at the time I could preach my thesis or, better still, dance it.

I was discovering how much the Father wants to release the creative into the wider church. Many churches in Africa and around the world worship like this. A friend of mine would sometimes bring his pottery and make things as part of his worship. We had some people painting prophetic art, which they would sometimes then gift to people at the end of the service.

My bond with the pastor grew strong during these years. He was incredibly special to me, especially as my relationship with my own mother and father was faltering at the time. He was very supportive and walked with me to help me understand what was happening with the prophetic call I felt on my life. I was particularly moved when everything was unraveling with my parents that he took the step to declare over me that he would be my father and take the place of my own father's inability to be so for me.

There were many visiting speakers and conferences that were also deeply impacting for us as a family. People like Danny Silk were pivotal for me, as I processed developing boundaries not just with my family, but also as a mother. His book on parenting, *Loving Your Kids on Purpose*, was revolutionary. He was clear and had many practical ways to handle everyday parenting problems. I cannot recommend this book highly enough (and it is listed it in the bibliography). One of my favorite phrases I picked up in one of Danny Silk's seminars was: "Never forget that you cannot work harder on someone's problem than they are willing to work." I cannot count the number of times this phrase has saved me.

This season at this church was special for us in so many ways. Because of this, I was surprised one Sunday morning in January 2014 to hear the Lord say to me repeatedly on the way to church that I would be "deeply betrayed." I just could not fathom by whom and why. I got to church and was so concerned about this that I informed a friend of mine. This friend is not prone to emotional outbursts or reactions. When I told her, she fell to the ground and started groaning. I was so surprised. Then another friend came over and said, "I don't know what is going on, but God has got your back." I just hid the word in my heart because it didn't make any sense at all.

Proverbs 20:10, the verse the Lord had given me years earlier, was now being impressed on me in the present: "Differing weights and differing measures, the Lord detests them both." The impression was incessant. I felt the Lord wanted me to send it to one of the leaders, but I didn't want to. One, I didn't understand completely what it meant in this setting; and two, if it meant what it had meant for me before in my journey, I didn't want to be the one to say it. I was very happy in my position and place within this church family. I did not want to be the one to say anything that may have a negative aspect to it in such a strongly affirmative prophetic space. I had just lost connection with my father and mother, and I had very strong, beautiful connections in this church family; I was not going to risk losing that. Unfortunately, my Father kept insisting. This went on for over a month, and it was hard to ignore him.

We went north to visit our friends, and the impression became so persistent. I just said, "No, I am not going to do it!" Alas, I cannot deny my Father for long, and I sent the email with the word that had been on my mind for over a month to one of the leaders. That email would serve to be the beginning of the end of our time in this church. There was a host of misunderstanding and conflict over the Scripture that strained once-deep connections. I could not explain away what I knew my Father was asking me to say, and my pastor could not deny the way he interpreted the Scripture and my theological position in relation to it. My interpretation of the timing of the Scripture was that the Father wanted us, as leadership, to be careful not to label what he was doing in releasing creativity in our church as something we as a church were doing. As I explained in an earlier chapter, whenever we take what the Holy Spirit is doing and knowingly or unknowingly take steps to define it, decipher it, or own it so we can produce it as a manifestation of ourselves, the Holy Spirit's role is to discipline us to see that its origin is first and foremost in Jesus, and therefore belongs to Jesus. I believe the Father wanted to warn us, so the Holy Spirit could continue to release his creative fire to our nation. It felt similar to when I faced my mum. I had to decide between my Father and my pastor, who had been a father to me, and I knew if I chose my Father, I would lose relationship with this new father and possibly some of my church family. I suspect the pastor also felt betrayed by me. I have purposely withheld the name of this church and the people because they are still very precious to me.

This definitely was what the Lord said would happen: a deep betrayal that splintered my soul and left me feeling isolated. However, my Father was very strong for me and I felt his presence. He would say to me over and over, "I have got your back." This beckons back to the word my friend gave when my Father first warned me I would be betrayed. I realized later I should never have accepted this pastor's invitation for him to be a father to me. I had just lost my natural father, and my heavenly Father wanted me to cling to him, but I went from one earthly father to another and denied my heavenly Father the position he had been trying to plant in me since my youth.

I had once idolized my mother, and now I had to dismantle idolizing this pastor. I value his stand for what he believed to be the truth and what he fights for, for people's freedom. We are just on different paths in our understanding of some of the ways God does that, and that's okay. It is okay for believers to disagree and to still live full lives in desiring to see the kingdom come.

God's justice is that our enemies are also blessed and healed and restored. I cannot ask God for justice and not want to see him bless my enemy. This powerful truth was so important in what had transpired with my mother and father. The thesis I was writing on justice had been given hands, feet, and a heart. Knowledge was giving way to knowing. I had to live what I was writing. My thesis needed to be a *living thesis*. Yet, I still wasn't ready for what the Lord really wanted me to learn as a master's student.

There was another level of justice I had to face concerning my attitude toward the pastor. I had elevated this person to fill the void left in me by the lack of a father figure. My heavenly Father shone his light on this through the Scripture 1 Corinthians 3:21, which says, "So then, no more boasting about human leaders!" I had boasted in my secure position with this pastor, and my Father convicted me on this point. In Corinth, there had been conjecture over which leaders were more spiritually elite. Paul was aggravated by this, as he called himself a servant for the Lord's sake. I had been showing partiality, and my Father convicted me of this (Mal 2:9).

We were still attending the church in the early months of 2015. I remember, on one occasion, being down the front during worship. I had fallen to my knees as I was beginning to process the weight of all that was happening internally for me. I was crushed with wanting to know why doing the right thing felt like the exact opposite. I was grieving bitter tears, and they were rolling down my face. I felt a presence behind me, and someone wiped the tears off my face and comforted me with a deep hug. I sat weeping and processing with my Jesus, asking for his presence and help to surrender myself deeper.

After I gathered myself together, I walked back to my husband, who was sitting near the front of the congregation, and asked him who had come to comfort me through the worship. He told me that no one came near me. He said, "I was watching you the whole time and left you with the Lord, as it seemed you were deep in worship." I was in disbelief. "Was this an angel of the Lord that had come to physically wipe my tears?" I wondered to myself. What a beautiful Savior. God was comforting me in the midst of betrayal.

I was still deeply grieving leaving our church family and wept as I walked most days. I had been accused of saying things I had not said. I had given most of these to my Father because he is the only one that can bring justice. I also wept because of an overwhelming sense of my Father's faithfulness. There was nothing I could say to those who were slandering me. Some of it may even have been right. I was learning, in my research on Romans, that none of us has a place from which to boast. I, for one, knew I was not together, and, like Paul, I was learning to rejoice in my weakness. I needed God desperately, and I was beginning not to be ashamed to say that. The isolation of betrayal was turning into intimacy with my Father.

I found a lot of solace in my research during this time. There are times in your life when, before resurrection can take place, there is a crucifixion and you are left alone, naked, and feeling crucified before others and mocked for your silence. You know you are taking the heat for others, and you wonder where God is in it all, especially as he gave you the cup to drink in the first place. Yet you know you agreed to drink it, but in the meantime, everyone else scatters. "Why has God forsaken me?" I cried.

Sometimes we experience the isolation because there is more at stake than our own name or reputation. At times like this, lean into the God hidden in the cross, knowing that resurrection is coming.

I was beginning to fear the new season my Father was beckoning me into, and leaving was extremely painful. I was reading a very good book for my thesis called *The Healing Presence* by Leanne Payne. In it, she talks about the need as believers to lay our idols down in order to enter into the joy of being our true selves in God.[9] I felt God's hand on my shoulder one night, telling me this transition time was the perfect opportunity for me to finally let go of the desire to belong. I had never let God truly be my Father. I felt

9. Payne, *Healing Presence*, 88.

that this season was a good opportunity to let him. I was at ground zero. Instead of feeling lost as I had been, I felt my Father ask me to press into trusting him, especially since who I was had been questioned of late. When you doubt yourself, it is time to press into the one who doesn't doubt you.

In all of us, the betrayal we had experienced tested concepts of love and justice. I was pouring out my heart to my Father continually. My heart just hurt. I was so broken; I didn't even know if I could keep going (and I had been pretty broken before). However, the Lord said to me in my deep pain, "Do not drink the poison of another's offense." Yes, amen, Lord. It was hard enough as it was, without imbibing poison.

Digging Deeper

I am thankful the Lord had warned me nine months before the betrayal transpired. I would have found it very difficult to process this experience had the Lord not already indicated what was coming. I don't know why he didn't try and avert this situation, but in the end, this tested whether I would be obedient to give the Scripture he had given me, even though the cost would be high. That seems to be a common theme in my story. We cannot bring deliverance to others in places where we are still bound. What seems like sacrifice and cost can, in actuality, be God delivering us. We must be free from being bound to people and places to be able to release his freedom to them. We cannot serve where we are mastered.

I had acknowledged that I had felt deeply betrayed by people, but I was starting to grasp that I had also felt betrayed by my Lord. I felt like I had obeyed him and spoken what he asked me to speak, and then lost friends, a family, and, in the process, a reputation. In the midst of these musings, the Lord came to me and spoke the words he spoke to Peter, asking me the same question, "Do you love me more than these?" (John 21:15). I had to really sit with this Scripture. Did I love Jesus more than others' thoughts about me? More than my reputation? More than the people I felt I had lost through my obedience? The sheep, his people, are *his*. "Feed *my* sheep," he said. You cannot feed *his* sheep unless you first love Jesus *more* than his sheep. The Lord was indicating to Peter that it was not going to be easy, and he would suffer persecution and die for his obedience. The Lord asked Peter to face his betrayal when he failed to stand with Jesus. It was after a season of betrayal that Jesus came to Peter, not only to forgive him, but also to call him to lose his reputation and his self-promotion and to spend his life serving and feeding his Lord's people. After spending three years in the presence and the glory of Jesus and seeing the miracles that came from being his disciple, Peter did not see the fruition of what he anticipated Jesus' purpose was; i.e., Jesus did not fight the soldiers back and lead a resistance to overthrow Rome. Instead, Peter witnessed his master be killed.

I learned a lot through this process. I learned God's word does not return void. The more I have walked on from this time, the more I see what the Lord was trying to say all along. It has given me confidence that the Scripture I had, though seemingly packaged negatively, was in actuality a promise of what could be. I think we need to be careful as people of God not to be scared to present the truth and let it do its work. Not every word God gives us will sound positive. Sometimes we need seasons of pruning. Sometimes he will give us a promise in a package that sounds harsh. Are we open in those times to trust and hold on to the word and allow time to reveal the beauty within?

In essence, it taught me one of the biggest lessons I have ever received: justice. If we really want justice, it needs to be bidirectional. During the conversations I had as a repercussion of this Scripture, I desperately wanted everyone to see my side of the story. So much conversation was being had that I was not part of. I wanted so much to talk about it. I remember over and over wanting to rant online or to someone, and the Lord would say, "Do you want my justice or yours?" I would groan and say, "Yours!" and then shut my mouth (which in itself was a miracle).

A beautiful exchange happened between my daughter and me during this time. She was trying to explain to me how something I was doing was hurting her, and I just couldn't see it. In the end, she said to me, "Well, I will just have to forgive you and let it go." I said I was sorry and that I would try. That week, I suddenly saw so clearly what she had been trying to tell me. I was so upset that I had not seen it before. It was now so obvious. My Father showed me why I could suddenly see her pain. He said to me that her forgiveness released me to see what she was trying to show me. Her forgiving me released her from the consequences of my sins but also released me to see clearly.

Unforgiveness can sometimes tie us into the consequences of the other person's sin. Forgiveness opens the door for change in the other person. When my daughter forgave me, it opened my eyes to see why she forgave me. My Father then gave me the power to change what I needed to change. My Father showed me through this that if I am struggling to reveal my heart to someone (usually my husband!), to forgive them and ask for God's help— no strings attached. Of course, this will not always be that easy, but it was a very important lesson for me to learn.

Psychological Justice

It is hard to describe how dancing brought such deep healing to my identity. I almost cannot believe my Father knew what my soul needed and led me to a church where I could tap into the very core of who I was to be liberated. Within this space, all aspects of my identity were able to show their face again. The shame that had covered me was being brought into the light through dance. I was able to see the toxicity of shame, how destructive it had been to my psyche, and the effect this had on my apprehending my identity in Christ. This was my Father giving me *psychological justice* by showing me he was passionate about the creativity of his people in worship. This was so different to the academic image of God I had been building. Not that this is wrong; it is very necessary. However, the Father will not be limited to our understanding. The Father created the universe and is still creating. What was even more important was experiencing dance *in* God. There were so many times in my dance journey that I experienced a deep and profound presence of my Father; I can't even put these experiences into words. These were no mere mental apprehensions or even a mindset.

Treasuring the presence of God in the creative prophetic realm showed me there is more to know of our Father than we can ever dream possible. Our Father wants us to flourish in all our lived experience, in our work, in our creativity—whatever that looks like for you. Creative—that is what worship is, not some band singing upfront. We are poorer if all we experience in worship is singing some songs in church. We are called to be worshippers and priests. I don't believe this is limited to a couple of hours in a building with others once a week. I believe the Father desires so much more for his people than this. What I experienced in this church was just a taste of the vastness of our Father's heart for us in worship; it's our fullest experience of his love as God pursues us. *Psychological justice* is the manifestation of all our Father is in all spheres of our lives; a heavenly agenda that has an earthly purpose.

Psychological justice shows us that blessing our enemies will set us free. For me to know my Father's justice through betrayal, I had to give justice. I had to release those who were in pain through this situation from my expectation they would see what I was trying to say and do. I also had to let go of needing to be understood and vindicated. The only vindication that is true victory is when we can bless our enemies as our Father does. I am not saying this was easy, but the more we walk in *psychological justice* and understand its full implications, the more freedom our Father can release in us and through us to others. *Psychological justice*, in these moments, is a gift from our Father.

The betrayal tested my heart, and my Father wanted me to really count the cost of *psychological justice*. Did I love Jesus more than those who were against me, enough to love them more than I felt betrayed? There is a cost to walking in *psychological justice*, primarily because it is not a natural way to respond to injustice. We can see this because the world's justice system does not sometimes or in all ways reflect our Father's justice.

My loss of reputation was necessary to be able to come to the place where ministry was no longer about my desire to achieve something for my Father. I would come to understand that *psychological justice* would not be produced through my flesh. We are not able to walk in *psychological justice* in our own strength. It takes a strong person to be able to forgive those who have perpetrated a grave injustice against them. I needed the fullness of the Holy Spirit just to keep my mouth shut in the beginning. It would take time to forgive to the extent my Father required of me. I needed to come to the place where I could surrender the will of my flesh enough to let the Holy Spirit do it in me. *Psychological justice* needs to be supernatural to be life-changing.

What's Your Story?

God's justice is sometimes predicated on forgiveness. Where might you need to forgive another or an institution, in order to see God's justice be wrought in you or in your circumstances? Who is an enemy that you could bless today?

Season 6

Transition

I consider that our present sufferings are not worth comparing with the glory that will be revealed in us. (Rom 8:18)

THE SEASON FROM 2014 through 2018 was bookended by extreme polarities. It was as if two differing timelines were running parallel. For example, it is like a woman when she is at the point of transition in labor. It is the most painful, excruciating, and multisensory part of the delivery process, but it is just before the most glorious and joyful part of delivery. We were being stripped as a family in every way imaginable, but glory was shining amidst the darkness and confusion. This season touched every one of us in multiple ways at the same time. My relationship foundations would almost crumble. I am so very grateful for this now because I am placed in more solid and respectful places. These years were intense. They would have been hard enough on their own, but God placed a thesis in my lap in case I got bored, I suppose.

My master's thesis held grief, exhaustion, discouragement, and despair, but alongside these were insights from my research that were strengthening me in my journey. I felt like I was failing as an academic. This was particularly debilitating, as academia and my high grades had been a safety net for my fledgling confidence. It seemed like God wanted this branch dead, but I was desperately trying to reattach this branch to the academic vine. It was obvious what my Father was doing. I just didn't want to accept it was him doing it. I am so thankful my friend Sarah, who was one of my supervisors for my master's, did not give up on me as I waded through the tumultuous and yet at times invigorating journey of exegeting Romans. My journey post-thesis was traumatic but helped to shed more layers of constructs I had built to survive life.

John became very ill, and what we initially thought was a bump in the road became a deepening ravine that he is still walking. Most of this journey has been more like crawling, yet we also saw incredible breakthroughs in his hospital stays so that now when he goes to hospital, we often think, "Who needs John's wisdom this time?"

These years were horrendous to walk, though. Difficulties seemed to touch every single area of our lives. I lost my ability to flow academically. I got to know every hospital in our region intimately. We went through so many medical issues with different family members that doctors started asking if I was a nurse because of the medical knowledge I had acquired and the corresponding language I was using. Betrayal within church, encounters outside of church—suffering and glory, paralleling, dancing, weaving in and out.

It felt like my branches were being hacked off one by one, but others seemed to profit from this. The encounters I was having with those in the community, where God would just turn up and whisper in my ear what he was doing, revealed that no matter how dark, confusing, and life-sucking circumstances can be—God is at work. During this intense period of shifting, like an earthquake, light was emerging like beacons through the cracks. His glory was shining amidst my suffering, coincidently *outside* the walls of church. I will place these God encounters in callout boxes alongside my story to show how involved God actually was through this time.

In the midst of all of this, and a thesis, was the process of disownment from my parents. Basically, I call this period my ground zero. I thought I had got there with Ben. I was still processing Ben. I still hadn't really resolved my role in Ben's death and resurrection. How do I walk with dignity when I had been so neglectful? The Scriptures say that God holds all our tears: "You keep track of all my sorrows. You have collected all my tears in your bottle. You have recorded each one in your book" (Ps 56:8, NLT). I mused at the time that my Father must have thousands of bottles of mine stored somewhere.

These years would test the limits of my trust in God. I would come to a breaking point with the only one who had been faithful all these years. Keep reading. It gets interesting.

The Pond Revisited

Ben was diagnosed with post-concussion syndrome after a scooter accident, and the medical issues associated with this took me back in time to the intensive care unit at Starship Hospital when he drowned. Around the same time, I was contacted by St John's Ambulance Australia, as they were seeking a story to use for fundraising purposes and had asked the paramedics if they knew of any stories they could use. Nick, the ambulance paramedic first on the scene with Ben, told them about our story. They rang and wanted to know the story behind the miracle Nick had told them about. We were very excited! The St John's fundraiser was mailed out to all their supporters; Ben's was their main story and it included pictures from Ben's journey, as well as input from Nick and myself.

A couple of months later, I got this email from the general manager of St John's in New Zealand:

> I wanted to update you on the appeal we recently did featuring the incredible story of your incredible little boy—Benny. Firstly, thank you so much for allowing us to tell your story. Having a personal story to share makes our work more real to people. And I think Benny's story was a very special one. I'm delighted to tell you that our donors thought the story was pretty special too. It obviously connected with them because they have responded very generously to our appeal. In fact, this is the most successful appeal we have ever run. Today we reached $550,000 in donations. This will help us to purchase not just one, but two or three new ambulances. This success surpassed our expectation and has meant lots of our staff and volunteers have had to work extra hard to process it all. So, we would like to put on a morning tea to thank them and to celebrate the results. We would love you and Benny to be there (and whoever else you might like to bring along). It will be very simple, but having you and Benny would make it very special. Are you able to make a morning tea? I know Benny would normally be at school, but if you think it would be a worthwhile experience for him, we would love to make it happen.

Ben's story was getting feet and gaining momentum.

Not long after this letter, I was awake stoking the fire around three o'clock in the morning. My Father spoke to me saying, "You can't fix this." I replied, "I know." He said it a further two times, and both times I said, "I know!" Then he said to me, "You know what my favorite thing to do for you is?" And I replied, "What?" He said, "Fix your mistakes."

The next day, I was out walking and talking with my Father. As we talked, a shield over my heart was unearthed and the guilt over Ben's drowning faced me. It was a double guilt:

1. That I put Jessica, who was nine, in charge of a twenty-two-month-old boy near water.

2. That I was ordering a coffee at the time.

The symptoms associated with Ben's post-concussion highlighted my need for deeper healing in my journey over his accident.

This linked in with my master's thesis on *psychological justice*. Jesus didn't die to save saints; he died for people like me, who not only sin, but through their sin and weakness are perpetrators of injustice. People over the years had tried to console me that Ben's drowning was an accident and I shouldn't blame myself. I was once offered the platitude that I just needed to agree with Romans 12:2 and adopt a new mindset about what had happened. (I have an utter revulsion for this misinterpreted premise of "helping" people in trauma). This reasoning hadn't shifted anything over me; it only seemed to deepen the shame I felt because deep down I believed it was my fault. God's justice for me was in calling out my deepest fear, which was that if it were my fault, the Father would not fix it, but rather I would be punished. I had perpetrated the greatest injustice on my own child, yet my Father's answer was, "I got this. I can fix your mistakes." His promise to me in this was that no matter how badly I blow it in life, he has my back; his justice is greater than my injustice. This was not punishment; this was grace unmerited. I need to reiterate here that I am not saying this means every situation will be resolved the way we want it to be. I did not receive Krissy back to me alive. Yet, my Father has put me right in psychological terms through healing and strengthening me through the grief process in response to her death.

> I was in Melbourne, Australia, attending a conference where N. T. Wright was speaking. The most wonderful thing happened one afternoon after visiting the zoo. I saw a cheap poncho rain jacket and went to buy it, but I felt my Father say I would not need one. I didn't buy it, but the heavens opened after I left and I groaned, "Oh no, I got that wrong!" I went to buy an umbrella, but they were expensive. I started venturing out of the museum to torrential rain outside, and a lady walking past me asked me if I had an umbrella. I replied that I didn't. She said to me, "I have a spare. You can have it." My Father said to me, "I told you so!"

On May 28, we received an email, sent so close to Benny's ten-year memorial coming up on June 5 that none of us believed it was a coincidence:

> I manage the fundraising and marketing for St John's Central Region. Just recently, St John's used Benny's story to mail out to potential new donors and guess what—as a direct result of Benny's story, we have had a family want to donate a fully kitted ambulance. They have also asked if I could seek permission from you to name the ambulance "Benny" and to see if your family and Benny would like to attend the dedication.

To say we were excited for Ben would be an understatement. We all saw God in the timing and the gift for Ben, who had been going through some very difficult struggles. Of course, we said yes.

We were given a launch date for the ambulance named "Benny" in Katikati. Benny's miraculous story was continuing to ripple. Later we were staying with friends about three hours south of us, and a young man came to the door with a brochure featuring fundraising for St John's Ambulance Service. He was blown away when John told him Ben was his son. We told him the whole story and about the launch of Benny's ambulance in Katikati that was coming up. This made his day and ours. When we got back home after our trip away, I was out doing my walk around our local estuary and came across another person raising money for St John's. I said, "That's my son," and told him the story of God's miracle. God was continuing to use what the enemy meant for harm for others' good all over the country. November 9 came, and we felt extremely blessed that the dedication of Ben's ambulance was through a service led by an Anglican vicar. He anointed Benny and the ambulance with oil. The family who dedicated the ambulance were beautiful people. It was a very special day for all of us, remembering God's miraculous mercy. We got to share our faith and tell people some of the details of Ben's story.

Digging Deeper

Ben's post-concussion was a present circumstance that was being compounded by my past psychological trauma at the pond. I can see my Father's justice for me in his promise that he could fix my mistakes. In my Father's great love, he was able to take the deep pain I was in, watching Ben struggle, and bring deeper psychological healing to my heart. My Father was also strengthening deeper theological roots, and I came to understand that he is not fixated on punishing me for my mistakes but is full of mercy toward me.

Psychological Justice

I can't begin to describe what the success of St John's fundraising meant for us as a family. Somehow, the Father saw fit to allow Ben's story to bring so much healing, hope, and financial provision to an essential medical emergency ambulance service in New Zealand. Having had several ambulances now dedicated in service due to Ben's story is so like our Father. Our Father can bring so much good out of our tragedies. This showed me that Ben would have justice come to his health as well.

What's Your Story?

When healing from trauma, you may find you are still triggered. Next time you are, stop and just sit with it and know you will be okay. Each trigger event can be an opportunity for more healing.

On one occasion, I was walking with my friend Tui when we stopped to buy some strawberries. We walked on, and I felt compelled to go back and pray a blessing on the lady and her stall. I argued with Daddy for about a minute until I realized it was pointless. Tui and I walked back to the lady, and I told her I wanted to pray a blessing on her business. She lit up and asked me to pray for her family and her work visa, which she was going to submit that afternoon (she was from the Philippines). So I did. I finished by giving her a hug, then I felt led to ask God for anything else. I got a picture of heaps of kids. I asked her if she had children, and she said she had two. I shared what I was seeing, and she recounted a long story about how her daughter was in year eleven at school and had been going to study computing but had decided to study early childhood instead. This lovely lady was so excited. I stated that God really loves her and her children and to encourage her daughter. I then felt compelled to give her some money for Christmas presents. She was so excited that she wanted my business card. I told her I didn't have one, and the money was a gift from Daddy God, who loved her so much. We invited her to church, and then another customer arrived.

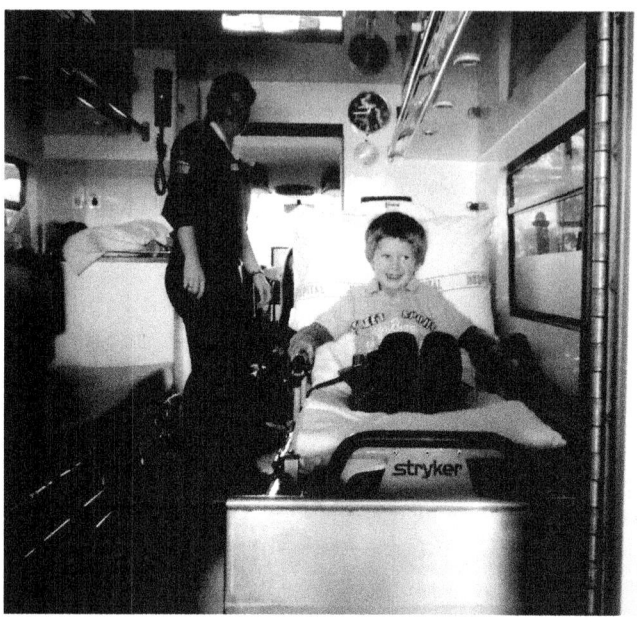

...every second counted.

Without kind people like you –
and the rapid response of St John
– Benny might not be here today.

first to care

St John

St John

ASB

Working Together

A gift from you today will save more
New Zealander's lives.

people like Benny life-saving care.

a new ambulance and keep giving

We must raise $200,000 to buy

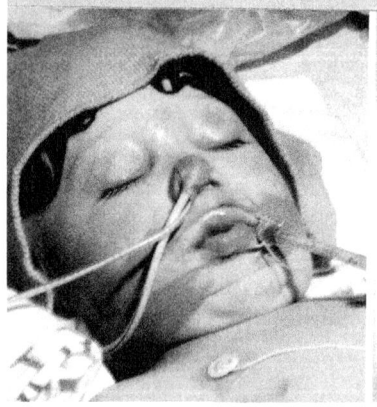

When a
tragic accident
almost claimed
Benny's life...

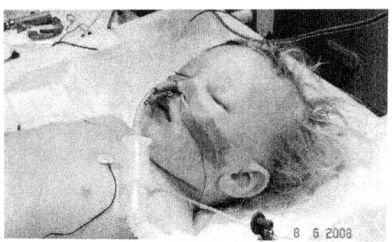

It was touch and go for little Benny.

"Benny was not responding when we arrived. He was completely unconscious and very, very blue, and showed no signs of life."
Nick Scott, Paramedic, St John Ambulance

Benny was close to death when he was pulled out of a pond. Thankfully, Nick was on the scene in minutes.

"If we'd been even a couple of minutes later, it's very possible Benny's outcome wouldn't have been as good. He may still be alive, but his brain activity would not be flash."
Nick Scott, Paramedic, St John Ambulance

Your previous gifts helped give Nick the equipment he needed to save Benny's life – from child resuscitation kits, to the state-of-the-art ambulance he used to rush Benny to hospital.

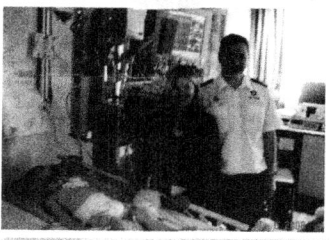

Lydia, Benny's mum, was just so thankful her son was alive.

Benny, his mum, and Nick - the St John paramedic who helped save his life.

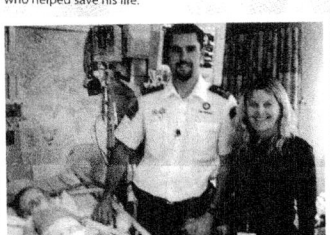

Without our rapid response – and the compassionate people like you who made it possible – Benny's mum, Lydia, believes she would have lost her baby boy that terrible day.

"If it wasn't for St John, Benny wouldn't be here. If we hadn't had the ambulance on the scene so quickly, he wouldn't have survived. We're just so grateful."
Lydia, Benny's Mum

We can only respond rapidly to emergencies like these because of caring people like you. And today – thanks to your kind gifts – little Benny is now a healthy, happy and extremely bright six-year-old.

With your help, we can buy a new ambulance for our region – and save more lives like little Benny's.

Please send your generous gift today.

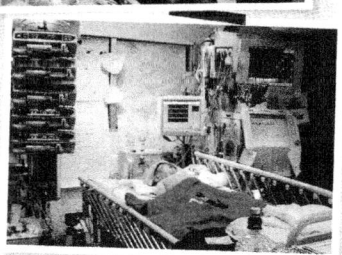

Benny in early days of his long road to full recovery.

Glory amidst Suffering

We don't really know what instigated the decade of illness that John has endured. After all the health issues our family had experienced, John was the last one we expected to get sick. At the end of 2011, John's health began to deteriorate. I was so worried about him that I asked our good friend Avinash to take him to the hospital because John did not think it was serious enough to warrant attention. He had severe pain down his trachea and had been experiencing a terrible cough for some time. The doctors initially diagnosed John with a lung infection, as the X-ray showed something on his lungs, but the cough remained, and now he was in severe pain. Up until this point, John had rarely been sick, so this marked a turning point. He also had atrial heart fibrillation, which they thought was causing emphysema.

The specialists were struggling to pin down a diagnosis. It was so stressful not having any idea what was wrong, and it seemed that whatever he did have would change from day to day, with new organs being affected in different ways. In the midst of this, I felt like I was a walking contradiction, trying to focus on the intense journey of doing a master's thesis while my husband was gravely ill. As the dichotomy got greater and John's health got worse, my response to God one night was this:

> John's health is really scaring me, to be honest. He's lost so much weight. Nothing we try seems to work, and now he has his cough back. I try hard to just get on with it. With four kids and a busy household and schedule, I try to do my best. But after we loaded a full trailer of what was cleared from our fence line today and seeing him tonight, I don't know how much more I can take of watching him suffer. After all that we have suffered together, I feel heartbroken. My head knows God is with us, but my heart just hurts. I am at the point that I feel I may need to surrender the master's, even though I really felt this was from God. I wish I knew what to do.

We were all deeply affected by John's health decline. The stress in the house and the constant dread that filled the air was exhausting. This was not an environment conducive to loving and building healthy, normal childhood memories from which the children would become equipped to function successfully in life.

In the midst of my grumbling and frustration, the Lord reminded me John didn't belong to me; he belonged to him. This was similar to John 21:21–22, where Jesus tells Peter he will be taken where he does not want to go. Peter asks, "What about him?" Jesus answered, "If I want him to

remain alive until I return, what is that to you? You must follow me." "Yes,"
I thought, "I get it, Lord. He is not mine to keep, but a little heads up and
a bit of help would be nice if you aren't going to tell me what will happen."
The Lord would not budge, so I gave up trying to pray or understand. I later
realized Jesus did this to protect me from worrying about John.

I had been busy doing my Greek analysis for Romans, typing up each
section where "righteousness" is used and stating my opinion on the case
Paul was building. Out of the blue, God asked me, "Do you believe this?"
My head hesitated, but my spirit instantly responded, "Yes." Then a surge of
resolve that I had to do this master's *for* John and myself and the children
erupted. I really did believe God is faithful and righteous; my head and
heart were really struggling, but my spirit knew it. In my struggle, I had an
encounter with my Lord:

> It is around three o'clock in the morning, and I am awake. I can
> hear John coughing in the other room. I am troubled with the
> content of my research and my present circumstances; how do
> I reconcile the two? Then I see Jesus coming to me with Com-
> munion. He places it on top of all my research materials spread
> out around me. He says, "Let this be life for you. It will be for
> you, my food and drink to sustain you." I have pondered this as
> we take Communion every night for Lent. Then a verse has been
> playing over and over in my head: "So that I may know him and
> the power of his resurrection and the fellowship of his suffer-
> ings, being conformed to his death, if, by any means I may attain
> to the resurrection from the dead" (Phil 3:10–11). The power
> of his resurrection is most manifested in suffering. I have been
> stunned to study Romans 5–8 and find that, over and over, Paul
> talks of reigning in life. 5:17 states, "How much more will those
> who receive God's abundant provision of grace and of the gift of
> righteousness reign in life through the one man, Jesus Christ."
> I am so thankful this morning that reigning in life is not for
> those with great faith in God. It is for those who, with their heart
> wrenched and their faith failing, can lift their eyes to the faithful
> one who will provide sustenance for them, so that through his
> faithfulness they can have overcoming resurrection life in their
> suffering. God can heal John. I know that. But his resurrection
> power is sufficient for us. I will boast more gladly, therefore, in
> my weakness, so that here in this place of pain, I can know the
> power of his resurrection to sustain not only me, but also John
> and the children. Blessed be his name. When I am found in the
> wilderness, when pain is my offering, blessed be his name.

Not long after this encounter with Jesus, the doctor rang early to say they wanted to see John urgently with the results of his CT scan and blood tests. There was some good news: the fibrosis of his lungs was stable and unchanged from a year ago. However, the CT scan also showed he had developed widespread bronchiectasis. Because of his lung disease, mucus had built up and bacteria had begun to grow in the pockets of his airways, leading to repeated, serious lung infections.

We were up visiting our friends the Schollums, and I was preparing for a presentation I had to give at Bible college on my research. I had written over seven thousand words and was working very hard, but John was extremely unwell. I was up late at night typing, and I said to my friend, "What am I going to do if John dies?" It was a very hard situation to be trying to write a master's thesis, not knowing if my best friend and husband would live to see me finish it. How on earth I kept going I will never understand.

I was writing my thesis from a bed of trauma.

> I had a supernatural supermarket encounter one night when I was feeling particularly shattered. I had reached the checkout after doing my shopping, and while my items were getting processed, the Lord indicated to me that the lady behind me needed my help. I asked him if she needed money. The Lord said, "No, but she needs you." After I had paid for my shopping, I packed my groceries nearby so I could watch what was going on out of the corner of my eye. The lady didn't get some of her shopping, so I walked over and said, "I would be happy to pay for those if you like." She said, "No, I am okay." I said to her, "I just felt God say you needed my help." She said to me, "I just got a call that my uncle has had a stroke." We prayed for her uncle, and I gave her some money to buy some sweets because she was in shock. I watched her little boy for her as she did that. Daddy seeks out his children wherever they are and, if we let him, will lead us to them. (There is another twist to this story; more on this later.)

John had lost twenty kilos since the previous January. A lot of that had been muscle, so his blood results were showing he was malnourished. I remember at the time being scared to hug him as he was skin and bones and I thought he might break. He was very gaunt and looked much older than he was. The Lord gave me a vision after this doctor's appointment:

> Jesus had a huge backpack packed and said to me, "I'll carry this for you. It has everything you need and when you are tired, I will carry you too." Then Daddy turned up, and I saw I was holding an alabaster jar in my hands and was fearful of sharing

it in case it wasn't enough. I saw Jesus weeping, and he said, "It's more than enough." Daddy poured his own tears into my bottle and said to me, "Don't be afraid to share it out. You are more than enough, and I will be more than enough. You will never run out." I think maybe I am the thesis that needs to be written.

At times, the ache of not having parents or siblings was so overwhelming. I felt so homeless, especially when John, because of his illness, was in bed early most nights. There were times when John was so sick that I would have to change him and tuck him into bed, say goodnight to the kids, then walk downstairs and write my thesis until one o'clock in the morning. Trying to keep the kids hopeful and not stressed was a real battle. Some days I fell apart as I tried to pick up the pieces alone. Feeling hemmed in from every side, it was hard to keep hope alive when it felt like life kept throwing mire at me.

I was bemoaning the fact that my once-sharp mind couldn't seem to write anything decent. At many points along the journey, I would try and surrender and wave my white flag; it felt like a part of me had been disabled, and I just could not switch it back on. I really believed in the thesis project and felt it was hugely important, but was too distracted and exhausted to put my full self into it. I felt like Jeremiah in the way God had given me a word to speak, and I felt like a fire was "shut up in my bones" until I spoke it (Jer 20:9). It was a humiliating place to be as I could not do what had always been so natural for me. All I knew was that my Father would not let me quit. The word was too strong in me. It was so painful to give birth to a thesis. I was in despair one day when my Father encouraged me with this word: "Your thesis is not a standard to be achieved; it is a life to be lived."

John's health was progressively getting worse. His esophagus was painful, his throat and mouth were swollen, and he was experiencing lung spasms. Living with sickness like this over a long period of time was hard on everyone, especially when we could not get any fixed answers from the medical professionals as to what was wrong. I often really doubted God's call to study while all this was going on. One night, I was thinking of my studies and the timing of my thesis research coinciding with John's illness, and I thought, "If God isn't *good* now, if he isn't *just*, then he isn't at all. If justice really is justice, and God really is good, then he is all that in my deepest valley. The highest of mountaintop experiences don't signify a great deal unless they are very present and real in the valley of the shadow of death." As I focused on his goodness, proclaiming the truth that he *is* good, I felt the everlasting arms underneath me, surrounding me, surrounding John and the kids. God is good—especially when the darkness desires to eclipse him from my heart. We often have energy to keep going when things are hard, as we have to, but our hearts get tired. Sometimes life hurts, and we just need a good cry. Sometimes I would visit Krissy's grave, as I found it easier to cry there, away from all I needed to keep strong for. I was missing BCNZ/Laidlaw, my family, and Krissy, and I was particularly missing my best friend, John, who was now covered in a cloak of sickness.

On one occasion, John had been groaning at night. He often does this when his lungs spasm. In this instance, I felt his symptoms resembled a heart attack. The next day, the doctor ordered some blood tests. Sure enough, his troponin levels were high; he had had a heart attack. He had an angioplasty not long after this. His main artery was 80 percent blocked and another was 70 percent. He had two stents put in, and we had hoped to see an improvement in his health.

Unfortunately, John's illness was about to take a drastic turn. My journal entry at the time was: "I am scared, Jesus. Scared of the progression of this disease that is taking John from me. Scared of his weight and the hollow in his eyes." My Father was about to make a drastic turn of events into a dramatic week of ministry—in hospital no less.

> After John's mum's funeral, I had a supernatural supermarket encounter. It started when the children and I went to get some fish food. We saw a man, aged about sixty, with two hospital canes pushing along his trolley with his body. He looked to be in incredible pain and it was slow going. People were rushing all around him; some even looked at him and kept going. I nudged Joseph to ask the man if he would like him to push his trolley, so he did, and we got to chatting with the man. He was on a waiting list for knee surgery, but in the waiting, his hip was now getting arthritis and was very sore. He looked like he had been a really hard worker in his life. We got to the checkout, the children put his food on the conveyer belt, and I talked to him about how I understood through John how pain robs more than just your ability to get around; it affects everything in your life. The Lord prompted me to pay for his groceries. I was like, "Really?" and the Lord was like, "Yes." I admit I watched diligently how much the shopping was costing. Anyway, when it came time to pay, the man was struggling to get his wallet out, and I said to him not to worry as I had this. He started crying, and then I started crying. The checkout lady wasn't sure what to do. I just hugged the man and said I understood. We took his groceries to his truck and put them in the back. We all prayed for him and went on our way. Heidi Baker says to stop for the one, as you never know; it

> may just change a life. Don't wait to be called. Don't wait for a
> prophetic word. Just start with the ones in front of you.

On July 15, 2015, John was admitted to the ED with pneumonia. His blood pressure was 80/40 and he had a rapid heart rate. In fact, all his vitals were pretty shot. His X-ray showed the pneumonia was not widespread, but the bronchiectasis had made his breathing labored.

The next day, John's blood pressure kept dropping, so they ran some blood tests to see if he had an infection in his blood or sepsis. Thankfully, he did not. What was amazing is that across from him was a ninety-seven-year-old man named *Mike. This gentleman's son and daughter were visiting and they had some really cool stories about him. The man next to him was a member of another Baptist church, and the other man was the father of a dear friend from another church. His wife was also there. We spent a wonderful afternoon talking about the Lord and hearing people's testimonies about how they had come to know the Lord and the healing they had experienced. I had a deep sense that I was very privileged to have met Mike, in particular.

I had spent years fighting for my children, and now, in this hospital, I had to fight for my husband. John's personal doctor said in his notes, which we gave to the hospital, that John was resistant to the antibiotic amoxicillin. I found out the hospital doctors had been giving John amoxicillin. I sat there all day trying to tell anyone who would listen that they needed to change the antibiotic. Finally, when they came to give him the amoxicillin again, we refused. This promptly got the registrar at his bedside, and I begged him to please listen to us. Finally, they gave him another type of antibiotic. It had been five days without John at home, and I was very aware of his presence and how much he did around the place. We were missing him terribly.

I had been telling the Lord that I just didn't know what to do, and he gave me Exodus 14:14: "The Lord will fight for you; you need only to be still."

John was doing much better the next day. We had been chatting with Mike over the last few days, discussing justice and my research of Romans. I did not know that the patient next to John, *Pete (a new patient), had been listening intently. When I got up to get John something, he asked me to come over. He said he was from Scotland and used to go to church when he was little. I asked him, "Do you miss God?" He cried and replied, "Yes." I asked him if he wanted to pray and come home. He replied that he did. We prayed together and he sobbed deeply, as did I. It was incredibly special. I had also been drawn to another lady in the next room and had bought her flowers the day before; the Lord prompted me to pray for her. She also cried and said she believed in God in her own way. John was doing much better and I was so grateful. I was also very grateful for the privilege of blessing people.

The next day, Pete, the Scottish man who had "come home" to Jesus the day before, had revived his childhood Sunday school faith and was now praying for John and anyone he could in hospital, fully expecting them to be healed. The story about Pete got even better that day. I went and got him a Bible from a Christian bookshop. On the way there, the Lord said to me, "Pete is another Wigglesworth." I responded, "What?" The Lord asked me to get Pete a book on Wigglesworth. I did so, and when I got to the hospital and gave him the Bible and the book, he was speechless. It turned out his grandmother and mother had both prayed he would become a minister like Wigglesworth and preach the gospel. Wow. He told me that when he was in his early twenties, he even preached at his church. He had so many stories. It made what John was going through bearable. It was awesome to see John evangelizing again. I think we made a great team, even when he was so swollen that he could hardly walk.

Another cool thing happened in the room that day. A man named *Jim had been admitted a couple of days before with alcohol withdrawal. He would scoff at our discussions and prayer times with the other two patients. This day was really sad, as Mike found out that he might have cancer. This new man saw Mike, his son and daughter, Pete, and John and I huddled, crying and praying together. Jim asked me to come over before we left and was crying. He said he had never seen so much genuine love between Christians before and wanted us to pray for him. We prayed with him and anointed him with oil. He then got up and about. He was going through his bag, found some alcohol, and gave it to me and asked me to take it for him. This was very brave on his part. I left him in Pete's capable hands and on the way out he said to me, "I may just be a Christian when you come back." I told him my Father would keep drawing him. On the way home, it felt like I was coming home from a mission trip in the hospital.

The heaviness of being informed that John's hospital admittance might be due to a connective tissue disorder had been buoyed by meetings like this. We had a long journey ahead of us with John's health, and it almost would have been better had John been diagnosed with pneumonia. This new diagnosis would require another stretch of our faith, but over a longer period.

The lung specialist had cautioned John that his lungs would not cope with many more winters where we lived. It was time for us to move to a warmer, drier area.

This illness had aged John hugely, and I kept getting asked if he was my father. This really affected me. I was his wife, and yet I was sometimes identified as John's caregiver. This also affected John deeply. It hurt to see him labeled in this way. I still saw the handsome man I married when I looked into his eyes. However, the rubrics of marriage and talking through our issues had changed. John was too sick to even get out of bed most days, so talking about any issues that were hurting, presenting, or damaging our marriage had been off the table for a long time. How do you get counseling for what seems trivial compared to keeping your husband from dying? The normal things we would talk about and resolve were no longer talked about and I carried the effects in myself.

There is a pressure that severe long-term illness brings to a person's psychological processing. I am able to function most of the time, but sometimes I watch my children and it hurts to see them trying to handle the normal interactions of life at school and relationships, then come home and deal with the weight of trauma that illness breeds in the home. I would often desire for people to understand the journey, not the immediate crisis.

This time in hospital for John was probably the sickest he had been. Friends came to visit, as we were not sure how much longer we had with him. It was an extremely difficult time, which was boosted by these supernatural encounters in the hospital ward.

We checked in on Jim, the alcoholic. His girlfriend, who hated Christianity, told us she had seen a remarkable difference in Jim since we had prayed with him. He told everyone we had prayed and anointed him with oil even though he wasn't a Christian, which he was puzzled by. He was so soft and gentle the next time I visited, and he looked so different. We prayed and anointed him again, as he heard us praying with Mike and wanted us to pray again for him. I peeked as I was praying, and he had a huge smile on his face. We asked God to give him an encounter of his great love for him. Mike's son rang to tell us that Mike had cancer in his lungs, liver, and backbone. It was very, very sad. I was so touched by this man of God.

We were still in the throes of getting our house ready for sale while all this was going on. I was overcome one day when my friend Nicky said she was going to bring a team of twenty people to our house to do whatever we needed in or outside the property to get ready to move. I was feeling particularly overwhelmed that morning with John's illness, as it seemed like nothing was working and the doctors didn't really know what was going on. I felt homeless, churchless, and family-less, and was really missing my husband and grieving for what was happening to him and us as a family. This was all a byproduct of sustained, accumulative stress.

On my way to visit John during another of his hospital admissions, I kept hearing the Lord say joy was my inheritance and that I should reach down and claim this. I was so angry with the Lord. I had spent the day going from one hospital to another and picking up my children left, right, and center, and on top of all of this, I had been getting hammered with texts from a person who just couldn't accept that I really could not help them at the time. This was not a time for the Lord to talk to me about joy! Anyway, you know by now, after reading this far, that the Lord doesn't quit with me. He got more persistent about this joy thing. As I was walking through the doors of the hospital, I stopped and said, "Okay God, I give up. I reach down and claim joy as my inheritance." I kid you not, the joy that welled deep inside of me and up I cannot fully explain. It wasn't a happy feeling; it was a feeling of being completely centered and anchored. I felt deep assurance and deep rest. This joy has never left me to this day. No matter what I am going through, I have this deep sense of calm. It definitely cannot be attributed to me changing my mind about joy. This was a gift from a Father to her daughter to help sustain her on her journey.

I hate to say it, but sometimes I wondered if God was preparing me to deal with life on my own.

John was finally home from hospital and was managing to work half-days, but I was finding it increasingly difficult watching him do so. He was getting thinner by the day; watching him deteriorate before my eyes was absolutely heartbreaking. I felt there was nothing I could do but pray. It definitely did not seem like the right time to leave the church we had been in for seven years, or get a house ready for sale, or move house, or do a thesis.

Getting the house ready for sale was exhausting. I spent weeks clearing out rooms and packing what I could. We had other friends come from another church, who worked extremely hard to get our yard under control. You could hear people all morning shouting, "No, John McSweeney, put that down!" Another friend, Owen, graciously offered to water-blast the driveway and path and take away any rubbish as I worked at finishing the back section.

I was still trying, in the middle of all this madness, to write a master's thesis.

Before we moved, I was given the opportunity of speaking at a local women's conference. The timing was perfect, as I had packed all I could, my thesis was with my supervisors, and I was really excited to put some feet to my thesis. God had a really awesome surprise waiting for me. My friend Ruth, who was running the conference, had asked me to share some of my stories as part of my message. I shared the story about the girl I felt led to give some money to and pray for at the supermarket late one night. At the end of my message, a lady walked up, chatted to Ruth, then came up on stage and said to everyone present, "I am that lady!" There was a collective gasp as she shared the beauty of our Father in what happened as a result of our encounter. It was so like my Father to arrange that testimony and confirm his message.

On August 31, 2015, our house was officially on the market. It would not be until March the following year that we would finally be in our new home by the sea. It is drier and warmer and much closer to the children's school. I was really enjoying living in our new home. I had joined a dolphin watch group, and there was a small mall three minutes up the road. It was lovely to be able to drop off and pick up the children. I also loved having a minimal garden with a small lawn.

The finishing of the thesis was exhausting. I was up very late most nights in the final weeks, checking thousands of footnotes and every quote. I often wished my bed would come to me.

I finally finished my thesis and had it printed, ready to hand in, as I wanted to hand it over before my birthday. I had been given a mid-December deadline, but I strongly felt the Lord say to me to get it in before my birthday. So, I pushed myself to get it in before then. I am so glad I listened to the Lord because in December, my computer was hacked. I opened an email that day that I thought was the documentation for Jessica's license I had just paid for. It wasn't. It was a fake statement that allowed an OSIRIS malware virus on my computer, which destroyed all my thesis files and everything else on my computer. It was an encryption virus, so there was no way we could get any of my work back.

This is going to sound strange, but I actually felt liberated that my files had been destroyed, as I felt I was finally free—as if my thesis was really over and done with, and I now could be free to live and enjoy other things. I still had my thesis on a USB stick, but that didn't feel as intrusive. My Father certainly knows how to turn everything to work for my favor. If this had happened prior to handing my thesis over, it would have been a totally different situation as I would have lost a host of other files that I still needed that were not on my USB stick.

This excitement and hope I had for my future post-thesis felt like it was brought to an abrupt end when, on March 13, I received my final grade. I read the email in anticipation, wading through the preliminary introduction. I saw the mark and my heart sank. Many of you will wonder why on earth I was disappointed. The reason was that I had achieved a 4.0/A GPA for my post-graduate diploma in theology in 2012. I had then spent four years giving every spare waking moment to my master's thesis, suffering immense anguish as I wrote. I honestly assumed unconsciously that my Father would reward my obedience with a decent mark. I am not sure why. That doesn't even make sense. This reveals a faulty image of who God was to me at the time.

I was left in utter distress as I read the email again. My masters thesis was awarded a grade of 79 percent, which equates to a 3.3/B+. The email felt like it was trying to make me feel better by writing that I had earned a Master of Applied Theology with Merit. I was so bitterly disappointed that with one percent more I could have been awarded an A-, which equals a Distinction. Over and over in my head, that one percent stared at me like it was mocking all the hours and hours spent researching and writing amidst so much pain that I could barely even function at times.

Given the circumstances over the course of writing the thesis and the complexity of my argument, I tried to conjure an image for other people of being happy and relieved I had passed. Deep down, however, was a fusion of anger and self-loathing, and I couldn't quite decide if I should celebrate or cry. I wasn't sure what to do with myself because I could not redress this situation by writing another paper. This was it. This was where all those years doing a degree and then a post-graduate study all led. This one mark is the only one, after all those A's, that would be noted in a library once the thesis was bound. One measly percent. It felt like a total kick in the guts.

However, I wanted to show my profound gratitude for what many had done for me through this complex journey, and I *was* profoundly grateful. Carey Baptist College went to a lot of trouble to make sure the presentation of the thesis to the library was a respectful and honoring moment for myself, John, and my friends. My wonderful supervisors spoke at the presentation, and it was lovely to hear their joy over my success. I definitely would not have passed without them. I presented my supervisors with a bound copy of my thesis for them to keep. They seemed delighted with this gesture. I did enjoy the process of having the book bound, and I chose a deep burgundy with some fine gold lines for the cover. On April 1, I graduated. John and the children were welcomed on stage with me as I was presented with my award. It was a very special time to have them with me, as they were the motivation for even attempting to tackle a project that massive.

After the graduation, I was completely obsessed with my final grade and the deep failure I felt, which was exacerbated because a few of my friends are academics with doctorates. They, of course, do not view me as a failure, but it was obvious that my past shame-based ways of being were still projecting into present events. I remember the Lord one day giving me a dream, as he often does when he needs to speak to me and get past my frustration. I saw myself in a cell with a very hard steel seat. Jesus came and sat next to me. I realized I was not in chains and the door was open. I had put myself in prison—again. I saw my Father come and hold my face in this pit and he said to me, "I just don't care what they think. I just don't care." By "they," he meant the generic "they" that I had conjured up in my performance-based construct of success.

I was viewing my four years of writing the thesis as a block of trauma. This indicated to me how enmeshed with my external world my master's had become. Writing was compounding my suffering. However, on another level, it strangely helped, as my research was absorbing some of the anxiety. I felt like I had post-traumatic stress disorder, and I made a joke to John that I had post-thesis stress disorder. For fun, I decided to Google if this was an actual thing. Would you believe?—it actually is.

I felt so stuck, and I did not know how to get myself out of the groove I was in. To diffuse some of my disappointment, I was encouraged to start a blog. I started to find my rhythm and enjoyed writing short but pointed messages. I was starting to feel more centered and more convinced that *psychological justice* mattered. In fact, I named my blog Psychological Justice Matters.

Digging Deeper

Receiving the final grade for my thesis was a huge disappointment and led to a period of prolonged despair. Starting my blog helped unclog my writing, and yet I still felt quite stuck. My Father had more to do in the multilayered psychological wounding I was carrying from my youth. Having strived for most of my Christian walk up until this point, I had processed a lot of this through previous trials, such as Ben's accident, but there were more levels to be healed. My academic abilities had always given me such confidence, and it was disabling to have such a sense of failure at the only thing left I felt I was good at. Past wounds were surfacing in the ways I was dealing with this grade in the present.

My Father would often turn up and invade my circumstances with his glory through these times, which I experienced as a tangible encounter, heavy with his goodness. I knew in my head he was good, but these encounters were different. This was like I had entered another realm. They were so heavy that I often couldn't get up off the floor for quite a while. The

Father knew I was struggling in my faith, and he brought himself. I am so thankful it isn't about my faith, but about *his* faithfulness. My faith in him grows when he tangibly reveals his faithfulness. I wrote this in my journal: "It is that dance of justice. I can't wait one day to write a book called *Dance of Justice*. One day I will, and one day it is going to bring life and hope to many. Daddy's just that good. He turns ashes into beauty. Show us your glory, Father."

As I was reading the Scriptures one day, a verse captured my attention: "The Lord will roar from on high!" (Jer 25:30). I heard the Lord say, "Enough!" I have only heard the audible voice of God once before, and that was when I had received a letter from my father ten years prior. This time, I saw the previous seven years as a block in time. My Father was roaring an end to this season. In Jeremiah 25:38, God is referred to as a lion leaving his lair. In this moment, I just knew I couldn't explain it any other way; I just knew God was rising up on our behalf against the enemy. Somehow, a season we had been in was turning. I didn't know how, or why, or what the season even was, but somehow I knew something had shifted. In the previous seven years, a persistent round of hospitals, doctors, diseases, and educational diagnoses had been thrown at us, labeled us, come against us, and harassed us. Somewhere, always lurking in the back of everything was my fight-or-flight mode, ready to kick in with the next crisis. I didn't even tend to react too much anymore, which I saw as growth, but I look back and wonder whether I was responding similarly to a frog in increasingly hot water. You have no idea you're in deep trouble because it's become your normal.

As I mentioned before, transition time is never easy, in the physical or in the spiritual. A woman in labor hates transition. It is usually at this point that a woman will scream at her husband or tell the midwife, "I can't do it. I want to go home!" It is, I think, harder when a period of transition is forced on you; it's a little like a woman who goes into labor early, when she isn't quite ready. That's how it felt for me. I love the Scripture the Lord gave to me in this time:

> "Do I bring to the moment of birth and not give delivery?" says the Lord. "Do I close up the womb when I bring to delivery?" says your God. "Rejoice with Jerusalem and be glad for her, all you who love her; rejoice greatly with her, all you who mourn over her. For you will nurse and be satisfied at her comforting breasts; you will drink deeply and delight in her overflowing abundance." For this is what the Lord says: "I will extend peace to her like a river, and the wealth of nations like a flooding stream; you will nurse and be carried on her arm and dandled

on her knees. As a mother comforts her child, so will I comfort you; and you will be comforted over Jerusalem." When you see this, your heart will rejoice and you will flourish like grass; the hand of the Lord will be made known to his servants, but his fury will be shown to his foes." (Isa 66:9–14)

Psychological Justice

Participating in these God encounters while John was in hospital was witnessing *psychological justice* in action. To see my Father seek out his children in this way was very heart-warming and strengthened my faith. We were in such distress watching John so ill while concurrently seeing our Father give so much freedom and breakthrough to others. It was incredible. Looking back, most of the encounters happened as people in the ward watched the way John and I and the other Christians were relating. As others watched the unity and love and, most importantly, the reality between us, they were drawn to see the Father as we did. They were impacted by the presence of our Father in our conversations. This led them, in their pain and fear, to be touched and open to the fact that maybe the Father wanted to be that for them. I am still deeply impacted by these miracles. You will find these God encounters scattered throughout this chapter as a representation.

Another huge moment of *psychological justice* for me was grasping that joy was my inheritance. There was no way I could ever have envisaged I would know such deep assurance and a knowing of being held in such a distressing period. This has never really left me. My Father did something in my psyche that is supernatural and permanent. There is no way I could ever manufacture what happened that day in those circumstances. I didn't even want to stop and let my Father do this for me. My Father was so faithful to pursue me until he could gift me this great deposit of grace. This is also *psychological justice* in the sense that my theological understanding of grace and joy had become a reality in my psychological being.

We were so blessed to have our Father's commitment to us during these very difficult months. I felt so much pressure during this year. I felt I was hemmed in by many circumstances that normally even one of would have been difficult to process. Having my Father so involved and committed to specifically leading me in this season profoundly impacted my image of him. After having lost my parents and then my pastor father, having my Father so actively involved was very precious. Whenever I needed physical help, he would send it. When I needed psychological help, he would bring himself, and the Holy Spirit would manifest what I needed in me. This year, more than any other, is where I see the outworking of *psychological justice*.

It was so grace-filling of my Father to gift me intimate encounters during such a difficult year—not only for me, but toward others in the community. Seeing my Father's desire to be involved in the community, with all sorts of encounters, gave me a respect for his deep engagement and knowledge of people and what they need.

The following year, I went to a wedding, and a dear friend got in my face about this book. Where is it? What's happening? I gave my usual excuses, but their prophetic insight and prayers started a healing process with my Father that culminated in another prayer time with another dear friend in Tauranga and an altar call. My father had given me the Scripture, "For in the same way you judge others, you will be judged, and with the measure you use, it will be measured to you" (Matt 7:2). At first, I felt convicted and tried to discern who I was judging and measuring. I couldn't, for the life of me, figure it out. I waited on the Lord, and then suddenly he came to me with a profound revelation. He showed me *I* was the one I was judging. I was measuring myself because of my need to feel significant and unique. I was choking and suffocating myself. I've measured myself against those I think are significant. Then it dawned on me: what if my significance is significantly different from them—significant in a way they cannot be? At the altar, I felt my Father ask me to lay down not only my master's, but my entire academic journey, where at the core lay my ambition to become a Bible college professor. When I did, I felt as though I had just been cut loose from a giant web. The result was that I felt excited about finishing this book.

What's Your Story?

I want to challenge you to ask God for joy. No matter where you are in your journey, you need his joy. Also, do you want more God encounters in your life? Ask God to open your eyes and ears to hear him so that you can express the glory he wants to release through you to others.

John and I had driven to pick up a dehumidifier, and afterward we headed to the beach. John got chatting to a man named *Peter at the playground. He felt God wanted us to pray, so I was listening in on the conversation. Peter's ancestry originated from the Morori in the Chatham Islands. Their claim was about to be put before the Treaty Tribunal of New Zealand in the next month, and Peter was their spokesperson. He'd had a relationship with the Lord when he was younger, and he knew the Scriptures. He showed us the prophetic call he gave his *whanau* (family) about a month previously as a call to walk in the covenant of peace his people had made in the early 1800s. We asked him if we could pray for justice for his people and the healing of the land in the Chatham Islands through this process. The Lord gave us such a detailed download for him that we felt like we had all entered a sacred space; Peter was blown away. After we prayed, he felt God's presence really strongly. This was another prominent moment in my walk with Jesus as Justice, as we prayed for the healing of the land, of the people, and for the integrity of the covenant his people had made. John and I said goodbye, then felt led to go and see our dear friends out south and had an amazing time of prayer with them. We came home feeling satisfied and fed by the Lord and his goodness toward his children.

Season 7

Coming Out of the Desert

Who is this coming up from the wilderness, leaning on her beloved?
(Song 8:5)

NOT BEING CONTROLLED HAD the reverse effect from what I was expecting. I suddenly felt deep anger at God because I had become accustomed to being controlled through familial abuse. Now that I was free, all this deep-seated anger that I had justified by saying or believing God had control erupted—I was now free to leave God.

I spent most of the summer of 2018 trying to figure out a way I could walk away from God. I woke one morning and my heart felt heavy. I was tired and felt emptied of faith and hope. John had a very important meeting with his leading autoimmune specialist (he has several specialists) and the news wasn't good. Recent blood tests showed his lymphocyte count was 150 when it should have been between 500 and 1,500. This meant he could be one serious infection away from death. This news compounded the hardening of my heart. I stopped venturing out and would panic at the thought of meeting new people or people I didn't know so well. I had withdrawn even from those close to me. There were a lot of questions, unanswered prayers, and situations from the past that were blocking my openness to my Father. I knew my heart was hard because I couldn't bear to feel anymore. I missed God, but opening my heart to him hurt. I had stopped trusting him, but I also hated living in a comatose state devoid of his intimacy.

In this space, I found myself trying to intellectually move my Father to the side so I could move on from the bitterness I felt toward him. I felt betrayed by him, lost, and hopeless. I think I decided that if I could take

God out of the equation, then I could somehow move on without him. Every time I thought I had intellectually sorted a way to move God to the side, Jesus would come and stand in front of me, saying he just wanted me to know he was still with me. I exhaled to myself one day, "What am I going to do with Jesus?" What was I going to do with Jesus in all of my intellectual reckoning of the death of God?

Then one day, as I mused on how hard this getting rid of God was becoming, I had a vision as I was walking. It was just like my Father to not take offense at my offense at him. In the vision, I was in a dark room full of people. I was trying to get to the stage at the front, where I and everyone in the room thought God was, but I kept getting pushed back. I was pushed back until I was forced with my back against the wall. A couple of times, I heard the Holy Spirit say, "Open the door." After a while, I gave in. As I turned and opened the door, there was God sitting outside, chilling out on a big comfy deck chair, reading a paper, and looking out over an expansive mountain range. He cocked his head and said, "Come sit with me. I am not in there." "Okay," I thought, "God is on a deck chair reading a paper." This was not how I was presently envisioning God. In my unconscious being, God was about ready to punish me for the minutest thing I may do wrong.

It was a simple picture, but it spoke volumes to me about my image of my Father. My heart had had enough of trying to belong to church, and felt implicitly that my experience with the church paralleled how I felt God had betrayed me. But my Father had not betrayed me; he was sitting outside on a deck chair inviting me to join him and rest while we enjoyed each other's company. He was waiting for me to leave the tangled mess behind. Betrayal opened a door to my understanding that my Father would always be my Father, no matter what his church or his people may say or do to the contrary. Because of my past, I had fused the two. I was starting to separate God and my perception of the church in my mind. At this moment, a transition occurred, and I knew God and I would always be okay. No one could separate me from the love of my Father (Rom 8:35). This was a profound shift away from a fear-based relationship with God into a place of security, hope, and stability in my Father.

When God Found Me Outside the Walls

Having experienced an intensely debilitating season in my faith journey, I was feeling vulnerable coming into Easter. I had come out of my last season having discovered my soul needed a revelation of deeper significance, but I was limping a little, like Jacob at the Jabbok (Gen 32:23–31). I was still processing my last encounter with my Father on his deck chair, inviting me into a more relaxed, grace-filled space, when on Easter Friday, I watched a video clip depicting Jesus dying. As I watched, Jesus drew to my side and sat with me. I heard him say clearly, "That was excruciating." It startled, disturbed, and shocked me. I was occupied with observing from my perspective—what his death meant to me. Jesus came and sat by me, watching with me. He interjected into my meditation with his vulnerability, and we sat in silence together, holding *his* story.

On Easter Sunday, during worship at church, I had an experience that was startlingly real. Jesus was on the cross. I saw the stripes on his back, deep and so exceedingly raw. I felt the atmosphere; I smelled the fear, the pain, the dirt. Then a couple of minutes later, Jesus came to me off of the cross, bloodied, dirtied, thin, torn, and weak. He came to me and held me. All the resistance and the blockages within me dismantled in that moment. The fight in me stopped. Like Jacob, I stopped fighting. I was touched in the socket of my resistance. This was what my Father was wanting all along. Not to win this fight with me, but to let it go on long enough that I would see that he was not fighting me. He was longing to bring me into a deeper, more intimacy-filled space, to change my perspective on justice being a right-for-wrong, win-or-lose consideration.

Jesus then asked me to wipe his tears away. The vulnerability of Jesus to me in this moment was and continues to be overwhelming. After some time in his bloodied embrace, his words came—like a flood, like a devastating wave. "Do I offend you? Does my suffering offend you? Are you ashamed to suffer with me?" No words. I can't even describe this moment.

Does Jesus' blood, dirt, sweat, and pain offend me?

Am I so used to focusing on my own suffering, on my own need for justice, that I have abandoned the one who suffered injustice for justice for me? His words came again: "I am not ashamed to suffer with you." It was time for me to stop fighting. The chest I was beating on was my Father's, and he was holding me close in his soothing embrace. He would not let me go, and when I stopped fighting, I felt his tears touch my face, and I knew I was changed.

Like Jacob's deceitful past, my past has been filled with performance. Like Jacob, my Father was ushering me into a new place. Although my name change had happened five years prior, I was still trying to apprehend what growing into Lydia, a noble person by birth, looked like. Jacob was given a new name, Israel. The angel of God came to reassure Jacob he wasn't who he once was, thought he may still be, and feared others in his past would still see him as. In an all-night encounter, Jacob fought for his life. When his hip was displaced, Jacob stopped fighting, and God promised to fight for Jacob.

This was me. I had fought for my relationship with God for a very long time and my hip was now displaced. I had a limp reminding me that God loves me more than my desire to prove to him how much I love him. I could stop fighting and let God fight for me. Whenever I get lost in the sea of pain, my Father seeks me out and brings me back home. The more I fell into the arms of Jesus' embrace, the more he became the perspective through which I started viewing my life.

I had not stopped attending church during this time, but I was finding it really hard to connect. One morning, the speaker read the passage about the Samaritan woman in John 4:4–42. I welled up inside and my eyes filled with tears. I had tried so hard to leave God; leaving all my disappointment, disillusionment, anger, grief and fear with him. I felt like this woman. I sobbed inside. "Shame," I sighed. Shame was why she came at midday. But Jesus knew her. He went outside religious walls to find her—for *her*. The dignity he wanted to release to her was overwhelming me. He did not care that the entire village she had left behind to gather water, when no one else was there, despised her. In the heat of the day, she came by herself.

She knew her place. She knew what Jews thought of her and her people. Not only was she a Samaritan woman, she was drawing water at midday. No woman—no respectable woman—would draw water alone at that time of day. So, not only was she from a maligned people group among the surrounding cultures as a Samaritan, but she was the least of her people group, and even less within her immediate community. She had tried to find love within her walls of shame, but it had only led to more shame, an increase in isolation, and a decrease in hope. Jesus drew this shame to the surface, and he was drawing mine. There is nothing worse than someone giving voice to your shame. Jesus was naming my shame. His response to her shame-filled predicament, and mine, was to locate the source of her pain and the source of the remedy—himself. Jesus proclaimed he is living water. This wasn't a religious encounter, this was my Father coming to a shame-filled, shame identified woman the only way my Father can, with love and a new name.

I was in church, but had never felt more like the Samaritan woman.

I sat there, thinking about how she must have felt, not hearing the sermon but absorbed in my thoughts as I looked out the window onto the beach below, with my sunglasses on. Deep down, my heart felt uncovered. Who wants to admit they are so shame-based in church that they don't want to come to draw water except outside the church walls, away from anyone who may see their shame? I was so aware of how much shame I carried, but I had felt shame most acutely within church walls or Christian groups. This was not the fault of churches or organizations or colleges. It was within me, a deeply felt religious isolation I'd had since my youth. When I did well in any religious endeavor, shame was replaced with confidence, and at times arrogance. When I failed, I could be deeply engulfed with shame, depending on the situation. The Samaritan woman gave me hope that Jesus comes to those like me outside the religious walls. Some of us are so ashamed to be present within church walls that we go to Jacob's well when no other upright religious people will be there. I am thankful Jesus sits there waiting for us to come. This is similar to the picture my Father gave me of sitting outside in his deck chair, waiting to spend time with me.

The woman at the well challenged me to continue to identify where I had allowed shame to warp my view of God's calling and place for me. Where were those places I needed to have courage and strength to stand against the Samaritan effect within me so I could radically change my response to the needs around me? Shame was stalking me, but so was love— radical love, with life-giving water, enough even for me.

I heard the Lord say, "The promises over your life have to be purged from your flesh, so they can be manifested by my Spirit."

Yes—that rang true. All the heroes of faith had their testing and purging. Joseph got a wild prophetic word over his life, then spent years being betrayed, imprisoned, and tested, and the testing purged and purified the promise. Moses was also sent to the desert, then at the right time (for God, not Moses—Moses was very happy in his home in the desert by this stage), God called him to leave his secure location and deliver Israel. Jesus was sent to the desert deliberately to be tested and then came back "in the power of the Spirit" (Luke 4:14). It was time to completely let my dreams be purged in his love, be manifested by his Spirit, and, most importantly, learn to *be* again.

There are seasons in our journey with God. Seasons are important in giving us quality of life. Winter is important in the natural world, as it lets the ground lie dormant for the next season of growth. In our busyness, there is often no time for letting the ground lay fallow. We are so busy trying to be purposeful and fruitful—yet lacking the ability to rest, the ability to see maybe our season is simply to sit, to *be*.

But then there are seasons of conflict that seem to go on forever. I was coming to a place where one season was ending and another was on the horizon—like Elijah, waiting after Mt. Carmel, who saw a small cloud, knew the rain was coming, and ran like the wind (1 Kgs 18:44–45).

I was beginning to feel that I was being led out of my self-imposed prison. Can you see a commonality in some of these terms during this time? Outcast, outside the walls, hidden in shame, religious structures, prison— they are all terms one could use to describe legalistic Christianity that has pushed God's children to the side, or down pits, or locked them in prison.

This whole season was about God redefining our relationship. Now that I was free to leave, I saw that my desire to leave was, in essence, not about leaving God—but his church. But it really wasn't the church either. It was the religious heartbeat of church that I had encountered in my past. I was really leaving the God of my mother, and returning to the God I had met when I was seven.

I felt like a dam was building in me. I doubted my ability to release what I felt my Father was placing in me, but I was groaning like creation for my Father's justice. The gap between what I had built internally and what I was able to release led to deep pain as I wrestled with what my Father had put in me. I felt pent up, but I could feel the passion of my Father in me for his children that was about to break loose despite me, despite my lack of confidence in my ability, despite shame shouting I was never going to be enough. Passion was about to give way to freedom and breakthrough. The dam was about to burst.

Digging Deeper

My thesis needed to produce an overhaul in my actions. I made a decision during this time that my learning, my knowledge, and my understanding *must* be an active pursuit of God and in God to others.

Romans 12:2 seems to be the gold standard for endorsing the teaching that transformation comes primarily through the mind agreeing with the Scriptures. I do not negate the importance of agreeing with who we are, our identity in Christ, and who the Trinity is to us, as declared in the Scriptures. I cannot stress enough how important it is to know the Scriptures. The Scriptures are foundational in everything I have discussed in this book. My life is built on the Scriptures and fueled by the truth they give. The Scriptures alone, however, without the infusing and guiding of the Spirit and our partnering with the Spirit, may result in a hollow reception, which robs or removes the power of Scripture from impacting or making a substantive difference in our lives. The Scriptures are not just another book we can glean information from to help us on our personal journey of healing and wholeness. They are life, and they are powerful. I have written of how my accumulation of knowledge, at one point, actually blinded me to how my spirituality was devoid of the Spirit's power, even though my activities in studying theology could be seen to be spiritual. In contrast, my activities were more likely being born from my flesh.

However, the converse can be true. I love living in the Spirit, but I really believe theology matters. We can sometimes grasp things with our spirit and we can have spiritual experiences, but do we know how to test if these experiences line up with the Scriptures? On the final day, it won't be either our spiritual experiences or our understanding of theology our Father is interested in; it will be how much we know his Son. We get to know Jesus through the Spirit and the Scriptures and allowing the Trinity access to every area of our lives. "For the Word of God is alive and active. Sharper than any double-edged sword, it penetrates even to dividing soul and spirit, joints and marrow; it judges the thoughts and attitudes of the heart" (Heb 4:12). The Scriptures help us discern what is of our flesh and what is of the Spirit. We can't labor on one and neglect the other. We need the Spirit and we need the Scriptures—and not just segments of the Scriptures we like, either. We need to understand what phrases mean within their context, then ask the Spirit to help us discern more meaning.

We are to be people who know the Scriptures and live in the Spirit. The transformation the Trinity wants to work in us is holistic, i.e., involving our mind, heart, and body. This requires more than an adjustment of our thoughts. Even though the teaching concerning the renewal of our mind is often couched in spiritual terms, the application is often done in neglect of the Spirit and without the Spirit's leading.

Psychological Justice

You may have noticed I have used the term "God" instead of "my Father" in the beginning of this chapter, revealing my heart response to my Father during this season as abstract and removed. Meeting "God" outside the walls led me back to my Father's heart.

I started 2018 with a state of being toward God I had never had before. I had never envisioned trying to leave God. I had spent my life striving to please him or escape his judgment by hiding in Jesus. I never gave thought to trying to leave him. My Father revealed that the core hindrance in my relationship with him was the fear he could not prevent evil. This was my father bringing *psychological justice* to me. He knew my resistance was rooted in a deep fear that he was not intervening in John's present health crisis.

I see my Father's *psychological justice* in how, through this period of time, he was able to deal with my long-term fear of not belonging. To have an experience of my Father on a deck chair was his way of coming into that fear-based lie and revealing his truth. To expound on this, Jesus came to me at Easter and sat with me and shared *his* story on his experience of the cross. I was trying to leave God, and my Father's response was to become more vulnerable to me. My Father held me closer, and let me beat his chest.

He held me and was not offended by my response because he knew the psychological root of why I was trying to walk away from him. A lot of people who leave church or seem to have left God may have a psychological, not spiritual or theological, root for their decision to walk away. We can pray for *psychological justice* for these people. The people I have prayed for who are struggling like this almost always have a situation in their lived experience they can point to that started their descent away from their Father.

I was starting to face head-on how shame, in its varied forms, had imprisoned me in so many ways throughout my life. The Samaritan woman, shame-based and outside her community, spoke volumes to me and gave me such courage. Jesus seeking her out and being present with her outside the gate resembled how I felt. Shame is isolating, and the shame we were experiencing as a family from long-term ill health was crushing our hope. I felt like Gideon when he was hiding in a pit. I could not envision ever getting out of this pit of shame. I had lived in this pit most of my life. The Samaritan woman being gifted a new identity was so life-infilling. I remember wondering if I could ever dare to hope for the weight of shame to diminish and to feel dignity. The story of the Samaritan woman shows a beautiful progression of *psychological justice* in action. Firstly, she had a religious response; secondly, a psychological response; thirdly, a spiritual renewal; and fourth, she was given her missional purpose. Similarly, my dreams were being purged in the flesh to be manifested in the spirit.

I cannot emphasize enough how important it is for our lived experience of the Trinity to personally invest time on a regular basis in reading the Scriptures. We need to read with an openness that is willing to hear what the Spirit wants to say to us on a regular basis. My experience of reading the Scriptures with the Trinity is fluid, but generally follows this pattern. Maybe it will help you.

I read the Scriptures, then I sit and meditate on what I have just read. Sometimes I read, then meditate as I walk. It doesn't really matter how or where we read, but it is important to meditate on what we have read. I consciously invite the Spirit in to speak to me. I also ask if there is any place where my gut doesn't really know the truth I have just read. Many times, there are blockages in my reception of the Scripture, deep enough to prevent substantial change. When this happens, we need to allow the Spirit to minister to us as we wait on him and invite his presence to come and aid us. Ask the Father where we may need to repent and put things right with others. Are there fractures we may need to resolve that are blocking our lived experience of the Scriptures we know or have just read? Be alert to where we may not necessarily agree with what we have just read and ask why. Where does a truth not register deep within us? Are the blockages mental, theological, or psychological?

I also think it is important to read widely and challenge ourselves to do some harder thinking. I suggest reading notable writers such as N. T. Wright or Craig Keener. They are some of my favorites. They are people who know theology and the Scriptures, but also bring revelation of the Spirit's active involvement and of the historical setting, in an accessible way.

I was beginning to recapture the heart of my thesis, which was *psychological justice*. I had come to a place previously where I buried the thesis in a bed of bad ideas. Now my Father was supernaturally reviving his heart for this, as *psychological justice* is his heartbeat. He gave me more insight into a section of the framework I had not fully explicated yet. I see the faithfulness of my Father to me in this. I had worked so hard on my thesis in such difficult circumstances that I really feel like I have been given *psychological justice* for having not been able to fully explicate the term in my master's.

What's Your Story?

Are there places in you where you need to find God outside the walls? What is your season right now? Knowing your season will help you rest in your season.

Finale

Tracing the Threads

YOU'VE MADE IT. You have read through to the end of my story. Thank you. I appreciate you sitting with me and hearing me. Yet, it really hasn't ended. There have been many traumatic events that I have not shared. There are some situations that maybe you hope to read have been resolved. Some have; many have not. This may be disappointing for some of you, and a relief for others. I was unsettled by this as I set out to write my story—troubled that there are many places in my walk that are not resolved, and people may not be satisfied by this disparity. Then my Father reminded me, this is reality. Unfortunately, we cannot tidy up every loose end in our lives. This is what life is—messy. There are some spaces or seasons that will only make sense once this life is over. So here it is; a list of my messy loose ends (there are many, so I will only bore you with a few).

Some things remain the same. I adore coffee. I enjoy long walks by the beach, rivers, or in the country, and talking to friends. One of my favorite winter escapes is watching movies, especially when it is stormy outside and the fire is on. I dream of traveling again and finding new quests to pursue.

I still feel minor panic when I hear ambulances. I quickly locate in my mind where all my kids and John are and instantly check my phone. Once I feel an immediate threat to my family has dissipated, I pray that the ambulance will get quickly to where it is going and arrive in time.

I am very proud of John's stubborn faith in God, despite being given a prognosis over ten years ago that he had less than five years to live. John still oscillates in his health. He has months of reasonable health, but within a day he can become acutely ill. Doctors have still not been able to narrow down any concrete diagnosis. It is an ongoing walk with our Father into rest. As the children get older, I find we cope with the bad times better. I am so very proud of them and their resilience.

Which brings me to mothering. Yes, I still waiver. Shame still nips unceasingly at my heels, speaking into present situations. However, its voice is not as loud or aggressive. I can hear it and it still makes me question myself. However, these dips into mothering shame are far less frequent. I am growing stronger in my trust in my Father and his ability to hold me close in my mistakes and fears.

What is most surprising, after all that has been said and done—and this in itself is shameful to still acknowledge—is seeing how much shame has disabled me through my life. It has been shame all along. I have noted throughout my story that it seems I flourish where I feel valued and have struggled where I have felt constricted. There is something more profound happening here. Both of these concepts, disabling and flourishing, are tied to whether shame from past wounding or from my shame-based identity is operating. Circumstances can act like triggers in the present for a shame-based person. The *psychological justice model* I hope to present in my next book is based specifically on this phenomenon. These triggers are getting less frequent for me, but they still happen—and are acute when they do. The shame spiral still operates. I am, through the model, gaining better processes to deal with them when they do operate in my present. Unfortunately, I have not been healed of shame—however, I am being healed to be freer in Christ when I am triggered by shame-laden events. Jesus is the master of dealing with shame. This is why I am committed to bringing you the shame-based model the Lord gave me over ten years ago now. Shame is crippling, but our Father's honor is life-giving. Who we are in Christ matters. I can't wait to share that with you, especially if you, like me, find you often stumble and are disabled by shame.

I still, at times, feel slightly disappointed in my thesis mark. I am learning to not measure myself, but it is hard to break the habit of performance. I have moments when shame likes to suggest to me what a complete failure I am. This despair is normally followed by questioning whether I should even be writing this book. Then the Lord reminds me why we are writing this book—to help others navigate their felt incongruence with God. I pretty much live in that space, so I do think I have something to add to that conversation. To be honest, I am not sure I would have written this book had I gotten that extra one percent for my thesis. I would probably have applied for a scholarship for a PhD and be busy for four years writing that. But here I am, thankful I am writing for you. I hope my perceived failure means that life has been breathed into your soul. It has led me into the arms of my Lord's embrace, which is a beautiful place to write from.

I miss my dad. He died on January 18, 2016. Yes, there is that date again. Strangely, I am infused with only good memories. In a way, I feel reconciled to him. Maybe that is what forgiveness gifts to us.

For some of you, this may grieve you, as it does me, but to date there has not been a reconciliation with my mum. Things are still where they were at over ten years ago. Many will doubt I have made the right call here. There are even those in my circle who seem to struggle with this part of my journey. I understand your disappointment. I am disappointed too. Perhaps because the narcissistic abuse came via my mother, it can be difficult for people to accept the decisions I felt led by God to make. I am not writing to vindicate myself or vilify my mother. As I noted, I have had to take responsibility for the consequences of discharging spiritual pressure on my own children. I have written about the relationship because you may have needed to hear my story through abuse to uncover your own. By doing so, this may enable you to face it squarely, erect some boundaries—or at least feel heard.

In any case, I wrote to my mother several months ago. I chatted about the children and included some pictures. I have not received any reply. My mother (or siblings, for that matter) may not have the psychological space to have me back in her life. I cannot demand they reconcile with me. Reconciliation, by its very nature, is an offer to reconcile. Sometimes it is too hard for the other party—too many memories, too much pain. There is, however, a place where we can be reconciled to God in those spaces. This may sound strange, but I feel that I have reconciled with God about my mother. I have been able to reconcile, through his eyes, that her past abuse was deeply rooted in her being abused. I have reconciled with the fact that behind her letter of disownment is a fiercely held belief that she was doing what she felt was right. I have also reconciled memories of her asking the Lord to grant her desire to die with dignity. I have reconciled most deeply that one day, when this earth is said and done for both of us, there will be a mighty reconciliation in our Father's deep embrace. We will both know as we are known, and it will be glorious. Dignity will envelop us both.

My relationship with my Father holds many questions, many still unanswered. There are always areas of incongruence I need to work on. I believe this is the nature of faith; the now and not yet of the kingdom of God, already here but not in its fullness. This disparate place where incongruity is really a part of life. It would be hard to find a believer who does not hold some form of incongruence between their circumstances and their relationship with God. All of us, at some point or another, will be faced with a season, or seasons, where God seems other than we thought, hoped, believed. Sometimes for better, and some for worse. But he is always faithful.

Despite all my angst in these areas that hold great incongruence, I am genuinely thankful for them. They cause me to go deeper, ask harder questions. In all of this, in my core, I tend to gain a more consistent center in God through these times. I am gaining more peace with regard to my past. Forgiveness, more than anything, has enabled me to feel at rest in many areas where seasons have been terribly painful and debilitating.

I gift you my story as a voice of hope from a fellow traveler that our Father is faithful in all our seasons to bring his promises to full fruition. I hope that I have offered you some depth, so those who are in the depths now or have known the depths will have a hand held out to them. I give you my heart and say, "You are not alone." Whatever season you are in, this too shall pass—and when it does, you will be stronger, you will be more whole, and you will know his justice for, in, and through you. For some of you, your season may seem unending and without hope. Our beautiful Trinity is faithful. I pray that some of what I have shared will help you find ways to bridge the incongruence you feel as you deepen your relationship with God.

For some, what is written may seem unrestrained. There is much emotion within these pages. It takes vulnerability to tell others your story. You place yourself in a position where others get to voice a response to your story, and it is a risk, for sure. But, the risk of vulnerability outweighs the destructiveness of keeping a story hidden out of fear of what others may say.

This is the risk I have chosen to take in writing this book. I know there are those of you who need someone to tell a narrative that resonates with your own in order for you to feel you have permission to begin to tell your story. The aim of my vulnerability is to help you find greater freedom, authenticity, and intimacy with our beautiful Trinity. I wrote this recently about the process this journey has been for me:

> There are times when, as you pour your expensive fragrant oil on the Lord's feet and wipe his feet with your hair and your tears, you will find others do not smell fragrance but may find your expression of love too extravagant and a stench in their nostrils. Be extravagant anyway. The Lord is deeply touched by the sacrifices of our brokenness, and the fragrance of an offering that has been pressed in the fires affects him deeply.

Don't be afraid to hear your own voice within my story. It is time the authentic you be heard.

My dance with him, the lover of my soul, who is justice, continues. It will continue for you too. I pray for all who are reading this that you may be blessed, encouraged, and inspired in your walk with your God into all the fullness he has for you. When the music stops, the lights are turned off, and no one is watching, will you still be dancing?

—*Lydia Rose*

Farewell, My Beloved Readers

Acknowledgments

To you who have suffered with and alongside us, this is your story too. Many voices that should have been heard could not because it would take many books to sufficiently thank each one.

There are some whom I need to specifically thank, as this book would not have come to fruition without them. To my husband, John, who with strength, tenacity, and loyalty loved me at my worst and without whom I would never have found freedom to be myself. To my beautiful, courageous children—Jessica, Joseph, Benjamin, and Rachel—you are my world, and this book is ours. I love you all to the moon and back.

A special thank you to Dr. Phil Halstead, who through his wisdom and encouragement believed in me and enabled me to articulate my psychological journey so thoroughly.

To my dear dedicated prayer group, who not only prayed each chapter into being but who read copious drafts and gave meaningful input and extensive editorial advice (and listened to my fear, doubt, crazy ideas, and excitement), I cannot thank you enough. I pray this journey has been a blessing to you. Thank you so much, Nicky, Tui, Lisa, Alison, Mike, Talitha, Anna, Brenda, Patrick, Rosie, and my beautiful friends from the Womb Room. A special mention to Sue and Teresa for their first edit and to Rachel and Nikky for their brilliant editorial skills on my final edition. You are all my most valued and faithful friends. To my dearest friend Jacqui, you are my signpost in an uncertain world. You are a safe place to run to and a stable home to rest in. Thank you.

To those whom I have written about within these pages, thank you for standing and walking this journey with us. Each of you have given your hearts to us, and we are deeply grateful for every one of you. For those who did not make these pages but have journeyed with us, we value the way each one has built into our lives.

To my beautiful Father, Jesus, and Holy Spirit—you are the only reason I was able to write this book. I cannot even fathom where I would be without you. Thank you for being faithful to me. Thank you for never giving up on me. Thank you for helping me find my true identity by seeing myself in your eyes. When all is said and done, the greatest honor in life is to be authentically known by you.

Reflections from Special Friends

Nicky's Reflection

I HAVE A CHERISHED memory of cuddling Krissy at North Shore Hospital when she was just a few weeks old. I was so honored that Lydia had trusted me with this precious baby. I loved that baby smell and the way a tiny baby snuggles in, so their wee body and yours interlock like a puzzle!

Fast-forward a few weeks, and that memory became even more special when I picked up the phone to hear Ruth's quiet, shaky voice at the end of the line. She told me the news that Krissy had passed away. I was stunned. I had a wee baby myself. He had been in the neonatal intensive care unit (NICU) after he was born, and Lydia had visited to pray and encourage me. Why was my baby home and doing well when her baby was no longer here? I felt guilty that my baby was okay and her arms were empty. I wondered how I would face Lydia at the funeral. I knew I couldn't possibly take James, but would my presence just remind her I had a baby to hold and she didn't? Would the fact that James and Krissy were so close in age mean the end of our friendship? I was in shock, so numb. I was completely at sea as to why the Lord would allow this to happen.

I sent flowers—white to represent the purity of a little one. I didn't want any colors; I was not celebrating this! I knew beyond any doubt that Krissy was with Jesus, but this was so unfair, and it felt like it could so easily have been me.

Action. I have to do something. Lydia told me she had very few photos of Krissy. I knew Krissy's photo had been featured in the *North Shore Times* in the "Welcome, New Births" section. I had to get that photo. I tracked down the reporter, called her and explained the situation, and she turned up on my doorstep that night. Through tears, she presented me with a copy of the photo. I was so grateful.

I got it framed, then placed it in my handbag to take to the funeral.

The funeral itself is quite fuzzy. My hormones were raging. I started crying as soon I placed my newborn in the babysitter's arms. I was wise enough to go without mascara! I do remember Lydia speaking. I could not believe it—what strength! She called for Ruth to join her for support but kept reading as she clutched her friend. My heart ached. I wished I could do something, anything, to remove the pain.

Krissy was lying in her casket. We were invited to walk past. She did not look the same. I stroked the side of her face. Was this okay? I remember saying to John, "She looks so peaceful," before we collapsed in tears. What a dumb thing to say. He didn't want her to look peaceful. He wanted her to look full of life! I retrieved Krissy's photo from my bag and placed it in Lydia's hands. She held it close and cried. Had I done the right thing? Was this causing her more pain? I didn't say anything, afraid my words might hurt. Was a hug enough? How do you support someone through a grief like this?

I left soon after the funeral service. I had to get home to breastfeed my baby. I was relieved I had a reason to go. I didn't want to go to Krissy's grave, as seeing the casket being closed was hard enough. It seemed so final.

Each anniversary of Krissy's Going-to-Heaven-Day, I sent something to Lydia. I can't remember what I sent—cards, maybe a poem, maybe flowers. I just felt the need to acknowledge her life and let her mumma know I had not forgotten her. After five years, Lydia visited me and gave me a small gift, yellow egg cups with gold trim. She told me it was okay; that I didn't need to send something on every anniversary anymore. At the time, I was puzzled, but she has since told me this was the conclusion of a phase of her grieving. It wasn't that she wanted to ever forget Krissy; she was moving on and honoring Krissy with the way she lives the rest of her life going forward.

Krissy's death impacted me greatly. No one in my circle of friends had lost a little one. Most deaths I had been exposed to were of old people or people who had been sick for a long time. I watched Lydia. Her faith, even under what I considered to be the worst trial imaginable, was incredible. She was so in love with Jesus. I wondered if my own faith would stand up if I faced a fire like this. I have used many parts of her story over the years as I have walked with people through the valley of the shadow of death. I have learned so much about grief, vulnerability, faith, and trust through this precious lady. Life seemed to come into focus, as Krissy's death had a way of casting off all that is not important. Krissy's life is a gift—to me personally, but also to those who read this book as they journey through life and face inevitable grief, injustice and death.

—Nicky

Jacqui's Reflection

Lydia is my closest friend. We met at a party at Ruth's flat in West Auckland. It was 1993. I had recently returned from London, where I had spent eighteen months working with Youth with a Mission, followed by a few months church planting with Ichthus Christian Fellowship. Lydia and John had recently returned to New Zealand after working with Operation Mobilization. Several others at the party worked with Open Air Campaigners. So, we were a group of like-minded people, some of us settling back into Auckland and finding church life a little frustrating.

In 1997, Lydia and John were married at Lincoln Road Bible Chapel, and Ruth and I, along with three others, were bridesmaids. Two years later Jessica was born, a beautiful baby girl with blond hair like her mother's. She was such a blessing. Then, just over a year later, Lydia gave birth to her second baby girl, Kristiana. Both John and I were at the birth. The umbilical cord was wrapped tightly around the baby's neck. We both held our breath and glanced at each other. We said nothing; just prayed silently. We did not want to frighten Lydia. The nurses worked quickly to unbind the cord and coax the baby to breathe. Eventually she did, and John and I sighed with relief.

Kristiana was a beautiful baby with dark hair like John's. Jessica loved to stroke her and give her hugs. Kristiana met all her Plunket milestones, but there were times when Lydia and I wondered if she was doing okay. She slept a lot, and sometimes she did not feed well. Then one day, when John went to get her up, he found her lifeless in the bed. Sudden infant death syndrome (SIDS). It was hard to believe. We were in shock. Lydia sat there on the couch cradling her child, and we sat with her. I felt numb and helpless. There was nothing to say. We made cups of tea and coffee as people came by to visit and brought flowers, meals, and baked goods.

We had the funeral a few days later. Kristiana was dressed like a princess and laid in a little white box. She was carried into the church and placed at the front. The church was packed with people and flowers, and they supported the family with meals for weeks. Lydia's brother and sister came from Australia to support her. From the church, Kristiana was carried to the cemetery, where we bade her farewell, believing this was not forever. We would be reunited again in the future.

This was a time of deep sorrow for Lydia and John, followed by several miscarriages. Lydia wrestled with understanding what God was doing. Was he angry with her over something? Was he punishing her for something? Could she really trust him? Such anguish intensified the grief and pain. People felt the need to offer advice: "God is in control"; "God knows what he is doing"; "It will all work out for the good in the end"; "There will be something we can learn from this"; "This will make you stronger"; "Keep on trusting in him." It reminded me of Job's friends, who had a lot of theological advice for him but only added to his suffering. People were trying to help. They wanted to alleviate the pain. I felt the same way. I wanted to have just the right words to say. But I began to realize that when we are in the depths of sorrow, we do not need pious platitudes or philosophical answers. I thought of Jesus weeping by the tomb of Lazarus, and I sensed he was weeping with us. It occurred to me that Jesus knows what it is like to suffer. Not only this, but God the Father knows what it is to suffer, for God was in Christ reconciling the world to himself. Being Christian does not make us immune to suffering. But it does mean that we are never alone in our suffering. We have a God who is with us no matter what happens.

In 2001, God blessed Lydia and John with a baby boy, Joseph. He was soon followed by Ben in 2006 and Rachel in 2009. Along the way, Lydia and John battled ill health. And Lydia's children had their own difficulties to wrestle with. Lydia fought for her children to get the assistance they needed to thrive. This was an ongoing battle. It did not help that some friends found it necessary to complain about her children or to tell Lydia that what she needed to do was correct them. How she managed to raise such wonderful children and complete a bachelor's and master's in theology while all this was going on is beyond me. She just kept going.

Everything came to a head on a cold winter's day in June 2008. The frost the night before gave way to a sunny day. Wrapped in coats and hats, Lydia, Jess, and Ben went for a walk through the Auckland Domain with Ruth. They spent some time feeding the ducks. Then, after a moment of distraction, they realized Ben was missing. They found him face down in the pond with his shoe above the water. His billowing jacket looked like a piece of rubbish floating on the surface. Ruth fished him out as fast as she could. He was lifeless, cold, and blue. His stomach and lungs were full of water. A nurse was jogging by at that moment and heard Lydia's screams. She ran over and began doing CPR. Ruth called for an ambulance. Within minutes, the paramedics arrived, and Ben was raced to Starship Children's Hospital. That's when Ruth called me.

I dropped everything, drove into town, and raced up to ICU. Ruth was there with John and Jess in a small reception lounge. Mark Strom was also there, and John's sister, Rita. John said, "Lydia wants to see you." I went through to the small room where Lydia was sitting beside Ben. He was lying on his back on a raised white mattress, wearing only his nappy. A tube was sucking pond water from his stomach and he was on a ventilator. A monitor tracked his heart rate and blood pressure. A doctor came in and asked Lydia if she would be willing to be part of a trial for a new medical procedure. They would lower the temperature of the body to prevent cell decay. John came in and they talked about this for a while. Eventually they signed a form granting their permission, and the temperature of the mattress was lowered. Ben's body was lifeless and cold.

John took Jessica home, and I sat with Lydia for a few hours. There was nothing much to say. I listened when she talked. Held her hand. Held Benny's hand. She cried. We prayed together for a time. She had no fight left in her. She could only pray, "Lord, have mercy." So, we prayed together, "Lord, have mercy."

As I was driving home that night, I kept thinking, "This is wrong. This is not God's doing. Lydia and John have been through enough suffering." I began to get mad (not at God, but at life, at death, at suffering, at the evil one). I started praying for a miracle. I started praying that God would raise Benny up. That God would restore him. That there would be a resurrection.

I texted and emailed all the people I knew who also knew John and Lydia, and I asked them to pray.

That night, I woke up at around three o'clock in the morning. I could not get back to sleep. I got up and started praying the same words as before, this time with more fervor and passion. I sensed that the Holy Spirit was in this. I paced back and forth across the room and prayed, "God, you can do this. You raised up Jesus from the dead. You raised up Lazarus from the dead. Raise up Benny. Don't let him die. Restore him to full health. Work a miracle. I know you can do this." As I prayed, I sensed that there were people around the world praying for Benny. It seemed as if my prayers were being added to the prayers of a thousand saints. The Holy Spirit was stirring his family to pray because God did not want Benny to die.

Lydia remained by Ben's side for the next ten days. I drove in as often as I could or babysat her children so John could be with her. A regular stream of visitors came to offer their support—Cindy Brickle, Kevin and Kaylene Tribe, and others from Vineyard West; Mark and Sue Strom and Miriam from Laidlaw; friends from Lincoln Road Bible Chapel; John's sister, Rita; and Ruth and Craig Scott. When Lydia and I were alone with Ben, we sang his favorite nursery rhymes and read him stories. He lay there still and silent with his Iggle Piggle toy beside him.

The doctors tried to prepare Lydia and John for the worst. They said children rarely recover from a drowning like this. They expected him to be in a vegetative state or severely handicapped. Once when we were praying, I overheard a doctor mutter, "As if prayer is going to make a difference. They are deluded." I was so angry. I was about to leap up and demand he show more respect and keep his philosophical beliefs to himself. He should know better than to mock people when they are in anguish. But I knew it would hurt Lydia if I got into it with the doctor. As I write this, I wish to point out that this doctor's response was not typical. Overall, the doctors and nurses working with Benny were understanding, respectful, professional, and caring.

After ten days, it was time to bring Ben out of the coma. They stopped the drugs that were keeping him sedated. They took him off the ventilator and he breathed on his own. The next day, Lydia washed Benny's face and gave his teeth a cleaning. Cindy was there and she noticed Ben's eyes open. He was tracking the toothbrush as it moved from side to side. He could see. Then he grabbed the toothbrush and started cleaning his own teeth.

I was so excited when I heard this. I thought, "You have to have brains to do that! Not only coordination, but memory of what a toothbrush is, and how to use it."

The next day when I went to visit, Lydia was sitting on the bed, and Ben was resting against her. She was eating from a packet of chocolate chip biscuits. Ben was looking at the packet. Then suddenly, he reached out his hand and grabbed a biscuit and started nibbling on it. Lydia and I looked at each other with wide-eyed excitement, but kept silent, not wanting to ruin the moment. We watched as Ben worked his way through half a biscuit. Then I poured a half cup of milk and gave it to Lydia to give to Ben. Ben reached out and drank it down. Then he sat there with a tired smile on his face.

Ben continued to recover, and his feeding tube was removed. Each day he was able to do more than the day before. He returned home a week later and celebrated his second birthday in August. I remember him sitting on the lounge floor, surrounded by presents and wrapping paper. Joseph was entertaining him and helping him unwrap his presents. Ben was laughing at his big brother. Later, Lydia held him up in front of his cake and he blew out the candles. Everyone was there—Cindy Brickle, Ruth and Craig Scott, Sarah and Craig Harris, Mark and Sue Strom, Miriam Strom and Rita Mc-Sweeney, and other close friends from church.

That was over fifteen years ago. Now Ben is an intelligent and healthy teenager. Every time I see him, I think, "He's a walking miracle!"

Benny's recovery was due in part to the swift action of the paramedics, the wonders of modern medicine, and the dedicated care of the doctors and nurses. But I do not think that was enough in and of itself. As the doctors said, people do not fully recover from drownings like this. Benny's recovery was nothing short of a miracle. The church prayed and God raised him up. But no matter what happens, God is with us and nothing can separate us from his love. So, we can continue to pray as Jesus taught us, "your kingdom come, your will be done, on earth as it is in heaven" (Matt 6:10 NIV). And when people's hearts are broken and they have no strength left to pray, we can pray on their behalf.

—Jacqueline Lloyd

Ruth's Reflection

At the time of writing, I am reflecting on the twelve years since I pulled Benny from the pond and marveling at the miracle that took place that day.

But twenty-two years ago, another miracle took place that I am deeply indebted to John and Lydia for. Following a miscarriage at the time of their wedding, in January 1997, Craig and I, over the next year, found that we couldn't conceive, so we went to Fertility Associates for advice. Their prognosis wasn't promising, and they suggested a costly intervention program that we couldn't afford.

John came to us and offered to pay for the program, which we were extremely grateful for and very blessed by his generosity.

Several months later, we set the plan in place and I was delighted to be pregnant on the first round of treatment.

In December 1998, at the age of forty-one, I gave birth to the first of three children, and we named him Joshua John, in honor of John's gift that brought life and children into our family.

With the pond experience being a small piece I played in their inspiring story, it is but one aspect of a bigger picture that God has been fabricating. It speaks of life and sowing with love into others, which John and Lydia have done so bravely, unselfishly, and with determination. Thanks for giving me the opportunity to be part of your lives for thirty years, and may there be many more for us to share.

—with love from Ruth Scott

The Last Scene

THERE IS SOMETIMES A scene after the credits have stopped rolling in a movie. I stay to the very end until, the music stops. If there is a scene, it almost always gives you a crucial clue with the introduction of a plot twist or another character for the sequel to come. Being a movie buff, I wanted to include one at the end of my book. I would call it not a plot twist but a plot amplifier.

Some of you have come to the end of my journey desiring greater practical help for issues that may have been raised for you as you have read my story. I have dropped seeds throughout to hopefully and meaningfully incite a desire for you to know more. In my next book, I want to be able to present in detail the *psychological justice model*, designed to help bridge the incongruence many of us experience between our intellectual understanding of justification—i.e., what it means to be saved—and our gut reactions to God, life, and others. The *psychological justice model* is a cyclical, continuous process with six steps crucially embodied through forgiveness. Corresponding questions are aimed at identifying those places in our journey that affect our process of developing stronger and more congruent life-giving constructs.

It can also be helpful as a practical step-by-step tool for processing specific events in our present that have triggered past wounding. Multiple aspects of our lived experience are explored through each stage of the model to provide psychological and theological support to engender a more engaged and deeply manifested lived experience of "Jesus as Justice." I want not only to help people deal with their responses to presenting triggers, which can result in shame-avoidant behaviors, but also offer concrete advice on how to locate core wounding that may have led to the development of these constructs.

I will endeavor to give a deeper exploration of *psychological justice*. I will provide the grounds upon which psychological healing is both legitimized and, more than that, proven essential to the development of a mature identity in Christ, both individually and corporately for believers, as presented in Romans.

Appendix 1

Vocabulary

Attachment style: A specific pattern of behavior in and around relationships. There are four attachment styles: secure, anxious, avoidant (dismissive or anxious-avoidant), and disorganized (or fearful-avoidant).

Identity in Christ: Jesus now defines our identity based on what he has accomplished for us on the cross. This also is the basis of the security we now have in our relationship with God.

Incongruency: Our core held beliefs are not consistent with our lived experience.

Physiological: Relates to the physical and chemical processes and responses of the body.

Psyche: The human soul, mind, or heart. From the Greek term *psuché*, meaning the vital breath of life.

Psychological: Affecting or arising in the mind and heart; related to the mental and emotional state of a person.

Psychological constructs: Ways to describe patterns of behavior or experience so that they can be explored, investigated, and discussed.

Psychological fractures: Where trauma leaves wounds in the psyche.

Psychological imprints: We hold within our attachment-style template many imprints. Psychological imprints are formed from a range of life-filling and traumatic events throughout our journey. These imprints determine our responses to and our understanding of our place in the world.

Psychological justice: Where injustices enacted on the psyche are given justice. In theological terms, predicated on the work of Jesus' cross and resurrection, through the Spirit, we are "put right" (utilizing N. T. Wright's vocabulary of "puting humans to rights").

Transitional spaces: A psychological transition is a three-step process: the ending of a season (grieving the loss of what was), a neutral period (a time of uncertainty between the old and the new), and a new beginning (instigating a new journey).

Triggers: A trigger is a stimulus that causes a painful memory to surface. A trigger can be any sensory reminder of a traumatic event—a sound, sight, smell, physical sensation, or even time of day or season.

Appendix 2

What's Your Story?

Mislaid Foundations

What attachment style do you think you may have had? Have a think about how that may have impacted your life, your relationships, and the image of God you hold.

Stolen Identity

What "unremarkable" events may have impacted your developing identity in childhood that you may have dismissed? They may hold the key to uncovering fractures in your psyche that are affecting your present.

Losing Hope

What was your role within your family dynamics? What constructs or ways of being did you develop that you would like to revisit?

The Great Escape

When has God brought you into transitional spaces or given you transitional people? What labels do you think you may have accumulated in your journey? Have a think about how they developed, so that you may be able to process these.

A New Family Is Forged

What prophetic dreams are you holding? Don't let go of them just because they seem like riddles right now. Like Mary, learn to hide them in your heart and let them strengthen your present. See them as deposits of hope.

The Great Sadness

Where have you seen, or do you need to see, God encountering faulty images you have of him amidst your journey with tragedy or grief? Where is pain hiding his face from you? Invite him into those spaces if you can.

The Pit of Despair

Where has grief, in its multisensory effects, impacted your physiological and psychological being? Are there places you have spiritualized your grief? Is it time to invite God to come in to heal and shine his light in your places of darkness?

Rebuilding Begins

Can you see God's hand in rebuilding your life either through or after difficult seasons? Take some time to discern ways in which trials have, in time, brought freedom. If you feel stuck, invite the Lord into this space.

A Broken Mother's Heart

Where is your striving a form of grace avoidance? Is the concept of God as mother disturbing or inviting? What do you think your response may be telling you?

The Promise Tested

Where have you felt disappointed or betrayed by God? Be like the Shunammite woman and go swiftly to God and cry out, "Why did you raise my hopes?" Where do you need *psychological justice* for the anguish of lost hope? Ask him. There is nothing too hard for the Lord.

Healing Journey

There are always deeper places in our psyche that need healing. Where might your rush to be healed mean that you have avoided deep, holistic healing? Where is shame drowning your cry to be heard?

Pride and Prejudice—Naming Pride

Have you used Jesus in your quest to be spiritual for him or for others? Where may you have used differing weights or measures? Have you had or could you be a transitional person for someone?

Master's Studies—Naming Shame

Does the description of shame resonate with you? Halstead's proposal that detailing specific sins to forgive may be helpful in processing unforgiveness. Where in your life are there situations that you may be able to appropriate this type of forgiveness? Where may Band-Aid's, i.e., superficial responses, be hiding shame in you?

Naming Abuse

Does my story highlight any types of abuse that may be operating in your life or in those you love? What steps can you take to start questioning these?

My Father Gifts a New Name

In what areas in your life do you need a new name from the Lord? What names have been placed on you that do not belong to you? For example, negative aspects of your personality, roles within family structures, or a traumatic experience.

Freedom through Betrayal—Renaming Church

God's justice is sometimes predicated on forgiveness. Where might you need to forgive another or an institution, in order to see God's justice be wrought in you or in your circumstances? Who is an enemy that you could bless today?

The Pond Revisited

When healing from trauma, you may find you are still triggered. Next time you are, stop and just sit with it and know you will be okay. Each trigger event can be an opportunity for more healing.

Glory amidst Suffering

I want to challenge you to ask God for joy. No matter where you are in your journey, you need his joy. Also, do you want more God encounters in your life? Ask God to open your eyes and ears to hear him so that you can express the glory he wants to release through you to others.

When God Found Me Outside the Walls

Are there places in you where you need to find God outside the walls? What is your season right now? Knowing your season will help you rest in your season.

Postscript

A WONDERFUL THING HAPPENED a couple of days before I sent this book to the publisher. A few family members reached out to me. We had some wonderful conversations. I was happy to hear that my mother is content and living independently in the same house I grew up in.

I am left feeling thankful for my Father's leading and guidance throughout these last ten years. I am deeply grateful for Jesus holding my hand and leading me out of the dance of control and chaos that enmeshed me with my past, and leading me ever so gently into an intimate dance of love and mercy with my Savior. To know the Holy Spirit as my lead dancer and counselor all these years is to know the hands of healing leading me in a dance so exquisitely choreographed that I could never have conceived I would be privileged to dance—one where my dignity soars and my heart awakens.

This, I see now, is exactly like the picture my daughter painted for me so many years ago that now graces this book. I am free. The scales are finally broken. My Jesus' delight over me is my inheritance. I can't wait to see where he leads our dance next. Wherever that is, let me be found in him (Phil 3:9).

Bibliography

Baker, Heidi, and Rolland Baker. *Reckless Devotion*. Grand Rapids: Chosen Books, 2014.

Bell, Daniel M., Jr. "Jesus, the Jews, and the Politics of God's Justice." *Ex Auditu* 22 (2006) 87–112.

Bradshaw, John. *Healing the Shame That Binds You*. Deerfield Beach, FL: Health Communications, 2005.

Bridges, Jerry. *Transforming Grace: Living Confidently in God's Unfailing Love*. Colorado Springs, CO: NavPress, 2008.

Cloud, Henry, and John Townsend. *Boundaries*. Grand Rapids: Cengage, 2004.

Comiskey, Andrew. *Strength in Weakness: Overcoming Sexual and Relational Brokenness*. Downers Grove, IL: InterVarsity, 2003.

Dupont, Marc A. *Walking Out of Spiritual Abuse*. Tonbridge, Kent, UK: Sovereign World, 1997.

Halstead, P. J. "Have My Parents Sinned against Me? Exploring the Concept of Sin in the Pastoral Context." *Journal of Spirituality in Mental Health* 12/2 (2010) 43–62.

Halstead, Philip John. "The Forgiveness Matters Course: A Theologically and Psychologically Integrated Approach to Help Churchgoing Adults Process Their Parental Wounds." *Journal of Spirituality in Mental Health* 14/2 (2012) 85–110.

Keener, Craig S., and Walton, John H. *NIV Cultural Backgrounds Study Bible*. Grand Rapids: Zondervan, 2016.

Kline, P. M. "Merton's True Self: A Resource for Survivors of Sexual Abuse by Priests." *Pastoral Psychology* 55/6 (2007) 731–39.

Linn, Matthew, Dennis Linn, and Sheila Fabricant Linn. *Belonging: Bonds of Healing and Recovery*. New York: Paulist, 1993.

Payne, Leanne. *The Healing Presence: Curing the Soul through Union with Christ*. Grand Rapids: Baker, 1995.

Silk, Danny. *Loving Our Kids on Purpose: Making a Heart to Heart. Connection*. Shippensburg, PA: Destiny Image, 2013.

Spurgeon, Charles. *Power in the Blood*. Columbia: Whitaker House, 2018.

Strom, Mark. *Reframing Paul: Conversations in Grace & Community*. Downers Grove, IL: InterVarsity, 2000.

Wright, N.T. *Paul and the Faithfulness of God*. Christian Origins and the Question of God 4. Minneapolis: Fortress, 2013.

Printed in Great Britain
by Amazon

37448038R00129